SOCIAL HOUSING
A European Dilemma?

Peter Emms

S·A·U·S

First published in Great Britain in 1990 by

School for Advanced Urban Studies
Rodney Lodge
Grange Road
Clifton
Bristol BS8 4EA

Telephone: (0272) 741117

British Library Cataloguing in Publication Data
Emms, Peter
    Social housing: a European dilemma?
    1. Western Europe. Housing.
    I. Title II. University of Bristol. *School for Advanced Urban
    Studies*.
    363.5094

        ISBN 0-86292-358-1

The School for Advanced Urban Studies was established jointly by the University of Bristol and the Department of the Environment in 1973 as a post-experience teaching and research centre in the field of urban policy. In addition to the dissemination of material in courses and seminars the School has established three publications series: **SAUS Studies, Occasional Papers and Working Papers.**

SAUS is open to the submission of manuscripts from outside authors within its areas of interest.

General enquiries about the School, its courses, research programme and publications may be addressed to the Publicity Officer.

SAUS is working to counter discrimination on grounds of gender, race, disability, age and sexuality in all its activities.

CONTENTS

PREFACE

The central theme of the work of the School for Advanced Urban Studies is a concern for public policy - its development, implementation and evaluation. Frequent and regular contact with senior politicians and officials in both central and local government is thus a normal part of SAUS activity. In 1984 Stephen Garrish, a civil servant in the Departments of the Environment and Transport, spent a year with SAUS looking at centralisation and decentralisation in England and France. More recently the School was fortunate to be able to replicate both the development of its European interests and linkage with a senior civil servant, through the association for a year with SAUS of Peter Emms, formerly Head of Estate Action in the Department of the Environment and currently Regional Director of the Eastern Regional Office of the Departments of the Environment and Transport.

In the light of the growing attention being given to housing management issues and drawing not only upon his experience with housing policy in DOE, but also on previously acquired language skills, Peter Emms decided to look at the differing approaches to social housing in France, West Germany, the Netherlands and the Soviet Union as well as in the UK. The award of a Leverhulme Nuffield Travelling Fellowship allowed for an extensive programme of visits and interviews in the countries being covered.

The School for Advanced Urban Studies is delighted not only to publish a contribution from a Visitor to SAUS (now the second such in our publications series) but also to provide an outlet for the research of a working civil servant. Peter Emms would want to emphasise that his approach has been very much that of someone who has worked extensively at the central/local interface, though inevitably from a central government standpoint, and he would not see himself as an academic researcher. His material relies predominantly on the extensive interviews which he undertook in the countries he visited and he was also able to make use of a great deal of unpublished material shown to him by his contacts as well as to draw upon documentation and statistics already in the public domain. His perspective is essentially that of the 'reflective practitioner'. We hope that this work will not only prove interesting reading but will also stimulate others to pursue some of the issues he raises for the future of social housing throughout Europe.

Since he completed his Travelling Fellowship, Europe, and eastern Europe in particular, has seen some momentous changes, which are still continuing. Wherever possible the text has been updated to reflect the situation at the time of publication - in late 1990 - but the account of housing in Germany is inevitably confined to the Federal Republic before reunification.

FOREWORD

This study originated from my discovery during a visit to France in 1986 that the French government's approach to rundown housing estates in the social rented sector had much in common with our own Estate Action (originally the Urban Housing Renewal Unit), which I was running at that time. Given the radical rethinking of housing policy which was taking place in the United Kingdom, the Department of the Environment decided to sponsor me on a Nuffield Leverhulme Travelling Fellowship to make a detailed and wider-ranging comparative study of the different approaches to social housing and its current problem in a cross-section of European countries of different sizes and political systems; France, the Federal Republic of Germany, the Netherlands and the Soviet Union, and to relate their experience to ours.

The material contained in this study was obtained during a series of visits covering over 10,000 miles - mostly by road - in 1987 and 1988, and concentrating on problem estates. Thanks are due first of all to the Department of the Environment for releasing me to undertake this programme and for funding the project. However, the work would not have been possible without the vast amount of help and cooperation which I received from literally hundreds of people from central and local government and housing organisations in all the countries covered, who generously gave their time to show me what they are doing, to explore their ideas and experience with me, and to comment on the emerging drafts of the report.

They are far too numerous for me to be able to list them all, but I would like to pay special tribute to Michel Amzallag, Patrice Dunoyer de Segonzac, Sylvie Harburger, Marie-Christine Leroy and Jean-Pierre Schaefer in France, to Claus-Jürgen Hachmann and to Toni and Ulrich Pfeiffer in the Federal Republic of Germany, to Loek Kampschöer, Jan van der Moolen and Hugo Priemus in the Netherlands, and to Dr Nikolayev and his colleagues in the Soviet Union. In the United Kingdom, Murray Stewart, Duncan Maclennan, Graham Hallett, Michael Harloe and Gregory Andrusz provided much invaluable advice and encouragement from the academic world, as did so many of my colleagues in the public service, in particular Michael Burbidge and Alan Holmans in the Department of the Environment.

Finally, a word on the structure of the book and a note of caution about comparisons. As well as giving a self-standing and comprehensive picture of housing in each country (with an emphasis on the social rented sector), the individual national chapters are organised so that readers can approach the material thematically, concentrating for example on financial systems across the various countries if that is where their interests lie. However, it would be dangerous to try to make detailed quantified comparisons.

Although 'purchasing power equivalents' rather than exchange rates are used to make financial comparisons, they are still only a rough and ready guide, while differences of definition - for example, of floor areas and empty dwellings in the various countries - mean that virtually all quantified international comparisons must be made with great caution.

introduction

COINCIDENCES AND BASIC COMPARISONS

The common origins of social rented housing

The 20th century has seen the emergence of social rented housing - that is, housing whose construction and in consequence rents are subsidised from public funds - in many countries around the world. This study considers the development and present state of the social rented sector in five European countries: the United Kingdom, France, the Federal Republic of Germany, the Netherlands, and the Soviet Union.

Taking the broadest possible sweep of history, the concept of decent but affordable housing for working people to rent emerged independently in each country at about the same time; towards and during the third quarter of the 19th century. However, as will be seen, it began to be implemented seriously only after the First World War, and then at widely differing rates and in very varied ways from country to country. Nonetheless, given the differing stages of urbanisation in the five countries at the outset and long thereafter, the many common factors in the development of their social rented housing programmes are bound to represent - according to individual perceptions of the historical process - either a remarkable coincidence, or a product of similar combinations of social and economic influences on national policy-making, such as reactions to the industrial revolution and to the First World War.

In this connection, it is perhaps significant that the protagonists of the new enlightenment seemed generally to see themselves responding to social needs rather than to demands of the market-place. Moreover, those needs were ill-defined, and have remained largely so, no doubt mainly because the response to them depended so little on economic forces.

It should, however, be emphasised at the outset that the original providers of social rented housing in all four western countries (and those who dreamed but did not provide in pre-revolutionary Russia) saw their clientèle largely as the 'deserving poor', such as skilled manual workers and clerks, rather than the really indigent. With the exception of the United Kingdom and the Soviet Union, in both of which countries the social rented sector increasingly came to assume a major role in housing families from slum clearance property or other forms of housing deprivation, social landlords have always been concerned to select tenants who were likely to be unproblematic both economically and socially.

Although many of the original social landlords had philanthropic motives, and had the backing of churches, charities, trade unions and other public-spirited bodies, there was also a strong thread of enlightened self-interest among employers who saw the benefits to themselves of having at least the less dispensable members of their workforce housed conveniently to their place of work and in reasonably healthy conditions.

Voluntary support, whether self-interested or not, inevitably had limited impact on its own in a late 19th century Europe where there was still enough housing for the great mass of the population to have a roof over their heads however poor the living conditions were. Government intervention by means of regulation, and above all with subsidies, was a prerequisite if social rented housing was to begin to make a significant impact on housing conditions. The following chapters on the five countries will consider the ways in which this process of intervention differed in form, speed and intensity from the late years of the 19th century onwards.

How the United Kingdom developed differently

The United Kingdom took a different road from the other countries in a number of significant directions from the end of the First World War. First, it embarked on a major social sector building programme, while the other countries did not do so until after the Second World War. There are various possible explanations for the early start in the United Kingdom, not least perhaps the successful lead given in this country by such crusading practitioners as Octavia Hill who had no real counterpart elsewhere. However, the main reason may be simply that the United Kingdom emerged from the First World War with relatively greater economic resources than the other countries.

As will be seen, this had major effects on the development of the United Kingdom's system of housing finance which distinguish it from that in other countries. It also meant that a much larger proportion of the United Kingdom stock (apart from Scotland) consists of houses as the main built form. To generalise again, the design of much social housing in England in particular was inspired by the 'garden city' ethos, while that of the rest of Europe, partly perhaps because of its differing housing traditions, came under the sway of the more grandiose mass housing ideas which came to dominate architectural attitudes after the Congrès Internationale d'Architecture Moderne (CIAM) in Athens in 1933.

For reasons which remain unclear, the construction and subsequent management of social rented housing in the United Kingdom was entrusted to local authorities as a direct responsibility. In other countries the development and management functions are carried out largely by other agencies, albeit with a substantial element of arms-length municipal influence.

There is little if any evidence to suggest that this historic decision after the First World War to make local authorities in the United Kingdom into major landlords has led tenants to benefit from a more coordinated and effective delivery of all the various housing-related services provided by their local authority than do their counterparts in other countries where the responsibility for providing these services is apparently more fragmented.

The United Kingdom also differed at an early stage from its continental neighbours in the decline of its private rented sector in the inter-war years, and the virtual elimination of private renting in the four decades which followed the Second World War. (Private landlordism, if not private sub-letting and owner-occupation, had of course been abolished in the Soviet Union after the Revolution.) Although all four western countries bowed to the political imperative of rent control after the First World War, private renting remained a major provider in France, Germany and the Netherlands. Indeed, in all three of these countries, it continues to offer a significant alternative to the social rented sector. In particular, it tends to cater for the poorest and most mobile households, most notably in West Germany and least significantly in the Netherlands.

The individual national chapters of this book consider the
continuing importance of the private rented sector in greater detail.
General speculation about the historical reasons for the contrast
between the United Kingdom and the other countries is perhaps of
little relevance to modern conditions, but it may be worth noting
that the United Kingdom, and the Soviet Union, were the only
countries to develop a major alternative to, or replacement for,
private renting in the form of the inter-war municipal programme.
Moreover, in both countries, slum clearance and the replacement of
existing housing played a major part in reducing the alternatives.

The development of the social rented sector after the Second World War

While the United Kingdom and the Soviet Union had been alone
among the countries covered by this study in seeking a large-scale
contribution from the social rented sector in the inter-war years,
they all took this route and on a vastly greater scale in the post-war
period. Whatever differences there may have been in the financial
arrangements and the landlord structures, the goal and basic
approach were the same; to promote the construction of the
maximum number of homes as quickly as possible by means of
government subsidies to bricks and mortar. The extent to which
this aim was achieved in the various countries, and the different
agencies and financial regimes which were adopted to do so, will
be analysed in later chapters.

Underlying the mass social rented sector programmes in all
these countries, however, was the apparently unquestioned
assumption that housing need was so great that the sellers' market
would go on for ever. Prospective tenants were seen as passive
recipients for a product whose design, quality, price, and location
were in practice almost entirely the prerogative of 'experts' -
administrators, planners and architects - who indeed usually
reached their decisions without reference to those who would later
be responsible for managing and maintaining the housing.

In fairness to the housing decision-makers, it should be
remembered that most commodities in short supply in the post-war
years were produced and allocated in a similar authoritarian way.
However, while most of the furniture, household gadgets and cars
of the first three decades after the Second World War have long

since disappeared, the housing legacy of this period (and later) will
be with us for many years yet.

With hindsight, it is all too easy to overlook the admirable
intentions of those who sought all possible short cuts to provide a
decent home for the millions of people who were in desperate
housing need throughout Europe in the post-war years, while at the
same time trying to improve the working conditions of those who
were building these homes, and to avoid consuming too much
agricultural land in a time of still chronic food shortages. However,
it is perhaps fair to wonder how far those who took the decisions
asked themselves whether they or anyone else would positively opt
to live in one of the massive high density systems-built housing
schemes which they variously caused to spring up on the fringes of
towns and cities all over Europe. It is also clear that little thought
was given - particularly in the United Kingdom - to how much
social disruption would result from the destruction of so much
sound existing housing and the communities which lived in it, in
order to replace it with similar mass housing estates in the inner
cities.

Despite the significant differences between the social rented
housing systems of the various countries, they had much in
common as far as the underlying ethos was concerned. The rush to
produce mass housing originated in the centrally planned
economies which were the order of the day as the programmes were
launched. The grateful attitudes of the consumers could be safely
assumed in a time of apparently endless shortage, to the extent of
there being no need to take the occupants explicitly into account.
Indeed, in the early days, tenants were suitably grateful to have
escaped from overcrowded and often poor housing into modern,
spacious homes.

The unacknowledged though real rejection of market forces can
be seen in several ways. Standards of space and amenity were
determined by balancing the claims of social and economic
advisers to the providers. Dwellings were (and are) allocated by
often arcane and sometimes barely rational criteria of priority laid
down by various combinations of central and local government fiat.
The groups for whom mass housing was destined remained as ill-
defined as they had been all along. Although there was some fine-
tuning on tenants' incomes in some of the countries, it was simply
assumed that the policy of centrally directed (and usually centrally
funded) subsidy systems to promote the construction of the rapid
mass housing programmes was inevitably and eternally matched

with a pool of tenants who needed subsidised housing. Low rents became and remained a tenet of political dogma, while at the same time reinforced the limitations on consumer choice.

Emerging discontent

It should be emphasised that in all five countries, the management problems which are the main theme of this book affect or have affected only a minority of the social rented stock. In the absence of any aggregated data about management problems in France, West Germany, the Netherlands, and the Soviet Union, housing experts there will only venture tentative and unattributable subjective judgements, in the range of 250,000 to 500,000 dwellings in France and Germany, and at the lower end in the Netherlands, while Soviet housing experts perceive their management problems as real but minor in relation to the need to deal with the continuing housing shortage.

In England, the annual Housing Investment Programme returns by local authorities habitually classify about a third of a million of their dwellings as "difficult to let", while the Department of the Environment's Priority Estates Project estimates that up to a million may be "difficult to manage". However, even on the higher of these estimates, more than three out of four local authority dwellings do not have significant management problems. Moreover, as will be seen in Chapters 1 and 2, periodic surveys of tenants in the social rented sector in England and France show only small minorities who are dissatisfied with their housing.

Nonetheless, perhaps the most striking historical coincidence in the history of the social rented sector in the four western countries is the almost simultaneous emergence of some unprecedented management problems in the early 1970s, despite the quite significant differences in their development, in their housing systems, and in the housing and the tenants themselves. As will be seen in later chapters, in all four countries, tenants began to move away from some estates, and there was a growing reluctance by new tenants to move in, even on to new estates in some instances. Costs to landlord organisations mounted as numbers of empty dwellings soared - thus exacerbating the poor image of such estates - and turnover increased. In some cases, landlords were faced with the additional costs of rising rent arrears and vandalism. Less significant though these problems may be in the Soviet Union, it is small comfort to think that this may largely be due to the still overwhelming overall housing shortage there.

The consequent accelerating spiral of social decline in the western countries was a new phenomenon for which many landlord organisations, whose experience and enthusiasms to date had been dominated by their role as developers of new housing rather than as managers and maintainers of their existing stock, were often completely unprepared. In this, they were hardly unique. By the early 1970s, many of those who had managed the massive post-war re-equipment programmes in several other parts of the public sector were facing a similar transition from managing capital investment to managing the assets which had now resulted from that investment.

The switch of emphasis from capital investment towards greater expenditure of money and effort on the management and maintenance of the existing housing stock received a considerable jolt forward with the effects of the first oil price explosion of 1973 on heating bills. At the same time, the older stock was beginning to feel the effects of age, with an increasing need for expenditure on modernisation and indeed on routine maintenance, to which landlord organisations were sometimes slow to adjust both psychologically and financially. These burdens were later to increase dramatically for many landlord organisations as the technical defects inherent in some industrial building systems became apparent.

While landlord organisations and tenants were starting to face a fundamental economic revolution, the social culture had been undergoing some radical changes too. The increasing prosperity of the late 1960s had given the individual family new expectations of choice, and a new range of consumer products - cars, household appliances, and televisions - with which to exercise these expectations. The self-assertion of the individual against collective authority was expressed most dramatically in the student disturbances and political events of 1968 in several countries of western and eastern Europe. However, above all, they were a symptom of a new-found will, especially among the economically and sexually emancipated younger generation, to make their own choices about how to conduct their lives.

By this time, the deficiencies of the planning approach to the supply of social rented housing were beginning to become apparent, at least in the western countries. The lack of consumer demand in some areas where the expected employment opportunities had failed to be realised, or competition from other tenures as more tenants were able to afford owner-occupation or found opportunities to move into privately rented accommodation, meant that here and there, market forces were beginning to play a part.

The oil price explosion which had been quick to affect tenants directly with escalating heating costs in buildings, which had rarely been built with thermal efficiency in mind, was later to reverse the until then apparently permanent upward drift in their general economic fortunes as the resulting recession began to take its toll on incomes and jobs.

As will be seen in later chapters, demographic and economic changes were also to start to exert a considerable influence. Although the national statistics vary greatly in the level of detail which they give about tenants in the social rented sector as such, it is clear that parts at least of the social rented sector in all five countries began to suffer from a general and growing tendency towards relatively high proportions of people dependent on public financial and social support. This included single parent families, older people, members of minority ethnic communities, as well as the growing numbers of unemployed. Changing family patterns - divorce and separation, growing numbers of single people and of childless couples - began to cause serious mismatches between the demand for accommodation and the size and nature of the dwellings which were available.

As in the United Kingdom, the shrinkage of the down-market end of the private rented sector in France, West Germany and the Netherlands created new pressures on the social rented sector in these countries from the poorer sections of society. Whilst at the same time the increasing lure of owner-occupation (and housing cooperatives in the Soviet Union) for those who could afford such changes of tenure, tended to draw off the more successful and self-reliant in all five countries.

Progress towards solutions

The late 1970s and the 1980s have therefore seen a growing tendency for the social rented sector in all four western countries - and in some parts of the rented sector in the Soviet Union - to be regarded as problematic and less desirable as a housing choice. This has faced landlord organisations and governments with serious financial burdens, compounding the increasing costs of ph̲ maintenance and modernisation of the stock. The radic̲ reassessments of financial approach which the western governments have undertaken are discussed in detail in Section V, 'The buildings', of the individual national chapters, which in particular will highlight that a common feature of all has been a change of emphasis from general subsidies on bricks and mortar towards social security and housing benefit payments more closely attuned to the needs of individuals. This approach involves a fine balance between rent levels and the social support system if the economic contribution by those tenants who can afford to pay is to be maximised. Comparative work by Department of the Environment's (DOE) economists and statisticians on rent levels for all tenants not in receipt of income related assistance in France, West Germany and England in 1985 suggests a remarkable similarity between real gross rent levels. That is, rents including property taxes and services except heating. This work also identified considerable similarity between the share of net income which is taken up by rent in the various countries, amounting to under 14% in England, and about 15% in France and West Germany.

As will be seen later in the book, there is a major difference of approach by government between France and the United Kingdom on the one hand, and West Germany and the Netherlands on the other as they approach the malaise in the social rented sector. Whereas the central governments in France and England have been directly involved in the development and promotion of new approaches to management and social and economic revitalisation of rundown estates since the late 1970s, the governments of West Germany and the Netherlands have intervened only to a limited extent, and usually only when the financial viability of landlord organisations appeared to be under threat.

The approaches to the social and management problems in the social rented sector in the various countries covered by this study are considered in detail in Section VII of the next five chapters, 'Management problems and solutions', and they are summarised and assessed in the concluding chapter.

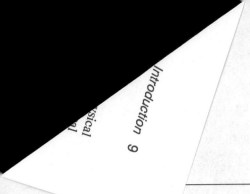

THE UNITED KINGDOM

I The general background

Population and housing stock

The Office of Population Censuses and Surveys puts the 1986 population of the United Kingdom at 56.76 million. This compares with a little more than 38 million at the beginning of the century, and a projection of just under 59 million at the end of the century, after which it is expected to continue to rise to about 59.6 million in the period from 2016 to 2021.[1]

In 1989, the estimated total of the housing stock in the United Kingdom was some 23.2 million dwellings.[2] The average size of household is estimated at 2.55 in 1986, compared with 2.91 in 1971.[3] A further fall to about 2.43 is expected by the end of the century.[4] In Great Britain, about 22% of households live in dwellings built before 1919, 24% in dwellings built in the inter-war years, 25% in dwellings built between the end of the Second World War and 1964, and 29% in dwellings built in 1965 and later.[5]

There are, however, some significant variations between the different constituent parts of the United Kingdom. According to the 1977 *National Dwelling and Housing Survey*, over one household in four in England and Wales lived in property built before 1919, just under one household in four lived in property built between the two world wars, with a similar split between property built in the 1940-1964 period, and that built in 1965 and later. The age profiles of the housing stock in Scotland and Northern Ireland are different. In 1984/85, one in five Scottish

families lived in property built before 1919, and a similar proportion in property built between then and 1945, while three out of five lived in post-war property. This is split equally between that built before 1965 and that built since then.[6] Out of a total housing stock of about 491,000 dwellings in Northern Ireland in 1984, one out of three was built before the end of the Second World War.

Tenure

The balance between the three main housing tenures has undergone two major changes in the last twenty years. The first is the dramatic increase in owner-occupation. In Great Britain (that is, England, Scotland and Wales), owner-occupation has increased from under half (46.6%) in 1966 to nearly two thirds (62.9%) in 1986.[7] The *General Household Survey* (*GHS*) shows owner-occupiers to be under-represented in housing built between 1945 and 1964 (50%), whilst the highest proportion of owner-occupation is to be found in pre-1919 stock (72%). A large proportion of those in recently built property were buying with the help of a mortgage. Owner-occupation tends to be mainly the preserve of the married, and the majority of men and women marrying for the first time lived with their parents until then. Increasingly, they then move straight into owner-occupation, and those who rent before buying keep their time as tenants as short as possible.[8] Owner-occupation is seen as an above average hedge against inflation, and a relatively safe way of making a (tax-free) capital gain on borrowed money. It has been actively promoted by all recent governments through mortgage interest relief against income tax, and by the present government through large discounts to encourage social sector tenants to buy their homes. Owner-occupation is higher in England than in Northern Ireland and Scotland.

The second major change has been the even more dramatic decline in the private rented sector. In 1939, private tenants easily outnumbered owner-occupiers and tenants in the social rented sector. They still formed nearly a quarter of all households in 1966. However, by 1986 less than one in twelve households rented from a private landlord. The main reasons for the decline of private renting have been the statutory control of rents and security of tenure which have existed for most of the period since 1915. This is coupled with the consequent poor image of private landlords who are understandably reluctant to do up their property if there is no prospect of a compensating rent increase, and who are just as understandably anxious to get rid of their sitting tenants if they can see a more financially attractive use for the property. It is also significant that the private rented sector bore the brunt of the slum clearance programme in the inter-war years and after the Second World War. Private renting also fares much worse than the other sectors for public financial support.

The present government has introduced measures to revive the private rented sector by creating two new alternative regimes for landlords. One involves the removal of rent control on new tenancies while retaining security of tenure. The other involves limited security of tenure, but some limitation on rents.

Table 1.1: Tenure (Great Britain, 1986)

	Number of dwellings (thousands)		%	
Owner-occupation	13,931		63.1	
Private renting	1,744		7.9	
Social renting	6,418		29.0	
of which: LA/new town		5,885		26.6
housing associations		533		2.4
Total	22,093		100.0	

Source: *Housing and Construction Statistics* **1977-1987, Table 9.3**

The social rented sector consists mainly of local authority landlords. It comprises more than a quarter of the total stock. However, housing associations have gained greatly in prominence in the last decade, and in 1986, they owned 2.5% of the dwellings in Great Britain, many of them acquired from the private rented sector. The social rented sector increased from less than a tenth of the overall stock in 1939 to peak at just under a third in the late 1970s before falling back through sales to sitting tenants under the statutory right to buy their homes introduced by the 1980 Housing Act. The social rented sector has since the 1920s been larger in Scotland than in England, Wales and Northern Ireland. In 1986, it still represented just over half of the total stock in Scotland. The

social rented sector is considered in greater de
sections of this chapter.

Conditions

According to *GHS* data, 80% of the housing stock in Great Britain consists of houses.[9] Of these, detached houses represent 19% of the stock, semi-detached houses 32%, and terraced houses 29%. Of the 20% of the stock which consists of flats, three-quarters are purpose-built flats, and the remainder are conversions.

Nonetheless, as with the age profile of the stock, the built form is subject to some significant variations in different parts of the United Kingdom. In Greater London, there are virtually as many flats as houses. In Northern Ireland, 91% of the stock consists of houses, most commonly the terraced house which accounts for about 40% of all dwellings in Northern Ireland. In Scotland, however, flats account for no less than 40% of the stock.

The 1986 *English House Condition Survey* (*EHCS*) showed a significant improvement in the proportion of dwellings lacking the basic amenities since the previous survey in 1981, but the proportion of dwellings in an unsatisfactory state of repair remained about the same. Table 1.2 gives comparative figures.

Table 1.2: Condition of the housing stock (England)

	1981	1986
	(thousands)	
All dwellings (excluding those built since 1981)	18,067	18,132
Lacking amenities	862	543
Unfit	1,116	1,053
In serious disrepair	1,178	1,113

Source: *English House Condition Surveys* **1981 and 1986 (HMSO, 1983 and 1988)**

The 1984 *Northern Ireland House Condition Survey* showed that the proportion of dwellings lacking basic amenities had gone down from 26.2% to 9.2% over the past decade, though one in four dwellings needed major repair (compared with one in five in

England). The 1985/86 *Scottish Abstract of Statistics* estimates that 56,000 dwellings, or about 3% of the stock, were below a 'tolerable' standard. The 1986 *Welsh House Condition Survey* showed that 7.2% of housing in Wales was unfit - some 1.6% lower than in 1981, while 4.3% were lacking an amenity - a reduction by almost half of the proportion lacking an amenity in 1981.

The 1977 *National Dwelling and Housing Survey* showed that four out of five people were very satisfied or satisfied with their homes and their surroundings, but tenants were two or three times more likely to be less satisfied than were owner-occupiers.

Household and dwelling balance

It can be estimated from the 1981 census data that there was an overall shortfall of about 100,000 dwellings in relation to households at that time, with two-thirds of that shortfall in London. Although there is no firm information to update the 1981 data, it is likely that the number of households has increased rather more than the number of dwellings.

II   History of the social rented sector

The foundations of the social rented sector in England were laid in the 19th century. The reasons were largely philanthropic, or at least concern during an era of growing social consciousness about the health of manual workers and their families, particularly in London and the industrial conurbations. Under the 1866 and 1867 Labouring Classes Dwelling Houses Acts, housing associations such as the Peabody Trust were able to borrow money at 4% from the Public Works Loans Commissioners, while the Artisans and Labourers Dwellings Improvement Act of 1875 and its successors (the Cross Acts) provided housing associations with opportunities to buy slum clearance sites at a discount from public authorities. By 1914, housing associations owned probably 50,000 dwellings, four-fifths of them in London.

Since the 1880s, local authorities too were becoming directly involved as landlords through the operation of the Cross Acts, though in a small way. Their powers were consolidated in the 1890 Housing of the Working Classes Act, but were purely permissive and there was no financial incentive to use them. It is therefore not surprising that by 1914, only 20,000 houses - or some 1% of the total stock at that time - had been built by local authorities under these powers.

The closing years of the First World War saw the recognition by government that the wartime imposition of rent controls would continue to be necessary, at least for a time after the war, and in consequence would deter a resumption of private investment in rented housing. A sizeable public rented sector was therefore an irresistible social and political imperative to meet the huge backlog left by the war and the build-up to it, and to fulfil the expectations of the returning troops and their families. Central government also recognised that the achievement of the target of half a million new homes would inevitably depend on Exchequer subsidy.

In the event, only a third of this target was built during the five years which followed under the 1919 Housing, Town Planning, Etc Act. However, this was still a massive advance on anything which had gone before, and not just in terms of quantity. Moreover, with the implementation of the recommendations of the Tudor Walters Committee in the 1919 *Housing Manual*, local authorities were obliged to build to unprecedentedly high standards of space, amenity and layout.

Thanks to these measures and the major development of public transport and the absence of serious planning restrictions on the use of land, the era of the cottage housing estates on garden city lines had arrived. However, London had already emerged as a special case before the First World War with the tenement housing which the London County Council (LCC) and housing associations such as the Peabody Trust had built for low-income workers, and the LCC resumed this programme on a large scale and for a similar clientèle in the 1930s.

The 1919 measures and their successors in the early 1920s created a crucial precedent for the future shape of social housing in Britain. Despite the existence and indeed the predominance of housing associations as social landlords before the First World War, the task of implementing the massive new public sector housing programme in the post-war period was entrusted decisively to local authorities.

This trend in the allocation of social housing responsibilities is part of a general pattern in Great Britain in the first half of this century of relying on the state directly rather than on state-supported agencies to provide welfare organisation. In housing as in other respects it therefore sets the British social rented sector totally apart from its western European counterparts, where socially rented housing is almost entirely owned and managed by organisations constituted on the lines of British housing associations, (and often coexisting with a still sizeable private rented sector). In the inter-war years, housing associations added a mere 24,000 to their pre-war stock of some 50,000 dwellings, while local authorities increased their stock from about 20,000 in 1914 to over 1,100,000 in 1939.

The ethos of the social rented sector has always been that it exists to meet needs which cannot be met in other ways. Before the First World War, the local authority role had been mainly to rehouse those displaced from clearance property. In the early years of the inter-war period, the emphasis changed to providing affordable housing principally for artisans in the "land fit for heroes". However, slum clearance continued to be an important local authority responsibility, and in the 1930s it resumed political priority under the 1930 Housing Act and 1933 Housing (Financial Provisions) Act, which between them provided subsidy for slum clearance while removing the subsidy on general needs housing. By 1939, 472,000 slum dwellings were scheduled for demolition under this legislation, though the programme was interrupted by the outbreak of the Second World War.

When house-building was resumed after the Second World War, the social rented programme was directed towards the same two needs as it had been before the war. The first priority was to make good the losses caused by war damage and to cope with the sharply rising number of families needing accommodation, which together meant that there was an immediate shortfall of some two million dwellings. However, in the 20 years between 1955 and 1975, slum clearance again came to play a major part in local authority programmes. In total, some 1,300,000 properties were demolished, mainly in the private rented sector.

There is no evidence to show that the development of the pre-war local authority hegemony was due to any deeply rooted policy of governments of any political persuasion. However, in the prevailing atmosphere of government dirigisme after 1945, there was no question but that the main brunt of the responsibility for providing housing should fall on local authorities, (and on the 32 new towns in the United Kingdom which since the first designation in 1946, have provided some 400,000 new houses and flats).

Although there has since been a fairly steady trend towards greater owner-occupation, and despite the huge relative increase in the stock owned and managed by housing associations to over

500,000 dwellings in 1987 following the introduction of capital subsidy in the 1974 Housing Act, local authorities have continued to reign supreme in the provision of rented accommodation, at least until the major question-mark which was raised about their future in the Conservative party's 1987 election manifesto. In 1987, after the Right to Buy introduced in the 1980 Housing Act had passed its peak, the local authority rented stock in England still topped 4.5 million dwellings. Table 1.3 summarises the development of the social rented sector from 1914 to 1987.

Table 1.3:   Development of the social rented sector

| | Number of dwellings (thousands) | | | | | |
| | Local authorities and new towns | | Housing associations | | Total* | |
	England and Wales	Great Britain	England and Wales	Great Britain	England and Wales	Great Britain
1914	20		50		70	
1939	1,180		75		1,250	
1953	2,400		90		2,500	
1961	3,528		150		3,700	
1971	4,803		200		5,000	
1981	5,361	6,442	435	466	5,796	6,908
1985	4,889	5,921	495	538	5,384	6,459
1986	4,814	5,833	509	554	5,323	6,387
1987	4,717	5,718	524	573	5,241	6,291
1988	4,569	5,541	543	597	5,112	6,138

Notes: *Totals rounded for 1971 and earlier. 1988 figures provisional

Source: Holmans, A. *Housing Policy in Britain*, pp 47 and 206, and Table V.1, and *Housing and Construction Statistics* 1978-1988, Table 9.3.

The table not only underlines the dominance of the municipal sector over housing associations, but also shows that the social rented building programme took off much more swiftly in Great Britain after the Second World War than in France, West Germany and the Netherlands. Indeed, there were 287,000 starts between April 1945 and the end of 1947. Completions continued at a high rate until the late 1970s, rarely dipping below 100,000 a year, and peaking at over 200,000 in the early 1950s, with second and third declining peaks in the late 1960s and late 1970s.   Table 1.4 gives annual public sector starts and completions (including building by housing associations, and by central government; for example, accommodation for forces personnel and police) in England and Wales from 1946 to 1987.

Despite the continuing resilience of the public sector building programme until the end of the 1970s, some serious problems were beginning to show a decade before then.   Housing managers were finding the large flatted developments of the 1960s to be particularly unpopular, and the difficulties in letting dwellings on such estates were made worse by the Ronan Point disaster in the London Borough of Newham in 1967.

With the election of the Conservative government in 1979, the social rented sector began to go through the greatest shake-up in its history.   The Housing Act of 1980 gave virtually all social sector tenants a statutory right to buy their homes at generous discounts. These discounts were further improved under subsequent legislation, which in particular sought to encourage the sale of flats. The original discounts ranged between 33% of valuation for tenants of 3 years' standing to 50% for tenants of 20 years' standing.   The 1984 Housing and Building Control Act raised the maximum discount to 60% and reduced the minimum length of time as a tenant to 2 years.   The 1986 Housing and Planning Act brought in a new scale for flats, starting at 44% with a minimum qualifying period of 2 years and rising to 70% for a qualifying period of 15 years.   Between April 1979 and December 1987, over 800,000 sitting tenants in Great Britain bought their homes.

The Conservative government's legislation has also greatly reduced the influence of social sector landlords, especially local authorities, by altering the relationship between them and their tenants, and by imposing new rules to govern the way in which they provide their housing service.   These changes will be discussed in Section III.

Table 1.4: Public sector starts and completions 1946-1987
(United Kingdom - local authorities, new towns, housing
associations, and government departments)

	(thousands)			(thousands)	
	Starts	Completions		Starts	Completions
1946		25	1967	222	211
1947	287*	99	1968	201	200
1948	133*	198	1969	186	192
1949	153*	177	1970	162	188
1950	159*	175	1971	146	168
1951	164*	176	1972	129	130
1952	213*	212	1973	117	114
1953	227*	262	1974	150	134
1954	228	262	1975	180	167
1955	190	208	1976	180	169
1956	162	181	1977	137	170
1957	153	179	1978	111	136
1958	124	148	1979	83	108
1959	153	128	1980	59	110
1960	131	133	1981	41	88
1961	127	122	1982	57	54
1962	144	135	1983	54	55
1963	175	130	1984	44	55
1964	185	162	1985	37	44
1965	189	175	1986	36	38
1966	193	187	1987	34	34

Note: * Starts exclude Northern Ireland 1946 to 1953

Source: Holmans, A. *Housing Policy in Britain*, Table A on p.157
(adjusted)
Annual Abstract of Statistics No. 88, Table 91 (HMSO)
Housing Statistics Great Britain No. 7, Table 2 (HMSO)
Housing Statistics Great Britain No. 24, Table 2 (HMSO)
Housing and Construction Statistics Great Britain 1970-
1980, Table 71 (HMSO)
Housing and Construction Statistics Great Britain 1978-
1988, Table 6.1 (HMSO)

III   The landlord organisations

There are 471 municipal, or local authority landlords, including 11 new towns, in Great Britain (England, Scotland and Wales). In April 1986, their average stock was 12,200 dwellings, ranging from 141 in the Isles of Scilly to just under 124,000 in Birmingham and just under 170,000 in Glasgow. The greatest concentration of large local authority landlords is in Inner London, where six boroughs have more than 40,000 dwellings.[10]

In addition, Scotland has the Scottish Special Housing Association (SSHA), a body established in 1937 and financed by central government to design, provide and manage social rented housing. SSHA now owns about 86,000 homes throughout Scotland. Despite its name, SSHA has a wide remit. In addition to providing housing for special needs, it also caters for general needs, and in particular provides new and rehabilitated housing in inner urban areas such as Glasgow, and housing for incoming workers in areas of industrial growth.[11]

Since 1971, all rented housing previously provided by local authority and other public sector landlords in Northern Ireland has been owned and managed by the Northern Ireland Housing Executive (NIHE). This is a body funded directly by central government and answerable to the Secretary of State for Northern Ireland who appoints six of its nine members (including the chairman and vice-chairman), and to the Housing Council which represents local authority interests and nominates up to three members of the Executive. In 1987, the total NIHE stock amounted to about 173,000 dwellings.

Including new towns, the SSHA and the NIHE, the local authority sector in the United Kingdom in 1985 amounted to some 6,150,000 dwellings, or about 27% of the total stock.

Local authorities

Local authorities in Great Britain have virtually no counterpart in other countries of western Europe as landlords of social rented housing. Nor do the political parties in other countries have anything like the same polarisation of attitudes towards housing tenure as exists in the United Kingdom. The British politically based social housing service answering directly to housing committees of municipal councils therefore sets this country apart from the others which are considered in this study. As will be seen,

the municipalities and sometimes the higher tiers of local
government in other countries may often have some say in what
social housing is provided, where it is situated, and who gets it, and
they often have some involvement in its initial funding. However,
apart from the relatively small-scale role of municipal landlord
organisations in the Netherlands (see Chapter 4, Section III), no
other country in western Europe has given its local authorities any
major responsibility as direct providers and managers of housing.

Relationships within local authorities

In later chapters, we look at the relationships between social
landlord organisations in other countries and the municipalities
where they operate. However, in Great Britain (but not Northern
Ireland, where social rented housing is largely in the hands of the
centrally run NIHE), the relationships are almost entirely within the
local authority itself. At first sight, the prospects for a soundly
based development programme are enhanced if planners, housing
managers, and architects are all part of the same organisation.
Similarly, tenants should be able to expect effectively coordinated
service delivery if lettings, repairs, rent collection, street cleansing,
grass cutting, and refuse removal come under the same head.

Reality has, however, often failed to match these apparently
reasonable expectations. Most housing managers can point to
housing of the wrong kind, or in the wrong place, built in response
to a political or departmental whim. Despite the more sensitive
local authority line management arrangements developed over the
past decade, many housing managers still complain of cumbersome
inter-departmental structures which have developed piecemeal, and
which exacerbate rivalries.

For example, rent collection and arrears chasing is often the
preserve of the treasurer's department with its own computer
system and little personal contact with those responsible for letting
the housing and dealing with the tenants. Similarly, tenants may be
required to request repairs from yet another department of the local
authority, the direct labour organisation. The parks department is
responsible for cutting the grass and maintaining open spaces,
while the cleansing department is often responsible for keeping
estate roads and pathways clean. Moreover, although the local
authority will almost inevitably have its system of internal
accounting transfers to charge the housing department for the
various ancillary services, the housing department just as inevitably

lacks any effective sanctions to ensure effective delivery of these services.   Nor - unlike housing organisations in the other west European countries covered by this study - do local authorities view their estates as 'cost centres', and still less do they have local estate budgets.

The diverse organisational and accounting arrangements of a selection of local authorities are described in *The Organisation of Housing Management in English Local Authorities* by Keith Kirby, Helen Finch and Douglas Wood (HMSO, 1988).   Section VII below looks at ways in which some local authorities are attempting to break down inter-departmental barriers and to introduce greater local accountability.

Relationships with central government

Municipal housing departments have close links with central government.   In England this is almost entirely through the ten regional offices of the Department of the Environment, and in Scotland and Wales through the Scottish Development Department and the Welsh Office respectively.   Until 1979, central government laid down detailed standards and cost limits for housing projects, and approved them individually.   With tighter overall controls on local government expenditure, with the progressive erosion of capital subsidies, and with the reduction in regional office staff levels, the emphasis in the relationship between municipal housing departments and central government in the 1980s has shifted.   It now tends towards more general concerns about financial resources, the implementation of the tenants' statutory right to buy their homes, the growing incidence of homelessness (for whom British local authorities alone among those covered by this study have a statutory responsibility), the deteriorating condition of the stock, management problems, and latterly, the role of local authorities as social landlords.   Insofar as they relate to the interests of an individual local authority, these issues are picked up in discussions with Regional Offices during the annual Housing Investment Programme (HIP) round, with ministers and officials at the DOE in London, with the Department's professional advisers in its Housing Services Advisory Unit (HSAU), and with its Priority Estates Project (PEP) consultants.   Both HSAU and PEP are key parts of the DOE's Estate Action team which is considered in greater detail in Section VII.

Relationships between local authorities

The main link between municipal housing departments on service delivery is in the mobility arrangements which have been set up to help tenants to move home within the social rented sector. The most important is the National Mobility Scheme, under which virtually all local authorities in the United Kingdom, including the NIHE, SSHA, and the larger housing associations, agree to reserve 1% of their lettings for people outside their areas who want to move for job or family reasons. Tenants throughout the social rented sector also have a widely drawn statutory right under the 1984 Housing and Building Control Act to exchange their homes.

In addition to the national mechanisms for brokering good housing practice and channelling the views of municipal housing departments which are discussed elsewhere in this section, the Institute of Housing (see below) has a well developed regional organisation in most parts of the country. There are also a few independently organised regional groups of local authorities, most notably the Northern Consortium of Housing Authorities, which fulfil a similar function.

At the national level, the local authority associations are a major source of advice and information to their member local authorities, and represent their views to central government. As their members tend to be concentrated among local authorities of different kinds, and from different geographical areas - large and small, urban and rural, Scotland or London - each has its own clear political emphasis.

The Institute of Housing

Although the Institute of Housing also acts as a lobby for the interests of the social rented sector, its main function is to lay down the professional standards for housing management. It approves the courses at colleges and universities which lead to its professional qualification, and itself provides training courses on specific issues. According to a survey which the Institute carried out among its membership in 1986, about 7% of local authority housing staff (and about 9% of housing association staff) have a professional qualification, most commonly that of the Institute itself.

In its main role as the body representing the professional interests of housing managers, the Institute is the successor to a peculiarly British tradition without any real counterpart in the countries covered by this study, although as will be seen, the larger of the umbrella organisations for the housing association movement in the Netherlands is beginning to move in the same direction. The history of housing management as a profession in the United Kingdom has been fully documented elsewhere, most recently in Anne Power's *Property before People* (Allen and Unwin, 1987) and need not be repeated here. In essence, what sets British housing managers apart from their European colleagues is the formal and specific professional qualification which is a virtual requirement for all who aim to reach the top positions in local government housing, and a strong sense of social mission towards the tenant, which may well override the business relationship between tenant and landlord.

Housing associations

There are about 2,600 'registered' (see below) housing associations operating throughout Great Britain, with a total stock of about 533,000 dwellings in 1986, or about 2.5% of the overall stock. In addition, the housing association movement provides about 38,600 bed spaces in hostels. As was shown in Section I, some of them were founded in the 19th century, but for the most part they stem from the late 1970s following the introduction of capital subsidies under the 1974 Housing Act.

Housing associations are non-profit bodies run by committees of volunteers. They cater for a wide range of people, but concentrate on the socially disadvantaged and groups with special needs including older people (who comprised 34% of new lettings by housing associations in 1988), single parent families (13% of new lettings), and minority ethnic groups (12% of new lettings). As will be seen in Section VII, housing associations also play an important part in the promotion of housing cooperatives.

Housing associations are nearly all locally based, and mostly very small. Nearly half of them own less than 100 dwellings. On the other hand, just over 100 associations own nearly 70% of the total stock, although only 7 of them own more than 10,000 dwellings.

Housing associations maintain close relationships with the local authorities in whose areas they operate, and their work is covered in the annual HIP returns which local authorities make to central government about local housing activity and needs. Local authorities can and often do finance some of their projects, usually in return for nomination rights to tenancies.

The bulk of housing association capital work is financed by the government-sponsored Housing Corporation, which is also responsible for approving, or 'registering' all housing associations which receive support from public funds (see Section IV), and for monitoring their continuing performance. For most practical purposes, the Housing Corporation is therefore the proxy for central government in dealings with individual housing associations.

Most housing associations are members of the National Federation of Housing Associations (NFHA), which - like its counterparts in the UNFOHLM in France, the GGW in Germany, and the NWR and NICV in the Netherlands (all of which are covered in subsequent chapters) - is an umbrella organisation acting both as a lobby for the movement as a whole, and as a source of advice to individual housing associations.

Home ownership

Although the main contribution by public sector landlords - local authorities, new towns, and housing associations - to home ownership has been with the introduction of the statutory right to buy their homes for most tenants under the 1980 Housing Act (see Section II), the public sector has long since had a significant role in promoting owner-occupation, and this activity has been stepped up since 1979. By the end of 1987, over 1,000,000 sitting tenants in Great Britain had bought their homes since the Act came into force, and in addition, some 51,000 households had become owner-occupiers under the 'low-cost home ownership' schemes promoted by the government.

In particular, housing associations are active contributors to home ownership. In the three years between 1983/84 and 1985/86, an annual average of over 7,000 dwellings were provided by housing associations for owner-occupation.

IV Finance

The history of local authority housing finance is comprehensively covered in Chapter VII of Alan Holmans' *Housing Policy in Britain* (Croom Helm, 1987). What follows here is a brief account of the financial arrangements which have had a particular bearing on the ways in which local authority housing has been produced, maintained and managed in the United Kingdom.

From the early years of this century, in this country as in the others covered by this study, governments have accepted the principle that in order to achieve rents which could be afforded by the people for whom social housing was intended, some form of subsidy on the cost of providing the housing was inevitable. From the time of planning the 'homes for heroes' who would return from the First World War, there has been a continuing tension between central and local government about the extent to which each should carry the cost of that subsidy. This tension has habitually sharpened during periods of high land and building costs, high interest rates, or wider economic difficulty. In the inter-war years, subsidies from central government normally took the form of an annual payment per dwelling (or per family rehoused under slum clearance legislation), with a further contribution from the local ratepayers where necessary to bring the rents down to an affordable level.

The 1935 Housing Act introduced, however, three financial policies which were to have profound effects on British social housing, reaching down to the present. First, it broke with the principle that housing provided under the various Acts should be treated as separate cost centres, and so paved the way for 'pooling', or cross-subsidisation, which distinguishes British housing financial practice so fundamentally from what is done elsewhere. Second, under the single Housing Revenue Account (HRA) arrangements which local authorities were now obliged to set up, rent levels became explicitly very much a matter for local decision, as long as they were "reasonable", and any deficit which might result could be made up by a subsidy from local ratepayers as a whole. Third, it gave local authorities wide powers to give rent rebates to individual tenants.

Rent pooling

Unlike its European neighbours, the United Kingdom emerged from the Second World War with a substantial stock of over 1,000,000 dwellings in the social rented sector, where as a result of the wartime inflation, the real running costs (and rents and subsidies) were at a very low level. Table 1.5 gives comparisons between 1938/39 and 1945/46.

Table 1.5:   Comparison of 1938/39 and 1945/46 HRA expenditure
and income per dwelling (1938/39 prices)

| | Expenditure (£) | | | | Income(£) | |
	Loan charges	Other costs	Total costs	Rents etc	Exchequer & Rate Fund subsidies	Total income
1938/39	29.0	8.2	37.2	20.9	16.6	37.5
1945/46	16.6	6.1	22.7	13.7	10.3	24.0

Source: Holmans, A. *Housing Policy in Britain*, p 318 (Croom
Helm, 1987)

This volume of low-cost, low-rent housing in itself offered a
firm foundation for the cross-subsidisation of the expensive
housing which was to come as standards improved, and costs and
interest rates escalated in the 1960s and beyond. However, the
scope for pooling was to be further increased by the low interest
borrowing for house-building which local authorities were able to
make - and indeed were obliged to make - from the Public Works
Loans Board in the late 1940s. In 1955, pooling (and rent
increases) became a staple feature of central government policy to
contain Exchequer subsidies.

The following year, the 1956 Housing Subsidies Act reinforced
the supplementary subsidies to encourage high-rise building,
particularly in order to further the slum clearance programme, and
to economise in the use of land. The height profile of the stock will
be examined in Section V.

Changes in rent levels

Between 1955 and 1970, rents almost doubled in real terms,
because of macro-economic policies and the declining scope for
financing the housing programme through pooling alone. The
absence of any perceptible gain to the existing tenants, and the
jerky nature of the rent increases, were a further cause of
dissatisfaction. The increases continued into the early 1970s as the
1972 Housing Finance Act sought to break entirely any link
between costs and rents, and to bring local authority rents by quite
steep phasing up to the fair rent levels of the private rented sector.

At the same time, the government introduced a national system of rent rebates and allowances.

The 1972 reforms, however, ultimately fell victim to the price and rent controls introduced by the Labour government of 1974 to combat the steep inflation of the mid-1970s. These put an end to the projected rent rises, while the huge increases in interest rates proceeded to inflate the Exchequer's subsidy bills under what had become in effect an open-ended subsidy system. Between 1975 and 1979, rents fell in real terms, followed by a sharp real increase in the early 1980s. Between 1975/76 and 1979/80, Exchequer subsidy rather more than doubled in cash terms, and increased by nearly 30% in real terms.

Local authority subsidy arrangements in the 1980s

The 1980s subsidy arrangements were introduced in 1981/82 under the new rules laid down in the 1980 Housing Act. Under these arrangements, the local authority receives the same level of subsidy as it did in the previous year, increased by an inflation factor (set by the government) for rising management and maintenance costs, and reduced by the aggregate rise in rent level which the government regards as appropriate in the coming year. Additional subsidy is also available to cover three-quarters of the loan charges on new capital expenditure on housing - new-build and renovation work - during the previous year. The government's assumptions about the appropriate levels of rent increase greatly reduced the number of local authorities eligible for subsidy. In 1981/82, 19 out of 20 local authorities were in receipt of subsidy; by 1986/87, this had dropped to 1 in 4 mainly metropolitan districts and London boroughs. However, the number has risen again following the introduction of the new financial régime (see below).

As will be seen, in principle, the 1980s subsidy system applies not only to bricks and mortar capital expenditure but also to some HRA running costs. It thus has something in common with the only previous measure which offered such support - the 1972 Housing Finance Act, under which management and maintenance expenditure reached unprecedented levels. However, in practice the only local authorities to benefit in this way, and indeed from subsidies at all, are inner city authorities with a large proportion of recent, high-cost loans to service, and with particularly high management and maintenance costs.

There was a radical shift in the 1980s from bricks and mortar subsidies to personal subsidies (housing benefit) coupled with a growing view that the HRA should be able to support itself without recourse to the local ratepayers. In July 1988, the government therefore published proposals to reduce the wide disparities which exist between local authorities in their receipts from rent and Exchequer and local subsidies, and to increase incentives to greater management efficiency.

These proposals led to the "new financial régime" which makes major changes to the existing system generally, not only as regards housing. From 1990/91, capital finance arrangements were changed in order to control borrowing rather than spending. HIP allocations under the new system specifically take into account the availability to a local authority of capital receipts for reinvestment. From April 1990, HRAs were 'ring-fenced' so that local authorities can no longer cross-subsidise their tenants at the expense of the local community as a whole.

Housing association subsidies

While bricks and mortar subsidies for municipal housing have effectively been a combination of rather lower than market interest rates on borrowed capital, combined with recurring deficit payments to keep rents down to affordable levels, the system which has applied to housing associations since the 1974 Housing Act relies mainly on a one-off capital grant; Housing Association Grant or HAG. This is payable on completion of a new-build or renovation project, and bridges the gap between the total capital cost and that part of it on which the loan charges can be met by the 'fair' rent after deduction of a set rate of management and maintenance allowances.

In practice, HAG typically amounts to some 90% of the capital cost of the project, and can be even higher in high cost areas such as London. Table 1.6 gives a simplified example of an HAG calculation.

The HAG system enables housing associations to break even on their new projects from the outset, and without further recourse to subsidy. However, when it was introduced, it made no provision for claw-back of excessive profits in the longer term if rents rise faster than management and maintenance costs. (Loan charges normally remain the same.) The 1980 Housing Act therefore brought in Grant Redemption Funds (GRF) to enable the government to recoup surpluses.   GRF proceeds have not been significant.

Table 1.6:   Housing Association Grant calculation

	£
Qualifying capital cost of, say, 10 units	500,000
Gross annual rental income (@ £19.16 weekly per unit)	10,000
Running costs (management and maintenance)	4,000
Net annual income	6,000
Capitalised net annual income (60 years at 12%)	5,000
Thus, HAG is capital cost	50,000
less capitalised income	5,000
	450,000

Source: Constructed from information supplied by Department of the Environment

Conversely, some housing associations, normally the older-established ones with expensively financed projects which were completed before the introduction of HAG, are unable to balance their books without recourse to further subsidy.   In these circumstances, Revenue Deficit Grant (RDG) is available to meet the gap between reasonable expenditure and the income from fair rents.   The rent increases which have taken place over the last decade have greatly reduced the incidence of RDG, which in 1985/86 amounted in total to £11 million paid to 131 housing associations, compared with £38 million to 494 housing associations in 1982/83.

Under proposals piloted in 1987 and the subject of a consultation paper in September 1987, the government is encouraging housing associations to mix private and public sector funding in order to expand their programmes with less recourse to HAG.   In 1987/88, £20 million was added to the Housing Corporation's programme to enable housing associations to

combine HAG at 30% with private funding (usually in the form of
a low-start mortgage) in schemes specifically designed to provide
decent interim accommodation for homeless families, and flat
sharing schemes for young job-movers. In a further move to
promote financial independence, housing associations have been
asked to use the discretion conferred by rent deregulation for new
lettings under the 1988 Housing Act to set 'sensible' rents, with
HAG fixed at set levels rather than being tied to fair rents.

The shift towards personal subsidies

The end of the 1970s marked the watershed between general bricks
and mortar subsidies and housing benefits to individuals. As has
been shown in Section II, there were already signs a decade earlier
that the mass programme of social rented housing was beginning to
run its course. As has been shown above, rent rebates existed
already in the inter-war period, and in 1965/66 nearly one in ten
local authority tenants were estimated to be receiving this form of
support. By 1974/75, the number had increased to one in five.

In 1979, the new Conservative government not only embarked
on a sharp reduction in capital expenditure, but also reverted to its
predecessor's policy in 1972 of encouraging large rent increases,
through the operation of the subsidy system (see above). At the
same time, tenants in need would be compensated by the
availability of housing benefits under the new arrangements which
were introduced at this time.

Table 1.7: Exchequer subsidies to the social rented sector (1985/86
prices)

	1979/80	1986/87
Bricks and mortar subsidies to local authorities and housing associations	3,900	1,700
Housing benefits	2,030	4,300
Totals	5,930	6,000

Source: Constructed from infomation supplied by Department of
the Environment

As Tables 1.7 and 1.8 show, the changes have been dramatic. While the total subsidy bill in England has remained almost static in real terms, expenditure on bricks and mortar subsidies between 1979/80 and 1986/87 has been halved, in contrast with housing benefits which have doubled in the same period. The increase in the bill for housing benefits is due not only to growing unemployment among tenants (see Section VI) but also to the sharp rises in rents.

Table 1.8:   Average rents in England and Wales (before deduction of rate rebates or housing benefit)

	Weekly rent	
	Current prices £	1986/87 prices £
1966/67	1.57	10.00
1971/72	2.48	11.85
1973/74	3.57	14.40
1976/77	4.91	11.70
1979/80	6.50	10.85
1982/83	13.58	16.30
1986/87	16.54	16.54

Source: Constructed from information supplied by Department of the Environment

The trend from new-build to renovation

As in the other countries covered by this study, there has been a significant shift from expenditure on new construction to expenditure on renovation and modernisation in the last two decades. Indeed, as will be seen, it has been much more marked in this country than elsewhere. In 1985/86, English local authorities renovated a total of 95,800 dwellings at a total cost of some £400 million, or more than £4,000 per dwelling. Table 1.9 shows the trend towards renovation work and away from new-build between 1971/72 and 1986/87. This trend has been no less marked in Northern Ireland, Scotland and Wales.

Table 1.9: Capital expenditure by English local authorities on new-build and renovation, excluding land, 1971/72 to 1986/87

	New-build			Renovation			Total	
Actual prices £(million)	Constant prices 1986/87 £(million)	%	Actual prices £(million)	Constant prices 1986/87 £(million)	%	Actual prices £(million)	Constant prices 1986/87 £(million)
1971/72	429.0	2,257.9	81.4	98.2	516.9	18.6	527.2	2,774.7
1975/76	1,159.4	3,238.5	79.1	305.6	853.6	20.9	1,465.0	4,092.1
1981/82	719.8	922.8	53.7	620.4	795.4	46.3	1,340.2	1,718.2
1982/83	685.2	819.6	41.6	962.4	1,151.2	58.4	1,647.6	1,920.8
1983/84	682.4	779.9	37.3	1,148.2	1,312.2	62.7	1,830.6	2,092.1
1984/85	729.5	798.1	36.3	1,280.1	1,400.5	63.7	2,009.6	2,198.6
1985/86	578.8	597.9	30.6	1,312.0	1,355.4	69.4	1,890.8	1,953.3
1986/87	457.5	457.5	23.2	1,511.6	1,511.6	76.8	1,969.1	1,969.1

Source: Constructed from information supplied by Department of the Environment

The renovation needs of the stock will be examined in greater detail in Section V.

V   The buildings

This section concentrates on the local authority stock in England, with supplementary information about the housing association stock and about the stock in Northern Ireland, Scotland and Wales wherever the position differs significantly from that in England.

The English housing stock differs from that in France, Germany, the Netherlands, and the Soviet Union in two major ways. First, in age profile it is older, with a much greater proportion built before the Second World War, and with the peak in post-war production coming earlier than elsewhere. Second, the majority of the English (but not the Scottish or housing association stock) consists of houses rather than flats. Tables 1.10 and 1.11 show the age profile and built form of the local authority stock in England.

Although local authorities bought in ('municipalised') significant amounts of old private sector property in the 1960s and 1970s, the proportion of their stock which dates from before the First World War is much smaller than the roughly one in four figure for the stock as a whole (see Section I).

Table 1.10: Age profile of the local authority stock in England

	Number (thousands)	%
Pre-1914	115	2.33
1919-1939	960	19.43
1945-1950	450	9.11
1951-1960	1,225	24.80
1961-1970	1,130	22.87
1971-1980	900	18.22
1981-1985	160	3.24
Total	4,940	100.00

Source: Department of the Environment estimates, based on completions

Table 1.11: Distribution of local authority dwellings in England by built form

	Number (thousands)	%
Houses	2,867	62.8
Low-rise flats and maisonettes	1,243	27.2
High-rise flats	299	6.6
Unclassified	155	3.4
Total	4,564	100.0

Source: Department of the Environment Inquiry into the condition of the local authority stock in England 1985, constructed from Table 1

The share of the local authority stock built between the wars is, however, much closer to the proportion in the stock as a whole. Housing associations, which provide about a third of their dwellings in housing bought from the private sector and then rehabilitated, can be expected to have a higher proportion of older dwellings.

As has already been shown in Section II, the 1950s were the high point for local authority housing in England, although the programme continued at a high rate through the 1960s. This was the time when flats and industrial building techniques took over from traditionally built houses as the most common form of housing in the local authority sector. The striking feature of the height profile of the stock is the way in which low-rise flats and maisonettes outnumber high-rise flats by four to one. We return in Section VII to the links between built form and management problems.

Obligatory standards for local authority housing in England were laid down in successive Housing Manuals dating back to 1919. They culminated in the "Parker Morris standards" which were published on an advisory basis in 1961, and made obligatory in 1967 in Circular 36/67 issued by the then Ministry of Housing and Local Government (MHLG). The Parker Morris standards were concerned not only with space and heating levels, but also with other amenities such as provision for car-parking, storage, children's play, adequate electricity points, sanitation, refuse disposal, lifts, and sound insulation. They fulfilled the post-war aims for decent standards in social housing, but also contributed to the steep rise in housing costs in the 1960s and 1970s. They were abolished in 1980 when the government made standards a matter for local authority discretion.

As Table 1.12 shows, according to 1984 figures, the majority of local authority dwellings in England have four or five rooms including kitchen. Two out of five have three bedrooms, and virtually all the remainder have one or two bedrooms.

Table 1.12:   Number of rooms: public sector dwellings 1984
              (England)

Number of rooms	Number of households (thousands)	Number of rooms	Number of households (thousands)
1	17	5	1,570
2	160	6	770
3	990	7 or more	97
4	1,430		
		Total	5,030

Sources: Department of the Environment Housing Trailers to the
           1981 and 1984 *Labour Force Surveys* Table 2.11 (HMSO,
           1988)

Table 1.13 gives the floor areas for different types of dwelling in
1977, showing that over half the stock at that time consisted of
dwellings between 90 and 110 square metres (measured externally,
including walls). Not surprisingly, houses are generally larger than
flats, which in turn accounts for the higher average size of English
local authority dwellings in comparison with their European
counterparts described in later chapters of this study. However, it
should be borne in mind that the distribution by area in particular
will have changed to some extent since 1977, mainly because more
houses than flats have been sold to their tenants under the Right to
Buy.

Local authority dwellings are well equipped, with 98% of them
having all the basic amenities, according to the 1986 *English House
Condition Survey*. This compares with 99% in the owner-occupied
sector, and 92% in the private rented sector. Similarly, the 1984
Northern Ireland House Condition Survey showed that 98% of
NIHE dwellings had all the basic amenities, compared with 93% of
owner-occupied dwellings, and 66% in the private rented sector.

Table 1.13: **English local authority dwellings by type and floor area (1977)**

Floor area in square metres	Detached and semi-detached houses	(thousands) Terraced houses	Flats	Total
<50	39	35	721	795
50-60	60	66	330	456
60-70	78	65	134	277
70-80	163	198	72	433
80-90	377	407	37	821
90-100	503	527	11	1,042
100-110	270	264	6	540
110-120	66	58	1	125
>120	37	43	3	83
Total of dwellings for which information was provided	1,593	1,664	1,316	4,572

Source: *National Dwelling and Housing Survey,* unpublished data supplied by Department of the Environment

Table 1.14 gives more detailed information about standards of amenity in the local authority stock.

Table 1.14: **English local authority dwellings: amenities (1986)**

	(thousands)
All dwellings	4,490
Of which: dwellings with all the basic amenities	4,418
dwellings lacking: inside WC	22
fixed bath in bathroom	23
wash basin	23
sink	0
hot water supply to bath, hand basin and sink	45

Source: *English House Condition Survey 1986,* Table A 4.1 (DOE, 1988)

As was shown in the financial trends given in Section IV, there has been a marked shift towards the renovation of the existing stock over the last two decades. Comparative unit figures for new-build and renovation by English local authorities between 1966 and 1985 are given in Table 1.15.

Table 1.15: Number of dwellings completed and improved by English local authorities

	(thousands) Units completed	Units improved
1966-1970	689	161*
1971-1975	489	376
1976-1980	472	291
1981-1985	168	381

Note: * 1966-1970 figures include Wales - estimated at 5% of total

Source: **Information provided by Department of the Environment**

Although the trend towards renovation of the existing stock is significant, progress in this direction is generally accepted as being far from adequate. According to local authorities' estimates for the Inquiry into the Condition of the Local Authority Housing Stock in England, carried out by the Department of the Environment in 1985, 3,836,000 dwellings, or 84% of the stock, needed expenditure totalling £18,844 million, at an average cost of £4,900 a dwelling. According to the 1985/86 *Northern Ireland Housing Executive Public Sector Survey*, 169,000 NIHE dwellings (95% of the stock) needed expenditure totalling £640 million, an average of £3,800 per dwelling.

There are considerable variations according to the age and type of property. For example, a smaller proportion of English local authority housing built before the Second World War needs improvement, probably because this is where local authorities have concentrated their energies and resources so far. However, where work is needed on these dwellings, the costs are relatively high.

Conversely, much more housing built in the first two decades after the Second World War needs improvement - mostly at costs rather higher than the £4,900 average - probably because few local authorities have as yet done much work on this stock. Overall,

improvement work on flats is more costly than on houses, and
dwellings built by non-traditional methods are more costly to
improve than traditionally built dwellings. Table 1.16 gives a
breakdown of the main categories of work which local authorities
consider necessary, with estimated total costs.

**Table 1.16: Local authority housing in England: renovation needs by
category of work and cost (1985)**

Category of work	£ (million) Estimated total cost
Repairs to structure and external fabric	7,306
Rewiring and plumbing etc	1,498
Asbestos treatment and fire protection	282
Heating, insulation and works to remedy condensation	4,028
Modernisation of plan arrangement, kitchens, bathrooms and WCs	3,610
Conversions, adaptations for elderly and disabled	773
Repairs and improvements to common parts and environment	1,304
Demolition	43
Total	18,804

Source: Department of the Environment Inquiry into the
Condition of the Local Authority Housing Stock in
England, 1985, constructed from Table 5

As will be seen, by far the largest item is major structural work,
followed by measures to provide adequate heating, and to
modernise the dwellings internally. Work on the common parts of
blocks and to the environment is also a significant item. Section
VII suggests which physical improvement work is most relevant to
management problems.

VI   The tenants

As was shown in Section II, the role of local authorities in the
United Kingdom has since the 1930s been to provide housing for
two distinct categories of tenant; members of the artisan class and

relatively well-off manual workers on the one hand, and former occupants of slum property on the other. Traditionally, the unifying characteristic between them has been that in the view of their local authority landlords, they were in 'need' of decent subsidised housing, and indeed, the 1949 Housing Act repealed the previous references to the working classes. In *Property before People* (Allen and Unwin, 1987), Anne Power outlines the subjective methodologies which local authorities have developed to evaluate the claims of their prospective tenants.

From the early days, this role of local authorities as providers to supplicants has left an enduring and adverse mark on the reputation of council housing in the country at large. With the better-off artisan class of tenants who continued to form the great majority of local authorities' clients from the beginning of the inter-war period, there was persistent popular suspicion that government subsidies were ill-directed and even unnecessary. The stereotype of the council tenant living in luxury at the expense of the rest of the community goes back to the Depression of 1926 and beyond. Similarly, estates populated by families cleared from the slums often became stigmatised with the 'coal in the bath' image.

The 1970s and 1980s have seen a major change not only in the composition of the body of tenants in the social rented sector in the United Kingdom, but also in the attitude of society as a whole towards them. Rising unemployment, the growing incidence of family breakdowns and single parent families, and the statutory Right to Buy have all led to a generally acknowledged concentration of the underprivileged in council housing, while the shift of subsidies from bricks and mortar to individuals in the social rented sector (and the growth in subsidies to owner-occupiers) have tended to reverse the old resentments between the tenures.

A detailed account of trends in family breakdown by tenure is provided by an article by Holmans, Nandy and Brown in *Social Trends 1987*. This shows not only that tenants are more prone to divorce than are owner-occupiers, but also that marriage breakdowns among owner-occupiers lead to increasing demands on the social rented sector, estimated at some 15,000 a year.

An indication of the extent to which the social rented sector caters for the underprivileged is provided by the trend in the number of homeless households accepted by local authorities. In 1987, just over 118,000 households were accepted by local authorities in England and Wales, 90% of them classified as "in priority need", such as households with dependent children, for whom local authorities are statutorily bound to provide accommodation. This compares with 97,000 in 1984, and - although the figure is not fully comparable because of a change in the reporting system - 83,000 in 1981.[12] The public sector houses a relatively higher proportion of households in groups which are generally considered to be socially and economically disadvantaged; the unemployed, single parent families, and those where the household head comes from a minority ethnic group. Table 1.17 gives comparisons of numbers and percentages in these groups.

Table 1.17: Heads of household who are unemployed, single parents, or members of ethnic minorities 1984 (England)

	All tenures Number (thousands)	%	Public sector tenants Number (thousands)	%
All households	17,940	100.0	5,030	100.0
Household head				
unemployed	1,240	6.9	670	13.3
single parent	1,370	7.6	700	13.9
member of ethnic				
(non-white) minority	660	3.7	220	4.4

Source: Department of the Environment, Housing Trailers for the 1981 and 1984 *Labour Force Survey*, Tables 2.5 and 3.2 (HMSO, 1988)

It should be noted that households headed by someone of West Indian origin are twice as likely to live in local authority housing than those with a white head of household, and four times as likely as those with an Indian, Pakistani or Bangladeshi head of household. Table 1.18 gives the distribution between tenures in 1984 by ethnic origin of the head of household.

Table 1.18:   Household tenure by ethnic origin of head of household, 1984 (England)

Tenure (%)	White	West Indian	Pakistani/ Bangladeshi	Indian	Other/ Mixed	All Non White
Owner-occupied	62	35	72	77	37	52
Rented from LA	26	53	16	11	29	29
Other rented	12	13	12	12	34	19
Total households (thousands)	17,140	190	80	190	200	660

Source: Department of the Environment, Housing Trailers to the 1981 and 1984 *Labour Force Surveys* Table 3.4 (HMSO, 1988)

   The total of 660,000 non-white household heads in England in 1984 accounts for just under 4% of all households. This is double the proportion in Great Britain in 1971/72 according to the *General Household Survey* report published in 1972. As Table 1.19 shows, as well as a significant shift by white households from both rented sectors into owner-occupation, there has also been a substantial movement by non-white households from private renting into the public rented sector.

Table 1.19:   Tenure of household heads according to colour in 1971/72 (Great Britain)

	Owner-occupied %	Local authority tenant %	Other tenant %
Non-white	50	19	32
White	49	32	19

Source: *General Household Survey* 1972, Table 2.36 (OPCS, 1975)

   As Table 1.20 shows, the overall number of housing benefit recipients tended to rise between 1983 (when the system was fully introduced) and 1985, although the numbers were affected by changes designed to contain the number of claimants on the 'standard' scheme.   That is, the category of householders who receive help only with their housing costs, as against 'certificated' householders, whose incomes are low enough to make them eligible for social security 'supplementary benefit' help as well. Three out of five of this least well-off group are local authority tenants, although the social rented sector represents less than a third of the stock as a whole.

Table 1.20: Housing benefits (Great Britain)

	1983 Cert. Stand householders		1984 Cert. Stand. householders		1985 Cert.Stand householders	
Type of rebate (thousands) Rent rebates and						
allowances	2,360	2,220	2,530	2,230	2,580	2,140
Rate rebates	2,980	3,660	3,210	3,620	3,310	3,540
Recipients by tenure (% rounded)						
Owner-occupiers	20	45	20	45	20	40
LA tenants	60	50	60	45	60	45
Private tenants	20	10	15	10	20	10

Source: Constructed from information supplied by Department of Health and Social Security

It therefore comes as no surprise that local authority tenant households are characterised by low income and low numbers of economically active members. Table 1.21 shows in particular a preponderance of low income, economically inactive people in the local authority sector, and a low proportion of households with gross incomes (in 1985) of over £200 a week.

44 The United Kingdom

Table 1.21: Tenure by gross normal weekly household income and by number of economically active people, 1985 (United Kingdom)

	Owner-occupied		Local authority/ new town	Rented Unfurn- ished private	Furn- ished private	Sample size (Nos)
	Owned outright	Owned with mortgage				
Gross normal weekly household income (%)						
Economically active heads						
< £100	17	19	40	15	9	313
£100-£150	17	37	29	12	4	519
£150-£200	15	47	25	9	4	676
£200-£250	13	62	18	4	3	735
£250-£300	12	68	15	3	1	609
> £300	13	74	8	4	1	1,407
Economically inactive heads						
< £50	21	2	60	13	4	782
£50-£100	34	5	48	11	1	1,054
£100-£150	42	10	36	10	1	393
> £150	55	13	42	7	2	524
Number of economically active people in household (%)						
None	36	4	36	11	2	2,281
One	18	44	24	9	5	2,043
Two	12	64	17	5	2	1,993
Three or more	19	55	20	6	-	695
All households (%)	23	38	29	8	2	7,012

Source: *Family Expenditure Survey 1985*, Table 5 (Department of Employment, 1986)

The gap between low-income local authority tenants and other householders, particularly owner-occupiers is further emphasised by their weekly expenditure on housing (see Table 1.22). These figures include payments as appropriate for net mortgage costs, rent after receipt of housing benefits, rates and water charges, maintenance and insurance. Local authority tenants with a gross weekly income (in 1985) of under £100 spend significantly less than the rest, largely because of the impact of housing benefits.

Table 1.22: Expenditure on housing by tenure and household
income, 1985 (United Kingdom)

	Gross normal weekly household income						
	<£100	£100-£150	£150-£200	£200-£250	£250-£300	>£300	All
Owner-occupiers							
In process of purchase	27.01	33.47	38.33	41.73	47.66	59.56	47.84
Owned outright	8.78	11.74	11.14	15.05	32.99	19.85	13.68
LA tenants	6.86	17.78	22.68	25.61	29.00	31.92	14.48
Private rented							
Unfurnished	9.57	19.00	20.65	22.11	24.42	25.16	15.44
Furnished	13.40	27.16	30.63	29.04	*	64.04	24.80
Number of households in sample	2,107	882	872	847	658	1,500	6,866

Note: * Too few households in sample

Source: *Family Expenditure Survey 1985*, Table 5 (Department of Employment, 1986)

Rent payments account on average for about 10% of council tenants' income (after deduction of housing benefit, income tax, and national insurance contributions). Table 1.23 gives a detailed breakdown of the proportion of income going on rent at 1986 levels.

Not surprisingly, the higher the household income, the lower the proportion going on rent. However, less than one in five households in local authority housing has a net income of over £8,000. Households with net incomes between £4,000 and £6,000 a year tend to spend the highest proportion of their incomes on rent, at a median level of 13%. However, rents of those with net incomes of less than £3,000 - who account for more than one in four households - amount to a median level of 11%. In all cases, these figures exclude the roughly one in three households whose rent is entirely covered by housing benefit.

Table: 1.23 Net rent as a proportion of local authority tenants' net household income (Great Britain, 1986)

<table>
<tr><th></th><th colspan="8">Number of tenant households (thousands)
Net rent as percentage of net income</th></tr>
<tr><th></th><th>Nil</th><th>Above zero but <5%</th><th>5% to <10%</th><th>10% to <15%</th><th>15% to <20%</th><th>20% or more</th><th>Total</th><th>Median % excl Nil</th></tr>
<tr><td>(£)
Annual net income
<3,000</td><td>850</td><td>150</td><td>200</td><td>150</td><td>100</td><td>150</td><td>1,600</td><td>11</td></tr>
<tr><td>3,000-3,999</td><td>450</td><td>100</td><td>100</td><td>100</td><td>100</td><td>100</td><td>950</td><td>12</td></tr>
<tr><td>4,000-5,999</td><td>300</td><td>150</td><td>150</td><td>250</td><td>250</td><td>100</td><td>1,200</td><td>13</td></tr>
<tr><td>6,000-7,999</td><td>100</td><td>100</td><td>250</td><td>400</td><td>100</td><td>-</td><td>950</td><td>11</td></tr>
<tr><td>8,000-9,999</td><td rowspan="2">50</td><td>50</td><td>200</td><td>150</td><td>-</td><td>-</td><td>450</td><td>9</td></tr>
<tr><td>10,000 and over</td><td>100</td><td>450</td><td>50</td><td>-</td><td>-</td><td>600</td><td>7</td></tr>
<tr><td>Total</td><td>1,750</td><td>650</td><td>1,350</td><td>1,100</td><td>550</td><td>350</td><td>5,750</td><td>10</td></tr>
</table>

Note: Net rent is net of housing benefit; net income is net of income tax and national insurance contribution

Source: Unpublished data from *Family Expenditure Survey*

Tenure depends not only on income but also on socio-economic group. Over half of heads of household in unskilled manual occupations are local authority or new town tenants, while people in non-manual occupations tend to be owner-occupiers even when their incomes are the same as those of manual workers. Table 1.24 gives a breakdown of tenure by socio-economic group.

Table 1.24: Tenure by socio-economic group and head of household,
1984 (Great Britain)

Socio-economic group of head of household (%)	Owner-occupied Owned outright	Owned with mortgage	LA/new town/HA	Rented privately or with job/business	Sample size (Nos)
Economically active heads					
Professional	10	78	2	9	442
Employers and managers	17	70	6	7	1,272
Intermediate non-manual	12	67	11	11	708
Junior non-manual	16	51	22	11	537
Skilled manual and own account non-professional	14	52	29	5	2,037
Semi-skilled manual and personal service	12	34	43	11	879
Unskilled manual	11	22	61	7	248
Economically inactive heads	42	5	44	9	3,338
All heads of household	24	38	30	9	9,461

Source: *General Household Survey 1985*, Table 5.13 (OPCS, 1987)

Local authority tenants tend to be concentrated at the higher end
of the age spectrum, though the sector also caters for rather more
than its share of very young householders (those aged under 25).
Table 1.25 gives a breakdown by age for the various tenures.

Table 1.25: Tenure by age of head of household, 1984 (Great Britain)

Age (%)	Owner-occupied Owned outright	Owned with mortgage	LA/new town/HA	Rented privately or with job/business	Sample size (Nos)
<25	-	34	35	40	453
25-29	2	60	25	12	804
30-44	6	66	20	7	2,796
45-59	22	43	28	8	2,312
60-69	45	10	39	6	1,677
>69	47	1	41	11	1,891
All heads of household	24	37	30	9	9,933

Source: *General Household Survey 1984*, Table 5.14 (OPCS, 1986)

The public sector houses a greater proportion of single-person households than average, and also a greater proportion of very large households. On the other hand, it houses a distinctly smaller proportion of four-person households. Table 1.26 provides a comparative breakdown.

Table 1.26: Household size 1984 (England)

Number of people in household	All tenures Number (thousands)	%	Public sector tenants Number (thousands)	%
One	4,410	24.6	1,660	33.0
Two	5,870	32.7	1,540	30.6
Three	2,890	16.1	720	14.3
Four	3,160	17.6	640	12.7
Five	1,130	6.3	310	6.2
Six or more	490	2.7	165	3.3
Total	17,940	100.0	5,030	100.0

Source: Department of the Environment, Housing Trailers to the 1981 and 1984 *Labour Force Surveys*, Table 2.4 (HMSO, 1988)

About two-thirds of new tenants housed by local authorities come from their ordinary waiting lists, with the remainder coming from special groups such as (declining) numbers of people displaced by slum clearance and the like, key workers, and increasing numbers of homeless households as described above. The number of lettings to new tenants has declined significantly in recent years, from 288,000 in England and Wales in 1979/80 to 257,000 in 1986/87. Conversely, the number of existing local authority tenants being rehoused through transfers and exchanges within the sector has increased from 172,000 in 1979/80 to 194,000 in 1986/87.

According to the 1984 *Labour Force Survey*, 4% of people in England eligible to be on a waiting-list for council housing (excluding transfers) said that they were on the waiting-list for local authority housing, but with a much higher proportion among private sector tenants, nearly 12% of whom were wanting a council house. Table 1.27 shows the existing tenure of waiting-list applicants, and the length of time they had been waiting.

Table 1.27: Time spent on local authority waiting-lists by tenure, 1984 (England)

Existing tenure	Total of people eligible to be on a LA waiting list	% on waiting list	< 1 year	% of people on waiting-list for 1-5 years	6 years or more
Ownei • occupied	15,190	1.6	36	46	18
Rented from LA/new town	1,760	8.0	45	47	8
Rented privately	3,010	12.3	30	44	26

Sources: Department of the Environment, Housing Trailers to the 1981 and 1984 *Labour Force Surveys*, Tables 7.4 and 7.5 (HMSO, 1988)

More recent information about those wanting and obtaining council housing is to be found in *Queuing for Housing: A Study of Council Housing Waiting Lists* by Patricia Prescott-Clarke, Patrick Allen and Catrin Morrissey (HMSO, 1988). This study shows that applicants were generally young or old, but that those who were successful in obtaining council housing were predominantly young. The majority of applicants (or their partners) were in full-time employment, but this applied to only a minority of successful applicants. A common characteristic of both groups was their low incomes and savings, indeed, most wanted council housing because they said that they could not afford anything else.

The incidence of overcrowding is low in all tenures, with rather less than 6% of tenants in both the public and private sectors below the 'bedroom standard', compared with slightly less than 3% of owner-occupiers. Tenants in both sectors are twice as likely as owner-occupiers to have accommodation equal to the bedroom standard. About three out of four owner-occupiers live in accommodation above the bedroom standard, compared with about one in two tenants. Table 1.28 gives detailed figures for all tenures.

Table 1.28: Households by tenure and difference from bedroom standard, 1984 (England)

(thousands)	2 or more below	%	1 below	%	Equal to standard	%	1 above	%	2 or more above	%	Total
Owner-occupiers	34	0.3	260	2.4	2,340	21.3	4,680	43.6	3,680	33.5	10,990
LA/new town/ HA tenants	31	0.6	250	5.0	2,360	46.9	1,710	34.0	700	13.9	5,030
Other tenants	12	0.6	100	5.2	780	40.6	620	32.3	410	21.4	1,920
Total	70	0.4	600	3.3	5,460	30.4	7,010	39.1	4,800	26.8	17,940

Note: Detail does not always add up to totals because of rounding

Source: **Department of the Environment, Housing Trailers to the 1981 and 1984 *Labour Force Surveys*, Table 2.12 (HMSO, 1988)**

Thus, in summary, overcrowding does not appear to be a significant source of management problems in the social rented sector. Nor in general terms does the presence of minority ethnic communities as such, although high concentrations of immigrants on some estates have perhaps contributed to tensions and a few-well known cases of violence. However, even these difficulties may just as well be due to the more widely felt social trends documented above; growing unemployment, rising numbers of single parent families, and the declining economic fortunes of tenants in the social rented sector, particularly in relation to the burgeoning owner-occupied sector.

VII   Management problems and solutions

Symptoms and causes of decline

Although earlier sections have shown that the great majority of council tenants are well pleased with their housing, a significant and rising minority of local authority housing is in trouble. In their annual returns to the DOE for April 1988, English local authorities

reported that a total of 103,000 council dwellings or
stock were empty, nearly 26,000 of them for more than
This compares with 100,000 empty council dwellings (2.
stock, which was reported empty at April 1980.   T
(dwellings becoming available for letting) in 1987/88 was 10.4
the stock at the end of the period, compared with 8.6% in 1979/
The proportion of dwellings regarded as 'difficult to let' was 7.1%
at April 1988, as against 5.5% at April 1980.

A further significant indicator of the extent of management
problems in the local authority sector is to be found in the rising
levels of rent arrears reported to the DOE in subsidy claim forms.
At the end of March 1980, cumulative rent arrears owed to English
local authorities amounted to £72 million, or 3.9% of the total
annual rents due, having risen from 3% in the mid-1970s.   By
March 1988, they had risen to about £230 million, or 5.8% of the
total rent due. The highest levels of rent arrears are to be found in
inner London and other large metropolitan areas, which also
contain a large share of the problem estates.

Rent levels are traditionally a major cause of tension between
central and local government, and a matter of significant local
political interest. Notwithstanding the extent to which they receive
help with their rents, local authority tenants are keenly aware of the
extent to which rents have risen since 1979 despite the efforts of
many local authorities to resist the upward pressures from central
government. Between April 1980 and April 1982 rents increased in
cash terms 75% and in real terms by 43%. Between 1982 and
1986, rents rose by little more than the general price level, but rose
again sharply with the introduction of the new financial regime in
1990. Table 1.23 in the previous section explores the relationship
between tenants' incomes and rents.

Rising rents inevitably create expectations of improved service,
which are widely accepted to have been disappointed. The climate,
if not necessarily the reality, of local authority manpower cuts since
1979 and the allegations by some councils about the effects of the
legislation affecting local authority direct labour organisations have
certainly contributed to the widespread perception of a deteriorating
service, especially of day-to-day repairs.   In part, the level of
service may also have fallen following the withdrawal under the
1975 Housing Rents and Subsidies Act of the subsidy on
management and maintenance expenditure which had been
introduced just three years earlier under the 1972 Housing Finance
Act. However, the most significant factor was undoubtedly the

.4% of their
12 months.
% of the
rnover
% of
0.

...uthorities found themselves with
...llowing the local government
..., and 1974 elsewhere, and their
...centralised bureaucracies to

...of rents (and local authority
...entirely offset by the housing
...costs is rare.   Having risen
...and 1974, heating costs -
...floor or ceiling heating systems
...orable climb in the later 1970s and the 1980s.

...tenants were particularly affected as they saw a disproportionate share of their incomes going on heating costs.   In 1986, households in the bottom two-fifths of the distribution of gross incomes (which include over 70% of local authority tenants) spent 10% of their total outlays on fuel, power and light, compared with 8.7% in 1978.

The difficulties in achieving comfortable levels of heating are one of the most evident symptoms of tenants' disillusion with the physical state of much local authority housing throughout the 1970s and 1980s.   Decayed window-frames which would not close, structural gaps and cracks which let in the rain and wind, faulty heating systems were, and remain, a major cause of dissatisfaction. Condensation is a frequent consequence of tenants' inability to afford to heat and ventilate their homes properly, which in turn adds to the decay.   These conditions are exacerbated and a significant safety hazard is introduced when tenants resort to oil and liquid petroleum gas heaters to supplement or substitute for inadequate or expensive heating installations.

No less real, though more difficult to quantify, is the growing incidence of crime on some local authority estates.   Police records are rarely kept in a form which provides statistical information at the estate level, and it is clear that many crimes against property or the person go unrecorded.   This applies particularly to vandalism and other abuse of lifts, stairways and common parts of blocks of flats and their environment.   Moreover, in practice, the fear of crime is almost as important as crime itself.   Underground garages provided at great capital cost are deserted by tenants who fear that their cars will be vandalised or that they will come under personal attack.   Many of them are now being demolished and the sites turned to grass.

The design of much post-war local authority housing seems positively to promote such crime, abuse and fears. Anonymous and drab buildings, depressing and inconveniently planned open space, entrances and staircases which offer easy cover for malefactors, and links and walkways which help them to escape, garages and car parks which no-one overlooks, all erode any remaining feeling of security among the often vulnerable people who live on these estates and sap their morale.

Inadequate services pose problems not only for residents on peripheral estates. Shopping and social facilities are often poor or non-existent. Low levels of car ownership and infrequent and expensive public transport add to the sense of isolation of families living in such housing and thus contribute to its growing unpopularity.

Dissatisfaction among social sector tenants has also increased because of their growing sense of awareness that they form an under-privileged section of society. For those who could afford it, owner-occupation has become the norm. As will be seen, this trend is not confined to the United Kingdom. This feeling cannot but be compounded by the growing concentration of the poor and socially disadvantaged - the unemployed, the victims of family breakdown, those accepted as statutorily homeless, some people from minority ethnic groups - in the social rented sector. As has been seen, bricks and mortar subsidies have decisively shifted to subsidies to individuals, and on an overwhelming scale. Two-thirds of local authority tenants now receive housing benefit, which accounts for no less than half of the total local authority rent income.

Although the trend towards social polarisation between owner-occupiers and tenants, and within the social rented sector itself, has become more marked in the 1980s, it was already emerging clearly in the early 1970s. This was the period when housing specialists began to discern that complex combinations of social factors, management, and location were at least as much to blame as the design and built form of the housing for increasing problems of the local authority sector. The most apparent symptom of the malaise at this time was the rising number of empty dwellings on some estates, and the growing reluctance of tenants to move on to them despite the persistent shortages of housing, often in the same areas.

In 1976 and 1977, the DOE therefore launched *An Investigation of Difficult to Let Housing* Housing Development Directorate (HDD) *Occasional Papers 3/80, 4/80,* and *5/80,* HMSO 1981. This study demonstrated once and for all that unpopular estates suffered from a complex and varied range of social and physical problems, and that social polarisation was growing, as poorer housing went to those with the least bargaining power. It also pin-pointed the deficiencies of housing management which was often impersonal and fragmented between different departments of the local authority.

The Priority Estates Project

As a result of this work, in 1979, the Department set up PEP to develop and promote new approaches to the management of problem estates. Initially, PEP set up three projects in agreement with the local authorities concerned: the Greater London Council, the London Borough of Hackney, and Bolton Metropolitan Borough Council.

The essential features of these agreements were first that the local authority's housing department should establish a local office on the estate, with responsibility for the main management functions - in particular, lettings and repairs - and second, that the residents should be actively involved in the development of the project and the running of the estate. The Department funded a team of three consultants to work full-time on the estates and to develop and promote the PEP approach more widely.

In the following years, PEP grew apace. In 1983, the Welsh Office set up its own PEP organisation in association with English PEP, starting with two estates and expanding to eight estates in 1987. In England, the programme had grown to 29 estates by 1988. In both countries, PEP has been able to demonstrate that its approach produces not only greater tenant satisfaction, but also a reduction in numbers of empty dwellings, rent arrears and turnover, with all round improvements in economy and efficiency (see the *PEP Guide to Local Management* Vol 2, 1987, and *Priority Estates in Wales - A Review 1984-1987*, Welsh Office, 1988).

At the same time as PEP was developing its approach, some local authorities were working independently to identify the weaknesses in their housing management arrangements and to develop their own PEP-style initiatives on unpopular estates. This activity has often been part of a general trend to reverse the process of concentration and centralisation of local authority responsibilities which had been so fashionable in the 1960s and 1970s. In the case of housing, this reversal was to reach its extreme with the decentralisation of Walsall's housing management to 32 virtually autonomous districts in 1981 (see *The Walsall Experience*, Rory Mainwaring, HMSO, 1988).

Estate Action

In 1985, the then Secretary of State for the Environment, Patrick Jenkin established the Urban Housing Renewal Unit (UHRU), later re-named as Estate Action, to promote the PEP approach as the core feature of a variety of packages to revitalise rundown estates.

Estate Action packages also almost invariably include measures to up-grade the estate physically, with the local authority normally finding the cost of any necessary traditional modernisation work - for example, the replacement of kitchen and bathroom fittings and standard capital maintenance - from its own resources, while Estate Action makes special funding available for more innovatory features or to enable local authorities to avoid piecemeal measures and encourage them to develop integrated and comprehensive approaches to solve the problems of the estate. Typical measures funded by Estate Action include, for example, concierge and entryphone schemes to improve security and to prevent crime, improvements to the environment and common areas such as entrance halls, and installations and insulation to provide affordable heating and to get rid of condensation.

On some estates with high levels of unemployment, Estate Action has sponsored Community Refurbishment Schemes as part of the revitalisation package. Such schemes draw on the skills and energies of unemployed residents to carry out environmental improvements and to reduce backlogs of repairs, with funding support from government programmes to pay for the work and materials. In this way, material conditions on the estates are improved, while at the same time, the residents benefit from some job-sharing and a boost to their personal income, while at the same time, their commitment to the estate is increased.

Wherever possible, Estate Action seeks opportunities to introduce the skills and resources of the private sector into the schemes which it develops with local authorities. Typically, the local authority disposes of unused land or empty buildings on the estate to a private firm for development or refurbishment, and subsequent resale to owner-occupiers. The proceeds are recycled to improve the remainder of the estate which is to be retained for renting. Increasingly, local authorities are also disposing of property on such estates to housing associations. As a result of these disposals, not only are there material benefits from the additional resources generated by the transaction, but there are also social gains from the increased diversity of tenure. In the longer term, diversity of tenure is also encouraged by increased take-up of the Right to Buy as the estate becomes more attractive.

Consultation with tenants on improvement proposals, and their support for the package of measures to be introduced on the estate is an essential pre-condition before an Estate Action scheme receives approval.

Beyond this, the Estate Action team is always on the lookout for suitable opportunities for the residents to take effective control of the subsequent running of the estate. This involvement may take a variety of forms. The most radical model tested to date is the tenant management cooperative in which the tenants take over responsibility for an agreed range of management and maintenance functions. Under such arrangements, the local authority retains the ownership of the housing, and remains responsible for funding major capital work. It agrees an annual budget with the cooperative. The cooperative takes on the responsibility for letting the housing, for collecting rents, and for carrying out day-to-day repairs and maintenance all within the budget agreed with the local authority. It therefore has strong incentives to run itself efficiently.

During 1988, PEP worked on an alternative model where it was intended that the responsibility for management and maintenance would be shared between tenants and Council representatives sitting on an Estate Management Board, operating under the terms of an agreement made with the Council, and with the tenants in the majority. Estate Management Boards are therefore less radical (and therefore possibly more easily established) than full-blooded tenant management cooperatives.

Starting with an annual budget of £50 million in its first year, Estate Action resources have increased significantly year by year to reach £190 million in 1989/90. By the end of 1987/88, some 250 Estate Action schemes were in progress or had been completed, in partnership with more than 90 local authorities, most of them in London, the Midlands, and the north of England. Examples of a comprehensive range of Estate Action schemes are described in detail in the annual reports from the unit, published by the Department of the Environment.

Other government initiatives

The effects of the statutory Right to Buy under the 1980 Housing
Act have been comprehensively covered in previous sections. This
has undeniably been the most significant housing measure taken by
the present government, and has visibly changed the face of many
estates. However, its main impact has been on estates consisting of
houses, and the Right to Buy has had limited impact on flatted
estates. Marion Kerr's *The Right to Buy: a national survey of
tenants and buyers of council homes*, (HMSO, 1988) gives a
detailed account of tenants' motivation and attitudes towards the
Right to Buy.

Following the Toxteth riots in 1981, the then Secretary of State
for the Environment, Michael Heseltine, introduced a series of
radical initiatives to tackle the social and economic needs of
Merseyside, including the transformation of one of England's most
seriously rundown estates, Cantril Farm (locally known as
'Cannibal Farm') in Knowsley. He persuaded the Abbey National
Building Society and Barratt Developments plc to join the
government, the Housing Corporation and the local authority in a
scheme to transform the estate by forming a non-profit making
housing trust. Re-named Stockbridge Village, the estate has
undergone large-scale physical remodelling and demolition, with a
totally new form of private renting from the trust for the remaining
existing housing, combined with a housing association new-build
programme. For social and economic reasons, there has been a
heavy emphasis on owner-occupation through Right to Buy sales.

The changing financial fortunes of this project are charted in
detail in the evaluation report *Stockbridge Village Trust: building a
community*, (HMSO, 1988). Costs proved substantially above
estimates, and the difficulties were exacerbated by unexpected
technical problems. As a result, further public funding has been
needed, and the original scheme has been modified. On the other
hand, the evaluation report shows a substantial measure of support
from the residents.

The 1987 White Paper *Housing: The Government's Proposals*
outlined major changes in the role of local authorities in housing.
One of them was a proposal to establish Housing Action Trusts
(HATs) to deal with the problems associated with major
concentrations of rundown council housing. The 1988 Housing Act
empowers the government to create HATs, if the majority of
tenants vote in favour to take over such estates from their local

authority landlords, to renovate them with resources provided by central government, and then to transfer them to another landlord. This could be the local authority which previously owned the estate, or a housing association, a tenants' cooperative, or a private landlord. In July 1988, William Waldegrave, the then Minister for Housing and Planning announced proposals for six HATs, three of them in London, one in the Midlands, and two in the north of England. There was £192 million of public money ear-marked for HATs, but following rejection of HAT proposals by the tenants on most of the estates selected, the scheme has been largely abandoned.

The White Paper also contained proposals - since enshrined in the 1988 Housing Act - to reduce the local authority hegemony in the social rented sector by giving council tenants the option to transfer themselves and their homes to other landlords. This is known as 'Tenants' Choice'. Here too, the broad options are housing associations, tenants' cooperatives, and private landlords. The legislation provides that a transfer may take place unless a majority of all the eligible tenants vote against the proposal. However, tenants who wish to remain with the Council may do so either by having their home excluded from the transfer if it is a house, or under a lease-back arrangement if it is a flat or maisonette.

There have also been a series of voluntary initiatives by some local authorities to transfer estates to other landlords, usually housing associations. In some cases, the tenants have reacted positively, and the transfers are going ahead. In others, apparently because of inadequate consultation arrangements, tenants have shown how the climate of choice and self-determination has enabled them to flex their muscles to defeat the proposals.

The government considers that housing cooperatives (both tenant management cooperatives and ownership cooperatives) have an important housing role in developing and sustaining local communities by providing opportunities for local management and control and by encouraging self-help.   In particular, it sees ownership cooperatives and community based housing associations as major options for tenants who are considering a change of landlord under Tenants' Choice.

There are over 120 tenant management cooperatives including those within Estate Action schemes (see above), mainly in London - where many date from the 1970s - and Glasgow. As has been seen, in this form of cooperative, the property is owned by a local authority (or housing association) which delegates the main management functions to the members.

There are also over 220 ownership or 'par value' cooperatives in England, some of them in property acquired from local authorities. In this form of cooperative, the cooperative both owns and manages the property, and the members pay a small fee to join but without any stake in the value of the property. In Scotland, Glasgow District Council is actively promoting this form of tenure on some of its housing estates, where six have already been formed (1988), while other local authorities are developing similar initiatives.

The government already supports the promotion and development of cooperatives directly through Estate Action and the Priority Estates Project (see above), and can make grants to them under Section 16 of the 1986 Housing and Planning Act. It also supports cooperatives indirectly, for example through the Housing Corporation's funding of 'par value' cooperatives.

The government is concerned, however, that the cooperative sector should expand on a sound base. In June 1988 it therefore launched a wide-ranging review of cooperatives in England. As a result of the committee's report *Tenants in the Lead*, in December 1989 the government launched a new grant system under which council tenants would be able to receive assistance direct from the DOE and from their local authority to develop housing cooperatives and other forms of tenant participation. The scheme was allocated £3.25 million in its first year.

Thus, in summary, the overall government policy towards management in the social rented sector in the late 1980s is to promote diversity of tenure and ownership, and with a special emphasis on breaking up the monolithic control of large estates. The reactions of local authority landlords have been varied, and by no means split neatly along party political lines, with Labour-controlled councils among those which have shown interest in voluntarily transferring their housing responsibilities to housing associations. As will be seen in later chapters, if the various parties - tenants, local authorities, and other landlord organisations - have the will to carry this policy through on a large scale, the social sector in the United Kingdom will tend towards that in the other western European countries covered by this report, but with a higher proportion of owner-occupiers and cooperatives among the social rented housing on estates.

NOTES

1. Annual Abstract of Statistics 1988, tables 2.1 and 2.7
2. 1985 based estimates of numbers of households, Table 2 (DOE, 1988) - refers to England and Wales
3. General Household Survey 1986, table 3.11 (HMSO, 1089)
4. Housing and Construction Statistics 1989 (HMSO, 1990)
5. General Household Survey 1985, table 5.32 (HMSO, 1987)
6. Scottish Abstract of Statistics 1985/86
7. Information supplied by Alan Holmans (DOE)
8. Population Trends No 24 (1981)
9. General Household Survey 1985, table 5.19 (HMSO, 1987)
10. Information supplied by DOE
11. Municipal Yearbook 1988
12. Information supplied by DOE

two

FRANCE

I   The general background

Population and housing stock

The 1982 census showed that the total population of metropolitan France - that is the French mainland and Corsica - was just under 53 million, occupying nearly 20 million main homes, three-quarters of them in urban areas, and just over one in six in greater Paris. As in the other countries covered by this study, average household sizes have decreased steadily, from 3.11 in 1962, to 2.69 in 1984,[1] (although it should be noted that the French definition of a household differs from that in West Germany, the Netherlands and the United Kingdom, in that the number of households in France is the same as the number of main residences).

In contrast with Great Britain and Germany, but like the Netherlands, the urban development of France has been recent and dramatic. In 1954, 42% of the French population still lived in the countryside, in 1982, the rural population had fallen to 25%.[2] It is therefore hardly surprising that nearly 9 million of the 11 million main homes built between 1949 and 1982 are in urban areas.[3]

The early post-war period was characterised by the legacy of acute housing shortages caused by the upsurge in household formation with the baby boom of the late 1940s, by the wartime losses of 452,000 dwellings totally destroyed and a further 1,436,000 damaged,[4] and by a cumulative deficit of some 2,000,000 dwellings from the inter-war period. This deficit was the result of neglect and failure to build, partly because of the rent controls and various degrees of security of tenure imposed during and after the First World War, but also because of the slowdown in economic and population growth in the period between the two world wars. Nevertheless, with an economy ravaged by war and occupation, and with continuing colonial wars, first in Indo-China and then in North Africa, reconstruction got off to a slow start, and it was only in the mid-1950s that the housing boom began in earnest.

Tenure

In the intervening period, apart from a major increase in the housing stock as a whole, there have been some significant changes in the overall tenure pattern, as is shown in Table 2.1.

Table 2.1:   Tenure 1962-82

	1962	1968	1975	1982
		(thousands)		
Owner-occupied	6,019	6,816	8,271	9,929
Rented unfurnished	6,105	6,535	7,199	7,746
Rented furnished	498	466	409	286
Accommodated by employer	1,271	1,216	1,032	784
Accommodated without charge	672	730	832	845
Total	14,535	15,765	17,744	19,590

Source: 1982 census, 'Logements immeubles', Table R.18

As the table shows, the growth in owner-occupation has been dramatic. In 1954, just over a third of main homes were occupied by their owners.[5] Thirty years later, in 1984, over a half (51.2%) were owner-occupied. One in six of all owner-occupiers in 1984 had entered the sector in the last five years, despite monthly repayments of between twice and three times as much as average rents. Most owner-occupiers start as tenants; over three quarters of them are over 40 years old.[8] Owner-occupation is less among white-collar workers (34%) than among blue-collar workers (41%),[9] probably because the latter are particularly favoured by the financial measures introduced by the state since 1977, although it is also probable that many blue-collar workers are outright owner-occupiers of cheap, low-quality housing. The table also shows that the rented sector as a whole has grown in absolute terms over the 20 year period, and has decreased only modestly as a proportion of all main homes.

Although the amount of furnished renting and renting from employers has gone down substantially, the private rented sector in total - at just over five million at the time of the 1982 census - is still firmly the largest sector after owner-occupation, with about a quarter of all main homes.[10] Reasons for this continuing strength will become apparent in Section IV which describes the forms of help available from the state. Nonetheless, the sector is in slow decline, falling by 6.7% between 1978 and 1984.[11] As will be seen in Section VI, this decline is having a critical influence on the social rented sector.

The social rented sector - known as HLM (Habitations à Loyer Modéré) - was only about half the size of the private rented sector at the time of the 1982 census. However, it has been by far the fastest growing sector in the post-war years, with over 95% of the social rented stock built since 1945. It had topped three million by the end of 1986.[12] Its characteristics, and those of its tenants and landlords are examined in greater detail in later sections. Table 2.2 shows the social rented sector as a separate component of the rented sector in 1982.

Table 2.2: Tenure breakdown in 1982, showing the social rented sector separately

	Number of dwellings	%
Owner-occupation	9,928,780	50.7
Private renting	5,103,080	26.0
Social renting (HLM)	2,643,320	13.5
Other (eg furnished renting, tied or free accommodation)	1,915,220	9.8
Total	19,590,400	100.0

Source: 1982 census, Table 301

The 1984 *Housing Survey* shows a general improvement in housing conditions since the previous survey in 1978, and an overall increase in satisfaction except in the social rented sector, as indicated in Table 2.3.[13]

Table 2.3:   Satisfaction with conditions

	HLM % 1978	HLM % 1984	Overall % 1978	Overall % 1984
Very satisfied	9.4	9.6	19.3	20.7
Satisfied	40.5	40.3	38.3	43.0
Acceptable	37.9	35.9	29.0	26.1
Inadequate	10.3	10.6	10.1	7.4
Very inadequate	1.9	3.6	3.3	2.8

Source: Institut National de la Statistique et des Etudes Economiques (INSEE), 'Premiers Résultats No. 70', Table 3

Conditions and housing balance

There is an increasing trend towards living in houses rather than flats, with the proportion of houses rising from 47.4% in 1968 to 52.4% in 1982.[14] This trend is particularly marked in the owner-occupied sector where three-quarters of households live in houses,[15] but the trend has more recently begun to affect the social rented sector.[16]

France has a high proportion of second homes, which rose from 7.8% in 1973 to 9.4% in 1984.   Many of them are holiday accommodation, much of them built recently (more than one in four of the second homes in the 1982 census figures had been built since 1975).   Second homes also contribute to the high overall rate of empty dwellings.   This remained roughly constant at 7.9% between 1973 and 1978, and with a slight decrease to 7.7% in 1984, which the Institut National de la Statistique et des Etudes Economiques (INSEE) puts down to increasing pressure on the housing market.[17]

Although there is no official view of the extent to which supply meets demand, in the general view of housing specialists, the market is in balance nationally, although with considerable regional variations. Pressure is particularly severe in the Paris area, while demand is slacker in the areas of industrial decline in the north and east.

II   History of the social rented sector

As elsewhere, the social rented sector in France originated in philanthropic concerns about physical housing conditions and particularly the risks to public health in the newly industrialised towns of the latter part of the 19th century. The movement gained its first statutory recognition in the Siegfried Act of 30 November 1894. The movement's product was now officially termed 'Cheap housing' (Habitations à bon marché). Before the First World War, the Acts of 12 April 1906 and 23 December 1912 already provided a legal basis for social housing for rent by non-profit municipal organisations, while the Ribot Act of 1908 provided a precedent for state subsidies for housing.   Although these were confined to owner-occupation at this stage, they were extended in 1919 to help the Habitations à bon marché sector to provide rented housing for large families.

It was such organisations, with their more recent private counterparts, which have since become the staple providers of all French subsidised housing for rent under the HLM system which is described in detail below.

The movement gained renewed moral legitimacy with the continuing concern in the 1920s with the poorly housed.   In particular, the Loucheur Act of 13 July 1928 provided for a programme of 60,000 social rented dwellings between 1928 and 1932, with state financing of up to 90% of the cost. However, its impact on the market was still slight, as was that of various other forms of financial aid which were on offer in this period. As has been seen, by the end of the Second World War in 1945, the total social rented sector contribution to the housing stock remained less than 150,000 homes.[18]

This period also saw a growing belief in the social, and even economic, virtues of garden city developments - a faith transferred later in the inter-war period to their more grandiose successors from the drawing-boards of Le Corbusier and his disciples. Large-scale central planning had come of age as the answer to the 20th century's persisting and growing social and economic problems.

As has been shown in Section I, following the Second World War, the overall housing programme was slow to start. This was particularly true of the social rented sector, which accounted for only 12,000 of the 199,000 dwellings built in the five years between 1945 and 1950.   During the same period, England and Wales saw the construction of more than ten times as many public sector dwellings, while by 1950 in Germany, social sector completions were running at more than 250,000 dwellings a year, and in the Netherlands, with a much smaller population, social sector completions had topped 30,000 a year.

It took the return to central economic planning in the early 1950s to turn the HLM movement into a major new source of low-cost housing, now with the benefit of substantial government subsidies (see Section IV).   This was the period of the new industrial zones which were to play a major part in France's economic regeneration. As early as 1953, the subsidisation of the massive new housing programme was recognised as a joint effort between employers and the state when the government imposed a payroll levy, the '1% patronal', to supplement its own subsidies.   As will be seen in Section IV, this levy - since reduced progressively to 0.77% - still exists as a major source of housing finance.

The Zones à Urbaniser en Priorité (ZUPs) - priority planning zones - launched by the Decree of 31 January 1958, and subsequent similar initiatives such as the Zones de Rénovation Urbaine and Zones d'Aménagement Concerté (ZACs), all of which were to play such a crucial role in providing the housing and communal infrastructure for this regeneration, were therefore first and foremost economic rather than social instruments.

That is not to deny an important element of social inspiration in the huge new high-rise and medium-rise housing developments - the 'grands ensembles' - which now started to spring up on a vast scale on the periphery of towns and cities.   They were intended to offer their occupants who came from the constriction, noise and squalor of the cities a life with views of the sky and countryside, with plenty of open space and convenient cultural, recreational, educational and shopping facilities.   However, in France, in contrast with the United Kingdom, the motive was not primarily slum clearance, and indeed, as can be seen from the previous section, many of the occupants of these great estates came from the countryside rather than the towns.

In the rush to produce new homes, industrialised building systems such as the Camus system soon became the order of the day, although apparently without anything like the same dire results as in the United Kingdom, in part no doubt because of the differences of climate. Although there is little quantified information about the condition of the stock, Union Nationale des Fédérations d'Organismes d'HLM (UNFOHLM) - the umbrella organisation for the HLM movement - claims that until 1970 at least, the balance between quality and quantity was successfully maintained.

Even if systems-built estates in France present fewer structural problems than they do in the United Kingdom, systems-building has had a pronounced and pernicious effect on the layout of numerous French estates. High-rise blocks are often to be found in closely packed groups of three, their spacing and height determined simply by the size of the cranes which were set up to lift components for as many flats as possible before having to be moved. Thus, from the 1950s, France played the numbers game as enthusiastically as her neighbours, and by the standards of that game, the programme must be counted a success. From a slow start between 1951 and 1955, when less than 100,000 dwellings were added to the stock, the next five years saw the addition of more than 320,000 dwellings. Thereafter, production continued to soar from one five-year period to another, reaching a peak of 682,000 between 1970 and 1975.

Table 2.4: Completions in the social rented sector

	Number completed	Cumulative total
Pre-1945	148,000	148,000
1945-1950	12,000	160,000
1951-1955	97,000	257,000
1956-1960	324,000	581,000
1961-1965	410,000	991,000
1966-1970	625,000	1,616,000
1971-1975	682,000	2,298,000
1976-1980	394,000	2,692,000
1981-1985	272,000	2,964,000
1986	66,000	3,030,000

Source: UNFOHLM, 'Aide-Mémoire Statistique' for 48th
            National Congress, Table 3.2

As can be seen from Table 2.4, the watershed was in the late 1970s, principally brought about by the 1977 reforms in the housing finance system which were designed to shift subsidy from new bricks and mortar to renovation and, above all, to people. Between 1981 and 1986, new-build completions averaged only about 56,000 a year, compared with an average of over 136,000 a year at the peak period between 1971 and 1975.

The late 1970s also marked a watershed for life on the large estates, as the economic changes of the previous decade took their toll. This was a period of general disillusionment, but it was particularly severe on the estates, where the 1960s dream which they embodied of a pioneering new way of life was transformed by the increasing harshnesses of reality. As early as 1973, the government acknowledged the inhuman scale of many of the new estates, when in his Circular Guichard, the Minister of the time put a limit of 2,000 units on new housing projects.

Most of the problems were, however, already there. Largely through poor coordination between the various agencies with responsibility for providing them, the promised social facilities - schools, shops, public transport, sports centres, community halls - arrived piecemeal if at all. The inadequacies of the buildings became increasingly apparent as they got older. Lifts and heating systems broke down, and the need for day-to-day repairs increased. Weathering made the gaunt concrete blocks even more unsympathetic. Heating costs rose sharply in the wake of the oil crisis, and were exacerbated by the poorly insulated buildings.

There were also growing social problems among the tenants. Although their influence was blurred, some former students from the era of the unrest of 1968 were now tenants on HLM estates. Other social trends were more obviously influential. Renting increasingly became seen as a stepping-stone to owner-occupation, and those who could afford to buy began to move away. At the same time, unemployment was beginning to rise. Growing numbers of immigrants from North Africa and the poorer countries of southern Europe - principally Italy and Spain - moved on to the estates, adding to the tensions felt by the residents who complained of their noise and alien cooking smells, all exaggerated by the form of the buildings. Existing and new residents on the estates increasingly saw themselves as trapped on dumping grounds for the under-privileged, while the popular image cultivated by the media in the outside world was one of crime, violence, and racial tension.

Recognition of these emerging social problems came earlier in France than in the other countries covered by this study. In 1971, a national conference attended by representatives of landlord organisations and government laid the foundations for the 'Habitat et Vie Sociale' initiative, which was set up in 1976 with the task of improving conditions on estates, with special funding from central and local government. Although - as its title indicates - the Habitat et Vie Sociale initiative was intended to tackle housing problems in a wider social context, it is generally agreed that the 80 projects which were launched under this programme concentrated in practice on physical improvement work, and made little progress on the wider social front.

The disturbances on several estates in 1981, notably on the Les Minguettes estate outside Lyons (see Section VII) spurred the government to take action on a wider front. Three major reports were commissioned: the Schwartz report on youth, the report of the Commission of Mayors on security, and the Dubedout report on problem neighbourhoods. The last of these, by Hubert Dubedout who, as Mayor of Grenoble had already been responsible for some pioneering housing neighbourhood initiatives, was to form the basis of the 'Commission nationale pour le développement social des quartiers' (The National Commission for Community Development of Neighbourhoods) which was formally set up in 1982. Section VII considers the National Commission's approach and achievements in detail.

III   The landlord organisations

Structure and size

At the end of 1985, there were 646 HLM landlord organisations, managing a total of some 3 million dwellings, or an overall average of about 4,600 dwellings each.[20] This compares with an average of about 12,500 for English local authorities and 2,000 for housing associations.

There are also about 100 cooperative housing organisations, which have allocation rights on roughly 250,000 dwellings built by themselves or owned by conventional HLM landlord organisations. A similar number of cooperatives build dwellings for rent or owner-occupation or make loans to purchasers.[21] Although the legal status of cooperatives goes back to the Act of 12 April 1906, and has been updated several times since the Second World War,[22] they are widely regarded as a spent force. They exercise less than half of their allocation rights, and the turnover of their management operation on renting in 1985 was a mere FF 110 million (equivalent to £8.6 million).[23]

Of the 646 conventional HLM landlord organisations at the end of 1985, 276 were 'Offices publics' (OPs) sponsored by local authorities at the level of 'communes' or municipalities (of which France has a total of about 36,000) or 'Départements' or counties (of which there are 95). OPs gained their original legal status through the Bonnevay Act of 23 December 1912, which has been updated by various 1970s legislation. Their area of operation is limited mainly but not altogether to the area of their sponsoring local authorities.

They are governed by 'Conseils d'administration' (administrative boards) whose composition of 20 members is laid down by statute. Six members are elected by the sponsoring local authority. Two members are nominated by financial interests (the 'Caisses d'Epargne' or savings banks, and the 'Caisses d'Allocations familiales' or family allowance funds, both of which, as will be seen, have an important role in the social rented sector). Two members are elected by the tenants, though they often have the reputation of being political activists whose chief allegiance is to their cause. Ten members are nominated by the 'Préfet' or senior official responsible for the delivery of central government functions within the local Département. The majority of his nominees are selected on their ability to speak on local issues which run wider than housing as such. For example, they typically represent bodies with family and conservation interests, and wherever possible, include a member with specialist expertise on minority ethnic community issues.

There is a considerable difference in size between the municipal and Département HLM organisations. Municipal OPs have an average stock of rather less than 5,000, while Département OPs manage an average of slightly over 8,000 units. Both types of OP have the administrative limitation that they depend on their sponsoring local authority for their accounting activity, which in particular can lead to slowness in identifying tenants with rent arrears.

An offshoot of the OP sector is the OPAC or 'Office public d'aménagement et construction', of which 16 had been formed by the end of 1985, all by transfer of status - on their own initiative - by existing OPs. They received their legal status in the Act of 16 July 1971, and although they are geographically based, they can spread their net more widely than OPs. To a great extent, they are a product of the decentralisation of functions from central to local government in the early 1980s, which involved the creation of an intermediate - Regional - tier of administration, and some of them are sponsored by the 22 Régions. The original OPACs were typically larger than OPs, managing an average stock of over 17,500 units, but more recently formed OPACs have been smaller, as more OPs have changed their status.

The main differences between them and OPs is that OPACs are organisationally much more independent of central government and their sponsoring local authorities, and so can operate more flexibly in terms of pay levels and financial control. They are claimed to be more adaptable to changing economic and social circumstances, and to have a more explicit economic and social remit. Their administrative boards consist of 28 members, appointed on broadly the same basis as their counterparts in OPs, but with a greater emphasis on the representation of social, cultural and economic interests.

The 292 OPs and OPACs described above are bodies constituted under legislation applying to the public sector. The other 354 HLM landlord organisations at the end of 1985 are non-profit limited liability companies - 'Sociétés anonymes' (SAs) - with their legal status set out in the Act of 24 July 1966 and the Decree of 23 March 1967 (which apply generally to private companies), and in subsequent legislation which applies specifically to HLM organisations. Their constitutions are subject to the safeguard that any one shareholder has a maximum of 10 votes. For the most part, they are sponsored by private sector firms, and also by public enterprises and even local authorities, with the primary aim of providing low-cost housing for their employees. Thus, although they are entitled to public financial support in the same way as their OP and OPAC counterparts (see Section IV), they often also may have recourse to funds from the appropriate employer through the '1% patronal' payroll levy (see Section II). They are typically much smaller than OPs and OPACs, with an average stock of about 3,500 units, but some of those sponsored by firms are considerably larger. Table 2.5 shows the total stock held by the OPs, OPACs and SAs.

Table 2.5: Stock held by HLM organisations (at end 1985)

	Number	Stock (thousands)	%
OP	276	1,489	49.4
OPAC	16	281	9.3
SA	354	1,243	41.3
Total	646	3,013	100.0

Source: UNFOHLM

The SA sector described above includes a major special case, SCIC, the Paris based property arm of the Caisse des Dépots et Consignations, the state sponsored funding agency which is described in rather more detail in the next section. Among its activities, SCIC has built and manages 180,000 HLM dwellings throughout France, mainly in areas without a local HLM organisation. It is therefore in the same bracket as the now defunct Neue Heimat organisation in Germany, whose problems and fate are described in the next chapter, and indeed in some ways it has modelled itself on Neue Heimat. It also shares some of the financial problems which afflicted Neue Heimat, in particular, relatively high but unviable rent levels and large numbers of empty dwellings. SCIC is also a shareholder in other SA landlord organisations, and provides an agency management service to many others, mainly those which are too small to provide an economic management service of their own.

As in Germany and the Netherlands, the social rented sector in France has traditionally had a small up-market component of rather higher standard accommodation at higher rents, for example by the 'Sociétés d'économie mixte' (SEMs), which are privately constituted companies not unlike the SAs described above, but with a high level of municipal sponsorship. Although this type of provision has been on the decline since the 1977 reform of housing (see Section VI), it has recently been given new prominence by the government under its 'Prêts locatifs intermédiaires' (PLI) scheme to provide rented housing for those whose incomes are too high for standard HLM accommodation but who cannot afford private rents.

In principle this is a reversion to the inter-war policy of developing a two-tier form of social housing.

In practice, however, this is largely limited to the housing market in Paris, where demand is high. In areas of lower demand, landlord organisations can let their existing housing to better-off people at higher rents. According to government forecasts there would be 12,000 dwellings under the PLI scheme in 1987 and 12,500 in 1988.

Building for sale

HLM organisations can also build for sale, and their output for this purpose since the Second World War comes to over a million dwellings. Both on building for sale and sales to sitting tenants, the remit of the largely privately sponsored SA sector means that it is more active than its municipally sponsored OP and OPAC counterparts, although sales activity in both sectors has declined greatly in recent years. In 1985, there were 3,200 SA completions for sale, compared with 600 in the OP/OPAC sector.[24] However, with the financial difficulties which many of them are now encountering (see below), sales are increasingly being seen as a way of breaking even.

As a further plank to his government's policy to boost home ownership, the then Minister for Housing, Pierre Méhaignerie told the HLM conference in 1987 that he was introducing a range of new measures designed to encourage HLM organisations to boost their hitherto negligible sales to sitting tenants, which amounted to a mere 6,000 in the whole of the period from 1965 to 1983. The age of dwellings eligible for sale was reduced, government approval procedures for sales simplified, and the financial regime made more attractive to landlords.

The market for HLM housing

In principle, standard HLM housing is intended for the broad mass of those who cannot afford to buy or to rent privately, and - as in Germany and the Netherlands - there are therefore formal income ceilings, varying according to whether the property comes within the pre-1977 or post-1977 financial regime (see Section IV), its geographical location, and the family circumstances of the applicant.

In practice, however, the ceiling is high enough for perhaps seven out of ten households to be eligible for HLM accommodation, and landlord organisations are known to make exceptions. Indeed, as in Germany, landlord organisations can accept tenants whose incomes are above the ceilings, especially in areas of low demand. These tenants pay a rent premium of between 5% and 25%, which in itself is attractive to landlord organisations who may also find such tenants attractive for social reasons and their greater ability to afford the rent.

Unlike Germany and the Netherlands where the responsibility for means testing rests with the municipality, it is the landlord organisation itself in France which checks the eligibility of the applicant. This makes it relatively easy for landlord organisations to identify applicants whose resources are low enough to make them likely to fall into arrears with their rents, and it is widely accepted that many landlords operate an informal income floor to avoid accepting such applicants, despite the disapproval of government, municipalities and their own umbrella organisation. The largely privately sponsored SA sector is generally considered to be more selective than OPs and OPACs.

This is borne out by the example of two HLM organisations in eastern France, both with a stock of about 11,000 dwellings with a similar size-profile, one an OPAC and the other an SA, which provides some interesting comparisons and contrasts between the two types of landlord. Both have a high turnover rate of over 16%, and a quite high vacancy rate, although that of the SA is worse, especially for dwellings empty over three months.

The proportion of tenants who are over two months in arrears with their rents is, however, much worse with the OPAC than the SA. This is hardly surprising when 42% of the OPAC tenants draw housing benefit, compared with 23% of the SA tenants; 44% of the OPAC households have incomes below 80% of the national median, compared with 23% of the SA households; 18% of the OPAC households have two incomes coming in, compared with 62% of the SA households and 14% of the OPAC tenants are single parents, compared with 8% of the SA tenants.

Allocations

In principle, applicants for HLM accommodation can apply to as many landlords as they wish, and there are no formal and few informal geographical limitations. A study of local waiting lists carried out by the municipal planning department at Marseilles in 1985 showed rather less overlap between the waiting-lists of different HLM organisations than might be expected with increasing numbers on waiting-lists. Out of about 7,500 applicants, one in five had applied to two organisations, but only one applicant in 250 had applied to three organisations. It is therefore not surprising that landlords show little interest in setting up clearing-house arrangements.

The practice on allocations tends to belie the freedom in access to waiting-lists. As elsewhere, some HLM organisations are sponsored by employers such as the Post Office or Air France, and so restrict perhaps half their waiting-lists to their own employees. This is particularly important to the employers in areas of high demand. More significantly, as has already been shown, some HLM landlord organisations are reluctant to accept the very poor, mainly because of the inherent financial risk.

Municipalities have extensive nomination rights, formally because of the guarantees which they give on the loans taken out in particular by the OP and OPAC organisations, and informally because of the presence of the mayor and other elected members on the board of management. The complex web of overlapping appointments and patronage which is a characteristic, although declining, feature of French political life (le cumul des mandats) can have a major influence on allocation policies and individual cases. It is therefore understandable if the OP landlord organisations often feel that they come under undue pressure from their municipal sponsors to accept problem families.

Even municipalities which do not have their own OP landlord organisation can play a political role on the housing stage. For example, the communist mayor of Vénissieux near Lyons is reported in the Rhône-Alpes pages of *Le Monde* on 16 September 1987 as accusing the local upper-tier metropolitan authority, the Communauté Urbaine de Lyon (COURLY) of meddling in the affairs of local HLM organisations, while he himself is well known for his efforts to stop them accepting more tenants from minority ethnic groups on the Les Minguettes estate (see Section VII) which lies in his area.

Relations with central government

Central government also has a substantial role in the allocation process. The Préfet, central government's representative at the

Département or county level, has formal nomination rights on up to 30% of lettings, some for government employees and some for people in priority categories of need. Landlord organisations can refuse to accept the first two of the Préfet's nominations but must then accept the third. In practice, there is rarely a confrontation on these lines, and all cases are dealt with by negotiation. Nor does the Préfet normally exercise anything like the number of nomination rights to which he is entitled.

Central government rather than local government has traditionally had a dominant influence on the building programmes of HLM organisations, as programming and finance of projects is a matter for central government through the Préfet. Indeed, in the post-war boom in HLM housing, although the HLM organisations were responsible for the actual construction process, it was central government which said how much housing should be built, where, and by what building method.

Under decentralisation, the municipalities are encouraged to produce their individual strategies for dealing with local housing needs, and to send copies to the Préfets in support of their claims for resources to be directed towards organisations in their area, but the executive relationship remains between the HLM organisations and central government through the Préfet. As will become clear, it is central government rather than the local authorities who pay the piper, and the local authorities make only a very limited financial contribution to the provision of HLM housing.

Traditionally, with the exception of a few large organisations, the individual HLM organisations have little direct contact with central Ministries in Paris, and dealings on such matters as normal scheme approval are handled by central government's officials at the local Département level. The creation in 1982 of the National Commission to develop initiatives on rundown estates brought central government officials into much closer contact with individual HLM organisations, and although much of the work on scheme development was subsequently devolved to the regional and Département levels, it would seem that a lasting closer relationship has been forged between Paris and some local organisations.

Less happily, Paris steps in when HLM organisations run into financial difficulties, as apparently is increasingly the case in the largely privately sponsored SA sector, whose debt profile is more vulnerable than is that of the OP and OPAC sector (where in any event, organisations in trouble can usually be helped by their sponsoring municipalities). According to some estimates, up to a fifth of the SA organisations are in trouble. The normal course is for ministry officials to negotiate a recovery plan with the HLM organisation. In serious cases, the ministry can put in its own temporary administrator, and typically about five organisations are subject to this arrangement at any one time. Liquidation is seen only as a last resort, in which case, the assets would be transferred to other HLM organisations (as has happened in the case of the Neue Heimat company in Germany - see Chapter 3, Section III).

Relationships with the municipalities

Apart from the local authorities formal and informal role in allocations which has been described above, there is a vital interface between local authorities and HLM organisations in matters of day-to-day service delivery. Although there are considerable local variations, broadly, the HLM organisations are responsible for what goes on within the curtilage of their buildings; caretaking, cleansing of common areas, ensuring that there are effective arrangements for getting refuse to collection points, and repairs. Although there are some local initiatives to promote tenant self-help in such areas as cleaning of landings and staircases, they have not yet had much success, but tenants have long since been responsible for specified running repairs and decoration. Other minor repairs are done by the caretaker (who is usually resident), while major repairs are put out to contractors unless the HLM organisation has its own maintenance service.

Although the demarcation lines between HLM organisations and municipalities vary from place to place, local authorities are normally responsible for such services as street cleansing, lighting, and collecting refuse, although the HLM organisations often do this themselves. Maintenance of flowerbeds, grass and landscaped areas presents most demarcation difficulties, and those HLM organisations which are responsible for this work are often negotiating with the municipality to take over the land and the responsibilities which go with it, particularly on problem estates.

Fraught with potential difficulties as these relationships may seem to those familiar with British council estates, it is rare to find a housing manager or local government officer in France (or West Germany or the Netherlands, which have similar arrangements) who would claim in practice to suffer significant demarcation difficulties except on the most problematic estates. As far as the local authorities are concerned, the provision of services to HLM estates is usually financially and operationally the same as to owner-occupied and privately rented housing, though it is not entirely unknown for HLM organisations to accuse their local authorities of unfair discrimination. The quality of delivery by different HLM landlords and local authorities certainly varies, but the gap between the best and the worst is clearly much narrower than in England.

Relationships within the HLM movement

Rather different issues arise in the case of relationships between HLM organisations themselves, especially where more than one owns and manages housing on the same estate. The extreme case is Les Minguettes near Lyons, where 11 HLM organisations are involved, some of them responsible for more than one parcel of the 9,000 dwellings on the estate. Although there are overall coordinating arrangements between them to implement the measures to rescue the estate, the management approaches of the various organisations, for example on tenant consultation, differ vastly. Examples will be considered in depth in Section VII.

At the same time, on the large estates, there is less conscious sense of competition between HLM organisations for tenants than might be expected, given the still major problem of empty dwellings, and despite the considerable scope which exists for different permutations of rent levels, service and amenities. Where rivalries are apparent, they seem to be in the form of broad generalities such as pointing an accusing finger at the remote management and financial irresponsibility of the municipal HLM organisation which has simply abandoned a large parcel of empty housing at Les Minguettes, or jockeying for position against one another in the battle for resources.

Individual HLM organisations are increasingly preparing their own standardised information systems, often as joint ventures with other local HLM organisations. A typical arrangement provides for a profile of the organisation's housing stock; the number of units with a breakdown by age and size (area, number of rooms and intended size of household), with management information such as turnover rates, vacancy rates (in total and over three months), rent arrears and average levels of rent and charges. Information about the tenants includes a breakdown by household size and age of head of household, with incomes in bands in relation to national median income, and the proportion who are in receipt of housing benefit. The HLM movement has considerable political influence which cuts across party lines. The former socialist housing minister Roger Quilliot as president of the movement's umbrella organisation UNFOHLM, and his right-wing successor Pierre Méhaignerie were on very similar wavelengths in their speeches to the national HLM conference in May 1987. Even though the minister took a robust line on financial resources, his references to his ambitions for a breakthrough with sales of HLM dwellings to their tenants were studiously delicate.

Apart from its lobbying role, the UNFOHLM is a major source of services and advice for its member organisations. In particular, it is the driving force behind housing management training. Housing managers come from a variety of backgrounds, and few of them as yet have any formal professional qualification. In 1986, UNFOHLM started to sponsor a two-year course at its own headquarters and at one of the major Paris colleges, the Institut pour la Formation de la Maîtrise d'Ouvrage. It accepts 60 students a year at various stages in their housing career. UNFOHLM also lays on a wide range of short courses and seminars on current management issues, including workshops on measures to turn round problem estates.

Another recent development has been an initiative funded by the Ministry of Housing at a cost of FF 25 million a year to provide a consultancy service for HLM organisations needing to improve their organisational and housing management. Between 120 and 160 organisations a year are benefiting from this scheme.

IV Finance

HLM organisations are independent cost centres, mostly smaller than the average English local authority housing department, and because of the limited variation of age and built form within their stock, mostly with little scope for cross-subsidisation or pooling of costs between their tenants. Indeed, the advent of 'conventionnement' (see pages 82-83) automatically hives off new and improved housing into a separate financial régime. Nor is there any equivalent of rate fund contributions to subsidise HLM housing costs.

Thus, the French housing finance system lacks the two features of the British system which have historically broken the links between rent levels and the quality of housing provision, both in the minds of tenants and in the minds of landlords. Under the French arrangements (as also under the arrangements for financing social rented housing in Germany and the Netherlands), any improvement to the quality of the housing or to the level of service provided by the landlord almost inevitably and directly involves an increase in rent which is rarely entirely offset by the bricks and mortar subsidies and housing benefits described below. HLM tenants (and German and Dutch tenants in the social rented sector) therefore see their housing and proposals for improvements to it in clearer value-for-money terms than do their British counterparts.

Nonetheless, there are rigidities within the rent fixing arrangements, which can put considerable strains on the finances of HLM organisations, as has been seen in Section III. Initial rents are fixed at a viable level for the individual project, and below a maximum level per square metre which is laid down by the government according to geographical area. Thereafter, apart from special increases justified by major capital works under the conventionnement rules (see below), rents can be increased only in line with increases in the cost of living. In time, this system can lead to some major distortions, with wide variations between rents for similar properties, and some rents which are uneconomic because they are held down by the ceiling levels.

Overall expenditure

According to Ministry of Housing estimates, about half the FF 34,000 million expenditure by the HLM organisations in 1987 was on debt repayment and interest. Expenditure on management amounted to about FF 10,500 million (or FF 3,500 per dwelling, about £280 in terms of actual purchasing power). Day-to-day maintenance came to FF 3,000 million in all (or about £80 per dwelling), with a similar amount spent on major maintenance work.

As has been seen in previous sections, the new-build programme peaked in the 1970s. Major maintenance work has however increased steadily from the early 1960s. Table 2.6 shows the differing trends between these two categories of capital expenditure between 1965 and 1985.

Table 2.6:   Gross fixed investment 1965-1985 (FF billion in out-turn
prices and in 1971 prices)

	New-build Actual prices	Constant (1971) prices	%	Major maintenance Actual prices	Constant (1971) prices	%	Total Actual prices	Constant (1971) prices
1965	26.53	33.96	81.4	4.95	7.78	18.6	31.48	41.74
1966	29.14	35.96	79.7	6.04	9.15	20.3	35.18	45.11
1967	32.08	38.67	79.9	6.73	9.74	20.1	38.81	48.41
1968	36.44	41.52	70.3	7.71	10.32	20.7	44.15	51.84
1969	39.40	42.23	79.2	9.33	11.09	20.8	48.73	53.32
1970	42.08	43.08	78.7	10.71	11.69	21.3	52.79	54.77
1971	47.50	47.50	79.9	11.94	11.94	20.1	59.44	59.44
1972	53.28	50.49	79.6	14.04	12.90	20.4	67.32	63.39
1973	63.16	54.67	80.0	16.45	13.67	20.0	79.61	68.34
1974	76.76	57.48	80.1	20.98	14.29	19.9	97.74	71.77
1975	82.39	56.38	80.3	22.94	13.83	19.7	105.33	70.21
1976	91.69	54.96	79.4	27.23	14.27	20.6	118.92	69.23
1977	94.70	52.54	78.2	30.92	14.61	21.8	125.66	67.15
1978	99.89	51.02	77.3	35.22	14.96	22.7	135.10	65.98
1979	115.41	52.92	77.4	41.60	15.43	22.6	157.01	68.35
1980	122.66	49.59	75.8	49.85	15.86	24.2	172.51	65.45
1981	131.87	48.45	75.1	57.41	16.10	24.9	189.29	64.55
1982	130.63	43.13	72.5	67.89	16.37	27.5	198.52	59.50
1983	133.16	41.18	71.6	74.84	16.37	28.4	208.10	57.55
1984	128.23	37.84	69.9	81.53	16.29	30.1	209.66	54.13
1985	127.81	36.36	68.9	88.06	16.45	31.1	215.87	52.81

Source: INSEE, 'Les Comptes de Logement en Base 1971', Tables
12 and 14; 'Le Report sur les Comptes de la Nation', Vol
2, Table 64

Bricks and mortar subsidies

The acute housing shortage which France faced at the end of the
Second World War inspired a range of subsidies to bricks and
mortar (aides à la pierre).   These subsidies applied to the
construction of private rented housing as well as the HLM sector
and owner-occupation. Despite numerous modifications since their
introduction in 1947, the principle of long-term loans at interest

rates heavily subsidised by the state has continued throughout the post-war period in all three tenures.

Loans to finance rented property in both the private and HLM sectors are made under an arrangement known as 'Prêts locatifs aidés' (PLA) - assisted loans for renting. There are two government-backed lending institutions which provide a pool of low-cost finance for housing activity which the government wishes to promote, such as PLA and PLI (the scheme for up-market but subsidised rented housing which was described in the previous section). Private landlords, developers and owner-occupiers obtain such finance through the Crédit Foncier de France. HLM organisations go to the Caisse dés Dépôts et Consignations which provides finance for public sector bodies, usually on rather better terms than does the Crédit Foncier de France.

Although they are probably unaware of it, the savings of small private individuals in 'Livret A' accounts at the Caisses d'Epargne or savings banks are a major source of finance for PLA (and PLI) loans made by these two lending organisations. A further important source of finance for the social rented sector is the '1% patronal' or employers' payroll levy. At a current actual rate of 0.77%, the total generated by the '1% patronal' levy in 1985 amounted to FF 13,465 million or £1,052 million, of which FF 4,593 million or £359 million went on HLM projects, three-quarters of it to the mainly privately based SAs, and a quarter to the municipal OPs and OPACs.[25]

The Act of 3 September 1947 originally enabled HLM organisations to borrow money at an interest rate of 1% over 65 years. Gradually, the terms became less favourable, with the period of the loan being reduced first to 45 years, then to 40 years, and the interest rate rising to 3.6%.

A radical change in direction came, however, with the financial reforms of 1977 which shifted government support towards personal subsidies in the form of housing benefits, and also tightened the terms on which bricks and mortar subsidies were provided. The interest rate rose in the first instance to 5.5% with a progressive adjustment factor which brought the effective rate up to nearly 6.6%. Subsequent interest rates have varied on PLA and PLI loans, but the overall effect has been a sharp increase in rent levels for HLM dwellings involving loans under the new arrangements.

The key feature of these new arrangements has been the introduction of '**conventionnement**'. This is a legally binding agreement for the duration of the loan between a landlord and the state which links bricks and mortar subsidies to rent levels and to tenants' eligibility to housing benefits (see below). It applies to two classes of HLM dwelling. First, new dwellings built after 1977 under this less generous bricks and mortar subsidy regime - but still with the state help which it implies - are automatically subject to conventionnement and thus to higher rents. Second, as a condition of state help towards the renovation of existing dwellings (about 80,000 a year at recent levels), HLM landlords have to accept conditions laid down by the state about standards of amenity and occupation levels, as well as rent increases.

Although the 1977 reform was intended to reduce the total level of bricks and mortar subsidies, in the event, they have continued to increase. Between 1978 and 1985, the total bricks and mortar subsidy bill doubled from FF 10,000 million to FF 20,000 million at 1985 prices. Even when the major distortion of help to owner-occupiers is removed, which rose from nothing in 1978 to nearly FF 7,200 million in 1985, there is still a substantial upwards trend in bricks and mortar subsidies to the rented sector. It can be safely assumed that most of this expenditure has been going to the HLM sector.

A major new source of bricks and mortar subsidy to the HLM sector under the 1977 reforms was the introduction of PALULOS (Primes à l'amélioration des logements à l'usage locatif et à occupation sociale). PALULOS consists of central government grants towards the renovation of HLM rented dwellings. The grant can cover 20% of the costs of such schemes (25% in schemes sponsored by the National Commission, the French initiative resembling Estate Action in England, which is described in detail in Section VII) up to a guideline unit cost limit of FF 70,000 (£5,600). It can be topped up by such sources as the 1% patronal to a maximum of 20%, and local authorities at the municipal, county (Département) and Regional levels. The balance - which determines the size of the rent increase after renovation - is borrowed from the Caisse d'Epargne at an interest rate of 5.8%. The PALULOS budget in 1987 was FF 1,290 million (£103 million). In 1985, about 191,000 grants were made for major schemes, averaging about FF 10,500 (£820) per unit. With contributions and borrowing from other sources, total unit costs therefore amounted to an average of some £4,000. Dwellings improved with the help of PALULOS automatically become subject to conventionnement.

Housing benefits

The 1977 reforms incorporated the existing housing benefit system of 'Allocations logement' (AL), while introducing a new system of 'Aide personalisée au logement' (APL). AL originated as part of the social security system, and has remained so in its principles. In consequence, childless couples - except in the first five years of marriage - and individuals between the ages of 25 and 65 - whether living alone or not - are not eligible for AL, irrespective of their rent or income. On the other hand, APL was in origin and intent a housing subsidy, and makes no such exceptions. All the conditions about entitlement are to do with housing.

The arrangements and levels of benefit under both systems should be considered against the background of the relatively generous social security support for those who are in work as well as for those who are out of a job or otherwise badly off (see Chapter 1). Perhaps most significantly, family allowances in France provide a major income supplement, which is largely unrelated to income, for families with two or more children. For example, a family with three children on the average male average annual earnings of FF 77,500 in 1983 would have drawn a monthly family allowance of FF 556 (about £45 in terms of actual purchasing power).[26]

As the new system is intended ultimately to supersede the old one, only those who are ineligible for APL can receive AL. However, as APL applies only to dwellings which have been built or have become subject to conventionnement since 1977, the new system will take a considerable time to replace the old one. Both apply to owner-occupiers who are buying their homes, as well as to private and HLM tenants. The levels of both depend on household size and income, and rent costs. APL is generally more flexible than AL, but older people living alone fare better under AL.[27] As far as HLM tenants are concerned, the key qualification for APL is that they must be renting a dwelling which is subject to conventionnement.

Taken together, the PALULOS bricks and mortar subsidy, and APL support to tenants in any property which is renovated with financial help from the state are a powerful spur to HLM landlords to do up their rundown housing. Table 2.7 (and Table 2.20 in Section VI) show the extent to which conventionnement has increased HLM rents in different areas and affected their affordability. Another effect has been increased competitiveness between private sector rents and the increased HLM rents, apart from Paris. However, competition is not entirely a matter of price, and it is generally recognised that the standard of the renovated HLM housing is higher than the average in the private rented sector.

Table 2.7: **Rent levels (1984, in FF)**

	With Convt.	HLM Without Convt.	Overall	Private rented	Rented overall
Rural	1,075	750	879	788	801
Urban					
less than 100,000	933	714	776	953	877
100,000-2,000,000					
peripheral estates	1,111	707	830	1,109	980
inner area	898	685	735	1,089	960
Paris					
outer	1,043	835	880	1,428	1,161
inner	1,051	895	920	1,632	1,517
Overall	985	741	805	1,123	1,003

Source: INSEE, 'Premiers Résultats No. 89', Table 3

The downside of conventionnement is that it contributes to the soaring cost of housing benefits. The Laxan report (see below) claims that only 18% of rent rises through conventionnement are borne by the tenants.[28] However, there are of course other important contributory factors to the rising bill for housing benefits. The number of claimants in the remainder of the rented sector also increased with the recession of the 1980s, as did the number of owner-occupiers needing help with their repayments. Between 1983 and 1986, the number of claimants increased by about 40% overall. Claimants rose from 3.65 million to 3.94 million, while expenditure rose from FF 24,000 million to FF 34,000 million or, also, by about 40%.[29]

In the case of AL, the number of claimants and expenditure within these totals dropped slightly overall, as is to be expected with the transition to the APL system. (Although the figures are not broken down fully, it is likely that the number of HLM tenants claiming AL also decreased.) On the other hand, the number of HLM tenants claiming APL more than doubled, from 281,274 to 596,663.[30]

Extrapolating from the incomplete figures available, an estimated 863,000 HLM tenants were claiming AL, making a total of some 1.46 million (or about half the total) HLM tenants claiming housing benefits of perhaps FF 11,000 million to FF 12,000 million. This is about 40% of a total annual HLM rent roll of some FF 29,000 million. (As a rough comparison, about two-thirds of English local authority tenants receive housing benefit, amounting to half the total rent roll.)

Faced with a housing benefit bill which in real terms had risen by a factor of more than ten since the 1977 reforms, in December 1986, the government commissioned a study by Max Laxan of the Crédit Foncier de France to find ways of containing the increases. His report, delivered in March 1987, contained recommendations which were mainly designed to discourage people with marginal incomes from over-extending themselves as purchasers. However, he also recommended some trimming of benefit payments to tenants.

The government's response to the recommendations applying to the HLM sector is to maintain the existing arrangements for those already living in dwellings subject to conventionnement, but to provide lower levels of benefit for those who move into dwellings subject to 'conventionnement' from elsewhere. In addition, in order to restrain expenditure and to prevent tenants from getting better housing at little extra net cost, for those rented dwellings which became subject to conventionnement from the beginning of 1988, the scale of assistance is the less generous AL scale but without the exclusion for childless couples and single householders (see above). As a sweetener, tenants in unimproved HLM dwellings all become eligible for benefit, but on the AL scale rather than the more generous APL.

V   The buildings

The most striking features of the HLM stock are its newness, and the overwhelming proportion of flats.   Some 91.7% of HLM dwellings were built after 1948, compared with 56.2% in the owner-occupied sector and 43.1% in the private rented sector.   Half of the entire HLM stock of three million dwellings was built in the 13 year period between 1962 and 1974 (see Table 2.8).

Table 2.8: Age profile of the HLM stock 1982

	%		%
Pre-1871	0.5	1962-1967	19.8
1871-1914	1.1	1968-1974	30.2
1915-1948	6.8	Post-1975	20.0
1949-1961	21.6		

Source: 1982 census, Table 301

Only 9.1% of HLM dwellings are houses, compared with 54% overall,[32] although houses form a much higher proportion of the most recent stock (24% of HLM dwellings built between 1981 and 1984).[33]

High-rise blocks of up to 20 floors are common, as are long straight or curved medium-rise slab blocks of 8 to 10 floors. Some of these slab blocks extend for up to a quarter of a mile. Typically, HLM high-rise and medium-rise blocks are served by lifts and staircases leading to two, three or four flats on each floor. Balcony or deck access is much less common. Entryphone systems and lockable main entrance doors are also rare, but are increasingly included in renovation schemes. Even so, the need for such security measures is a matter of continuing debate.

A national survey of the HLM stock undertaken by the Ministry of Housing in 1985, with the results interpreted by the Nancy-based research organisation Laboratoire-logement, provides information about 2.27 million dwellings in 18 of the 22 Régions of France. Although it is incomplete, this survey (which is updated annually) gives the best available recent and detailed information about the management characteristics of the social rented sector. Table 2.9 shows the distribution of these dwellings between individual houses and different sizes of blocks of flats. The survey shows that over three-quarters of flats are in blocks of more than 20 dwellings, while 15% of them are in blocks of more than 100 dwellings.

Table 2.9: Distribution of dwellings by units per block 1985

Number of units per block	Number of dwellings	%
1 (houses)	141,624	6.2
2 - 9	88,993	3.9
10-19	308,559	13.6
20-49	884,652	38.9
50-99	495,220	21.8
>100	350,834	15.4
Total	2,273,534	100.0

Source: MELATT/Laboratoire-logement Enquiry, Table 51

Another indicator of the extent of problematic HLM housing is the proportion to be found in priority planning zones, ZUPs, ZACs and the like. Although many of these initiatives, especially those developed within existing urban areas, have become successful communities with comprehensive facilities, some contain notoriously large and badly located estates with major social problems. According to the Ministry of Housing/Laboratoire-logement survey, a quarter of HLM dwellings are in priority planning zones. This picture is reinforced by the government's 1984 *Housing Survey* which, as is shown in Table 2.10, found a great preponderance of HLM housing - in relation to the distribution of the stock as a whole - in towns with between 100,000 and 2,000,000 inhabitants, and nearly as great a preponderance in the Paris area.

Despite the disadvantages suffered by many HLM estates in terms of size and location, the individual dwellings generally score well on levels of amenity and space standards. Although there is no information about their condition, about the state of their environment, or about levels of thermal and sound insulation, the 1984 *Housing Survey* found that over nine-tenths of them had all the principal amenities; internal WC, bath or shower, and central heating.

Table 2.10: Distribution of HLM dwellings and total housing stock
by type and size of municipality 1984

	HLM dwellings	All dwellings
Rural communes	3.6	24.9
Towns <100,000	34.7	28.7
Towns 100,000-2,000,000	37.4	28.4
Paris	24.2	17.9
	100.0	100.0

Source: INSEE, Constructed from 'Premiers Résultats, No. 89',
Table 1

The same survey found that HLM dwellings also fare better than
those in the private rented sector in terms of the number of rooms
(3.2 rooms, as against 2.7 on average) and of size (68.8 square
metres of usable space including bathroom and kitchen but not
entrance hall, as against 56.8 square metres). The 1982 census (see
Tables 2.11 and 2.12) provides a similar comparative picture about
amenities and numbers of rooms.

Table 2.11: Amenities 1982

	HLM %	Overall %
Bath or shower	96.5	84.7
Central heating	88.7	67.5
Inside WC	85.6	62.6
Telephone	68.0	74.4

Source: MELATT, 'Le parc d'HLM locatives, No. 84/233'

The size profile of HLM dwellings is significant, with a
concentration of three and four roomed accommodation, and
conversely, a low proportion of larger units in relation to the stock
as a whole, and a significantly smaller proportion of small units
than in the private rented sector. The next section considers the
match between household size and dwelling size.

Table 2.12: Number of habitable rooms 1982 (%)

	1	2	3	4	5	6 & +	Average
Owner-occupied	2.0	8.3	21.2	30.3	22.3	15.9	4.21
Private rented	14.3	25.3	29.0	19.8	7.8	3.8	2.95
HLM	5.8	17.1	36.6	30.3	8.8	1.5	3.24
Overall	7.3	14.8	25.7	26.8	15.5	9.9	3.65

Source: MELATT, 'Le parc d'HLM locatives, No. 84/233'

VI The tenants

The main mismatch between the profiles of dwelling size and household size in the HLM sector is the propensity of large families to move into HLM housing, and the shortage of large units in the HLM stock (see Section V, Table 2.12). Broadly, with a total of 13.5% of the stock nationally, and a lower than average proportion of large units, the HLM sector accommodates 22% of five-person households and 26% of six-person households. It is therefore not surprising that over-occupation in the HLM sector at 19% is higher than the national average of 15.8%.

Table 2.13 shows the comparative distribution of households by size in the HLM sector and overall. It will be seen that small households are slightly under-represented in the HLM sector, as also are small dwellings (see Table 2.12).

Table 2.13: Household size 1982

	Number per household %					
	1	2	3	4	5	6
HLM	22.4	24.7	20.5	16.4	8.4	7.6
Overall	24.6	28.5	18.8	16.1	7.4	4.8

Source: MELATT, 'Le parc d'HLM locatives, No. 84/233'

The figures for small households in HLM housing mask a striking contrast between the representation of the two ends of the age spectrum among HLM tenants. As Table 2.14 shows, older people are heavily under-represented, while young people are over-represented in almost exactly the same proportions (although they are even more heavily over-represented in the private rented sector). The tendency of younger tenants during the last two decades to regard renting as a stepping-stone to owner-occupation has contributed greatly to this age profile, and it is notable that the proportion of owner-occupiers overtakes the proportion of tenants at the age of 35. This trend is underlined by comparing the results of the 1982 census with the housing surveys of 1973 and 1978, which show the proportion of HLM tenants aged between 40 and 49 dropping from 21.1% to 15.1%.

Table 2.14: Age of head of household 1982 (%)

	< 30	30-39	40-49	50-64	>65+
HLM	23.8	25.8	15.1	20.1	15.2
Overall	14.1	21.2	16.4	25.1	23.2

Source: MELATT, 'Le parc d'HLM locatives, No. 84/233'

However, with the changes in the social composition of the HLM sector which are described in this section, the present age profile (and household size) are liable to radical changes in the future. A further possible complicating factor is the encouraging tendency noted by some housing managers for older people to move back to problem estates which have been turned round in recent years, usually to be nearer to their families. The statistical data available from the 1973 and 1978 *Housing Surveys* and from the 1982 census show a marked long-term trend towards an older population in the HLM sector, including an above average proportion of elderly people moving into this sector than into other sectors.

The 1984 *Housing Survey* shows couples with children and single parent families to be more heavily represented in the HLM sector than generally. This is of considerable relevance to the problem estates, where coping with high densities of children and especially of adolescents is one of the major issues. In 1984, 42.9% of HLM households were couples with children compared with 37.7% of households nationally, while 11.2% of HLM households

were single parent families compared with 8% nationally.
According to the 1982 census, 9.2% of HLM households were
single parent families, and the HLM sector housed 28.6% of all
such families. Bearing in mind that the private rented sector is
nearly twice as large as the HLM sector, Table 2.15, based on 1984
data, underlines the way in which the HLM sector caters for a
disproportionate share of families with children and single parent
families in unfurnished rented accommodation as a whole.

Table 2.15: Household type and the unfurnished rented sector 1984

	HLM %	Private rented %	All rented (thousands)	%
Childless couples under 60	32	69	1,234	16
Couples with children	43	57	2,917	38
Single parent families	53	47	617	8
One-person households under 30	24	76	516	7
One-person households aged 60 and over	33	66	1,037	13
Childless couples aged 60 and over	36	64	786	10
All households (including types not shown separately)	38	62	7,723	100

Source: Constructed from 'Le parc locatif et ses occupants',
            Table 4, in *Economie et Statistique*, September 1987

Section II referred to the way in which the media have
concentrated on immigrants in their sensationalist reporting of the
problems of HLM estates. The influx of people from the poorer
countries of southern Europe, and from North Africa with the end
of French rule there, has had a huge and continuing influence on
French social attitudes over the past two decades. According to
Données Sociales 1987 (the French equivalent of *Social Trends*),
the number of foreigners in France doubled between 1954 and
1982, from 1,765,000 to 3,680,000. Of the present population,
6.8% come from abroad. Immigrants live predominantly in urban
areas, and unemployment is particularly high among young people
in immigrant families. One in four immigrants live in HLM

housing compared with one in eight of the population as a w
No less than 41% of those coming from former French territories
overseas live in HLM housing. The 1982 census shows 10.8% of
HLM dwellings occupied by immigrant households, the vast
majority of whom come from North Africa and southern Europe
(see Table 2.16).

Table 2.16: Immigrant households occupying HLM dwellings 1982

Algerians	73,220
Portuguese	52,880
Moroccans	40,540
Spanish	24,060
Italians	23,040
Tunisians	16,300

Source: MELATT, 'Le parc d'HLM locatives, No. 84/233'

These groups are generally considered to be concentrated on
problem estates, and to be living in the worst conditions. The 1982
census showed that over-occupation among immigrants in HLM
accommodation is particularly severe at 45%, even if this is not
quite as bad as the 53% national average of over-crowding for this
group.

Comparisons of 1982 census data on the socio-economic status
of HLM tenants with data from the 1978 *Housing Survey* provide
little evidence of any real shift at that time, apart from a greater
tendency among people in the intermediate professional category
than among workers to move into the newest (and hence most
expensive) property. However, it was clear that families of manual
workers and lower-paid employees represented a clear majority
(58%) of HLM households, compared with rather more than a third
(36.4%) of households in the population as a whole. There is
additional evidence to support this trend in the 1984 *Housing
Survey*. As Table 2.17 which is drawn from this survey shows, the
HLM sector caters for a disproportionate share of manual workers
and junior white-collar workers in comparison with the private
rented sector.

Table 2.17: Employment status and the unfurnished rented sector
1984

	HLM %	Private rented %	All rented (thousands)	%
Employers and self-employed	13	88	443	6
Senior managers	16	83	554	7
Middle managers	27	73	872	11
Clerical staff	46	54	900	12
Manual workers and foremen	48	52	2,502	32
Other economically active	37	63	343	4
Retired	36	64	1,540	20
Other economically inactive	40	60	571	7
Total	38	62	7,723	100

Source: Constructed from 'Le parc locatif et ses occupants',
Table 6, in *Economie et Statistique*, September 1987

Table 2.18, analysing the changes in occupational status within
the HLM sector between 1978 and 1984, shows that there was little
change in the proportions of manual and junior white-collar
workers, but a substantial increase in the number of economically
inactive heads of household. Between the two surveys, there was
an increase of 800,000 in the number of economically inactive
heads of household, of which 280,000 (35%) were in the HLM
sector, even though this sector comprised only 13% of all heads of
household in 1978. On the other hand, although the numbers are
small (and the comparison as a whole is imprecise because of
changes in definition), there is also a noticeable increase in the
numbers of employers, the self-employed, higher management and
professional people.

Table 2.18: Occupation of heads of household in the HLM sector
1978 and 1984

	HLM (thousands)	%	Private rented (thousands)	%
Employers and self-employed	35	1	55	2
Senior managers etc	65	3	90	3
Middle managers	250	10	235	8
Clerical staff	285	11	410	14
Manual workers and foremen	1,150	46	1,195	41
Other economically active	180	7	125	4
Economically inactive	510	21	790	27
Total	2,480	100	2,890	100

Source: Constructed from 'Le parc locatif et ses occupants',
Table 6, in *Economie et Statistique*, September 1987

However, Table 2.19 comparing of 1978 and 1984 *Housing Survey* data shows that unemployment among HLM tenants has risen more than among private sector tenants, and even more than among owner-occupiers.

Table 2.19: Unemployment among household heads by tenure 1978 and 1984

	1978 %	1984 %
HLM tenants	2.9	8.4
Other tenants	3.3	7.8
Owner-occupiers with mortgages	1.6	2.0

Source: *Economie et Statistique*, September 1987, page 34

The 1984 *Housing Survey* provides some useful additional and more recent information in the form of the trend in household income in the HLM sector. In 1978, the proportion of households in HLM accommodation with incomes below the median was 48%. In 1984, it had risen to 59%, for those who had recently moved into HLM housing (that is between 1981 and 1984), the proportion was as high as 62%.

The most telling evidence of more recent trends towards greater social disadvantage in the HLM sector is provided by the soaring numbers of housing benefit claimants examined in Section IV. This evidence suggests that about half HLM households were claiming housing benefits in 1986. This is three times higher than the 17% proportion of claimants among the population as a whole, according to *Données Sociales 1987*.

The proportion of income which goes on rent varies considerably depending on whether or not a tenant is drawing housing benefit. As Table 2.20 shows, there are also significant differences between established HLM tenants and those who have recently moved into the HLM sector, especially those who occupy a new or renovated HLM dwelling, in effect one subject to conventionnement, and the gap is likely to widen with the new housing benefit rules (see Section IV).

Table 2.20: Proportion of tenants' income going on gross rent 1978 and 1984

	1978 (%)	1984 (%)
Tenants overall	10.3	12.4
HLM tenants	8.4	10.8
Recent HLM tenants	9.3	12.2
of which in new dwellings subject to conventionnement	10.4	18.3

Source: INSEE, 'Les HLM - une vocation sociale qui s'accentue', Table 4

Although HLM tenants generally devote a lower proportion of their income to housing than do tenants as a whole, those who occupy such dwellings and who draw housing benefit pay a higher than average proportion of their incomes on rent. This was the fastest growing group of claimants between 1978 and 1984, not least because their rents more than trebled in this period. Despite the greater payout which such tenants received from APL, the proportion of their incomes which went on rent increased by no less than 50%.[34]

Overall, between 1978 and 1984, rents both in the HLM sector and for tenants as a whole more than doubled. At the same time, incomes increased more slowly (by 78%), so that the proportion of tenants' income going on rent increased by 11% (from 6.71% to 7.46%).[35]

HLM tenants are less mobile than the population as a whole, and their mobility is tending to decline with the fall in the numbers of new HLM dwellings becoming available. As might be expected, younger people are more likely to move. Mobility is much lower in areas of high housing demand, especially Paris, partly no doubt because of the high rents in alternative accommodation in the private rented sector.

The relatively detailed statistical information which is available about tenants in the HLM sector therefore supports the widely held thesis that despite the marginal increase in the number of managerial and professional people in the sector, HLM tenants suffer greater economic and social disadvantage than the population as a whole, and that residualisation is increasing. In part, this is due to the continuing decline of the private rented sector, where as elsewhere, property is being sold into owner-occupation. This particularly affects the bottom end of the market which traditionally has housed the poorest families, and to an extent still does provide alternative basic housing for those unable to find a home in the HLM sector.

While the HLM sector is increasingly having to accept the severely disadvantaged, this is a relatively new role for its landlord organisations, and one for which they are not altogether prepared, either economically or as managers. They are making serious efforts to adapt their management practices to cope with tenants with problems to which they are largely unaccustomed. Moreover, as has been noted in previous sections, this shift is raising some major social and financial questions for the landlord organisations, for their tenants, and for the community at large.

To the extent that these problems tend to be concentrated on a minority of easily identifiable estates, they are the increasingly the concern of the National Commission, whose activity is considered in detail in Section VII.

VII Management problems and solutions

Extent of the problems

In France, there is nothing on the lines of the English Housing Investment Programme (HIP) system to inform landlords or central policy-makers about needs in the social rented sector, although in 1985, the UNFOHLM set up regional arrangements for monitoring management performance which are leading to the national compilation of statistical indicators. There is therefore limited statistical information to show the extent of management problems, such as English local authorities' estimates of their difficult-to-let stock, empty housing and turnover rates. Nor, despite the earlier interest in France in the problems of rundown housing estates, was there any early serious research similar to that in England in 1976 and 1977, which in 1979 led the DOE to set up its Priority Estates Project (PEP), which too in its turn has become a major source of information about the problems of rundown estates and solutions to them.

As has been shown in Section II, it was primarily hostile coverage by the media of conditions on the large estates, and the violent events on some of them in the hot summer of 1981 (which had their perhaps more serious English counterparts in Brixton and Toxteth) which spurred central government to mount a major expansion of its existing Habitat et Vie Sociale initiative. The launch of the 'Commission Nationale pour le Développement Social des Quartiers' - the National Commission - was therefore largely a political initiative to deal with an evident and serious problem, but one on which there was very limited quantified information about the nature and seriousness of the management problems which the HLM organisations were facing.

As has been shown in Section II, central government and the HLM organisations themselves had long since been acutely concerned about the growing problems. Indeed, the Habitat et Vie Sociale initiative in 1976 was the result of discussions which began in the early 1970s. Vast tracts of empty flats were not only grist to the mills of the media, but also represented a serious financial problem to HLM organisations - many of them vulnerably small - for which their rent income is usually the only source of money to balance their books. Similarly, less visual symptoms of social distress on the estates, such as increasing rent arrears and turnover of tenancies were beginning to take a serious financial toll. Growing unemployment in the economy as a whole was having a particularly marked effect on the social and economic fortunes of many estates, especially in the areas which are in structural decline in the north and east of the country.

Thus, although the National Commission had little in the way of statistics to show trends in aggregate for these various symptoms of growing sickness in the HLM sector when it began business in 1982, the discussions and experience of the previous decade meant that the list of estates which were clear priority candidates for its attentions was easily drawn up.

The subsequent survey in 1985 by the Ministry of Housing and the research organisation Laboratoire-logement (see Section V) reinforces many of the widely held views about where the greatest problems were to be found. Many of the main culprits are estates in huge priority planning zones (ZUPs, ZACs and the like) on the peripheries of towns and cities. These zones are described in Section II. They account for a quarter of the HLM stock. In ZUPs, the turnover rate is 16.5%, compared with a national HLM average of 13.8%, while in ZACs, it is 18.6%.

A similar picture emerges in the case of vacant dwellings, where ZUPs and ZACs have an average vacancy rate of 4.7% and 3.5% respectively, compared with a national HLM average of 2.9%. Even more striking is the number of dwellings which are vacant because of lack of applicants. In comparison with a national HLM rate of 1.1%, the proportion for ZUPs is 2.4%, and for ZACs it is 1.5%.

Vacancy rates also vary significantly in relation to numbers of dwellings per block, with a virtually consistent increase in the total proportion of vacant dwellings, and in the proportion vacant through lack of applicants, as the numbers of units per block increases.

The age of the property is often an important and usually consistent factor. The survey confirmed the common experience of housing managers in other countries that the most popular dwellings are those built before 1949, and by far the least popular are those built in the peak years between 1962 and 1974.

The National Commission

As will be seen, the approach adopted by the National Commission is very similar to that taken quite independently in England in 1985 by the DOE's Urban Housing Renewal Unit, later renamed as 'Estate Action' (see Chapter 2, Section VII). However, there are important differences. Whereas Estate Action was specifically charged by ministers at the outset to seek opportunities for private sector firms to take over parcels of empty housing on estates for improvement and onward sale to owner-occupiers, this has not been part of the National Commission's remit, at least so far.

Another key difference is that while Estate Action activity centres on the improvement of housing conditions - primarily by promoting better housing management on the lines developed in PEP, by diversifying tenure, and by helping with certain categories of physical improvement work - the National Commission (as its full title implies) is more broadly based, with social and economic measures playing a vital part alongside measures to improve the quality of the environment, of the housing and of its management. Thus, while Estate Action is firmly based in the DOE, drawing in limited ways on other departments such as the Department of Employment and the Home Office for resources and specialist expertise, the National Commission draws directly on 11 ministries which cover a wide range of interests including social affairs, employment, commerce, education, justice, economic planning, culture, youth and sport for their resources, expertise, and the staff for its secretariat. These ministries are represented on its executive committee, which also includes the UNFOHLM, the umbrella organisation of the HLM movement.

The launch of the National Commission came at a fortunate historical juncture for it to be able to adopt a broadly based approach. Although inter-ministerial initiatives were by no means unknown previously, they were usually bilateral partnerships. However, as has been shown, the disturbances of 1981 prompted the government of the day to set up three inquiries to tackle the problems on a broader inter-ministerial front. As a result, the National Commission does not come under the wing of any individual ministry, but reports directly to the Prime Minister. This novel feature of French administration makes it much easier than it would be in England for the National Commission to cut across the traditional boundaries between different ministries, especially in finding short cuts through procedures and in securing financial support towards the Commission's activities from a variety of ministerial programmes.

The launch of the National Commission also coincided with the major decentralisation of executive responsibility from central to local government (for a detailed account, see Stephen Garrish's *Centralisation and Decentralisation in England and France*, (SAUS 1986). Thus, while its predecessor Habitat et Vie Sociale consisted of officials at its policy-making level, the Commission has a much more varied membership of 25 people, including five mayors, academics, trade unionists, and representatives of local housing interests. It has throughout been chaired by prominent local authority mayors who have taken an active interest in its activities.

The National Commission started with the benefit of the long-standing existence of close-knit central government executive teams from all the ministries headed by central government's Préfet, and which traditionally provided a wide range of local services in the 95 French geographical Départements. However, the realignment of executive responsibilities between central government, the municipalities (communes), and the recently formed Régions which has taken place under decentralisation has coincidentally strengthened the Commission's hand still further. This realignment of functions has coincidentally favoured an operational structure on the ground which makes for an active partnership between central and local government in the development and implementation of individual projects, in the promotion of good management practice, and in the distribution of resources.

Like Estate Action, the National Commission is able to draw on ear-marked annual resources in support of its projects. Although the sums involved are remarkably similar, there are some important differences in the ways in which they are allocated and spent. In 1987, the total amount budgeted for projects supported by the Commission was FF 690 million or about £55 million. Of this, the largest amount was FF 500 million which the Ministry of Housing made available, principally through PALULOS (see Section IV), for physical improvements to the dwellings themselves.

The remaining FF 190 million came from the other ministries, and was directed towards a variety of capital and current expenditure programmes on the individual estates. Important as the physical measures may be, the National Commission sees its main role in matching comprehensive and coordinated packages of proposals with these limited resources in order to regenerate the social and economic life on the estates. Up to two-fifths of this money goes on current expenditure, for example on staff to promote tenant participation or to improve race relations. Other resources go on a wide variety of capital works, such as landscaping, the creation of children's play areas, communal facilities, and the promotion of small businesses. The development of better opportunities for young people and the unemployed is a high priority.

Although few of the 120 projects which were on the ground by the end of 1986 had then been completed, 40,000 dwellings had been renovated - with the emphasis on thermal insulation and common areas of buildings as well as on the individual dwellings themselves - at a total cost of some FF 3,500 million. This represents a unit cost of rather less than £7,000. In addition, special grants totalling some FF 600 million (£47 million) over the four years had come from the various participating ministries to help with non-housing measures on the estates. In many cases, this money has been matched by local authorities, Regional government, and other public bodies.

The process of allocating the resources from the various government programmes remains formally the responsibility of the individual funding ministries rather than of the Commission. In the first two years, when there were some 20 projects, project approval and resource allocation were coordinated centrally by the Commission. With the increase in the number of projects to about 150 projects, and with the strengthening of local structures under decentralisation, the Commission (like Estate Action) has devolved most of this work to the Regional level. On behalf of their HLM organisations, the municipalities develop and negotiate proposals with central government's Préfets in the 95 geographical Départements. On the basis of these negotiations, the Préfets put in bids to the 18 (out of a total of 22) Régions which are participating in the scheme. The Commission evaluates the Régions' bids and recommends allocations to the Regions from the various programmes. The subsequent share-out is the responsibility of an ad hoc Regional committee.

As with Estate Action projects, the voluntary partnership between central government's devolved structures and all the local agencies with an interest in the estate, and not least that of the residents is therefore of crucial importance. These interests are brought together into a formally constituted local committee which is responsible for developing and implementing the strategy for turning round the estate, and which reports ultimately to the Regional Council which with the Préfet of the Département has the joint responsibility for seeing the project through. Although the municipality is not the landlord, it always has a pivotal role in the Commission's projects, and is responsible for appointing and paying the project director who heads the project team. All sides attach considerable importance to the formal five-year contract which is always made between the various parties. It is seen both as an earnest of continuing political commitment to see the project through to a successful conclusion, and as the firmest possible guarantee that the various parties - including central government - will honour their financial commitments.

Les Minguettes

The estate known as Les Minguettes, which has already been cited several times in this chapter, merits a separate analysis not only because the disturbances there in 1981 were the launching-pad for the National Commission, but also because it is such a typical example of the large peripheral HLM estate.

Built in the late 1960s and early 1970s in the municipality of Vénissieux on the outskirts of Lyons, Les Minguettes at its peak consisted of 9,200 dwellings, four-fifths of them belonging to HLM organisations and the rest in private ownership. It was built under the priority planning zone (ZUP) procedures, which meant that from the outset, relations with the local council were remote. Although the municipality of Vénissieux is a party to the current recovery plan supported by the National Commission, it is clear that relations remain far from easy, and it is a frequent bone of contention that the municipality of Vénissieux lacks its own OP landlord organisation, and so its only direct involvement in the affairs of the estate is to provide supporting services such as street cleaning. It is also alleged that other local authorities in the Lyons conurbation which do have their own OP organisations have long since used Les Minguettes as a dumping-ground for problem families, and the local mayor's resistance to further lettings to immigrant families has already been noted (see Section III).

Although the continuing expansion of local industries guaranteed adequate jobs until the mid-1970s, the subsequent economic problems caused massive unemployment. The 1982 census showed that the estate had 13% unemployment, and the level has since risen. Young people are especially affected, with one person under 30 years of age out of three unemployed in 1982. The social composition of the estate contributes to the residents' low economic expectations. In 1982, one household in three was of foreign origin, mainly from North Africa, and two out of five young foreigners were out of work. Educational attainment was low, with half the population over 17 years of age having no qualifications. In 1986, over four out of five households on the estate were drawing housing benefit. Although the dwellings were generally good internally, heating costs were often high, as also were rents. Externally the estate presented a depressingly stark landscape of tower and slab blocks covering 550 acres. The sense of desolation was compounded by the poor standard of maintenance of the extensive open space, largely because of poor coordination of service delivery between the various levels of local government and the 11 HLM landlord organisations who own and manage blocks of housing on the estate. It is therefore not surprising that those tenants who could do so voted with their feet. By 1980, the overall vacancy rate was 20%. At the lowest point in 1984, one in three HLM dwellings was empty, and pressure for a programme of massive demolition was mounting. Indeed, three tower blocks totalling 180 flats were demolished, although it is argued with some justice that the objective was to reduce excessive density rather than to pander to populist demand.

The formal contract between the parties concerned in the regeneration of Les Minguettes was signed in 1986, but work had already been going on since 1982. First and foremost, it was necessary to develop networks of communication at all levels, not least with the residents, a task towards which the different landlord organisations have clearly adopted a variety of approaches, some considerably more intensive than others.

Just as crucial has been the need to coordinate delivery of the services provided by the various agencies working on the estate. Imaginative landscaping and the creation of children's play areas are an important feature of the scheme, and the high standard of maintenance of flowerbeds, playgrounds and open spaces testifies to the practical success of this coordination. Some, but by no means all, of the HLM organisations have set up local offices on the estate.

Although there has been some restructuring of dwelling sizes, most of the physical work has been to improve the external appearance of the blocks, for example by adding balconies, or in one experimental scheme by the architect Castro, by adding a spectacular entrance lobby to a tower block, with an enclosed garden area, and by training plants up its 16 storeys. Surprisingly, locking entrance doors are not considered necessary, even with an obviously spasmodic concierge service.

On the wider social and economic front, the low level of educational qualification on the estate, especially among the foreign population, has made education a high priority in the project. As with other schemes supported by the National Commission, it has been possible to bend some of the normal rules, and so to make up viable groups for teaching French as a foreign language.

Young unemployed people from the estate have been recruited on to parts of the improvement programmes, and in some cases have moved on to regular employment. Other unemployed people have gone into business on their own account in small shop units converted out of previously unused space at the bottom of tower blocks.

HLM organisations have been encouraged to market their dwellings widely and imaginatively. More radically, one HLM organisation has succeeded in persuading Bioforce, a national agency which trains personnel to work in Third World, to set up its headquarters in a previously empty block, and so bring outside money and some employment opportunities on to the estate.

The costs are high at Les Minguettes and there is still far to go. In the first three years, expenditure amounted to about FF 135 million, which is equivalent to rather less than £2,000 a unit of the remaining stock, although this initial expenditure includes the most expensive renovation and demolition work. Two lots of chronically empty housing comprising about 800 flats in all have been mothballed and their future remains uncertain. Although the HLM landlord of one lot seems to have abandoned them altogether, the other claims to be actively seeking alternative uses including possibly sale to the private sector. Of the roughly 6,400 HLM flats which remain in use out of the original 7,500, the vacancy rate at the end of 1986 was still as high as 21%. Nonetheless, that is a major improvement on a vacancy rate of 26% only a year earlier.

Other National Commission projects

Although Les Minguettes is the National Commission's most far-ranging project, some other examples present differences in scale and emphasis which are worth brief exploration.

Romans-La Monnaie presents a fascinating contrast with Les Minguettes, not only because of its relatively small size at a total of some 2,000 dwellings, but also because of the great differences within the estate. It is situated on the outskirts of a small market town to the south of Lyons. The estate consists of two distinct parts. The older one, the Ancienne Monnaie, consists of dreary and unimproved slab blocks in a bleak environment, with a high proportion of immigrant tenants. It sounded like a counsel of despair to hear that a decision had just been taken to demolish a block on this part of the estate simply to improve morale. It was on the visit here that we encountered our only example of tenant hostility, when a tenant suggested that we might be more usefully employed doing something about the estate instead of taking photographs. This was hardly surprising, given the sense of disadvantage which the tenants there must feel in comparison with those on the newer part of the estate, the Nouvelle Monnaie, where the improvements have been spectacular, and where the tenants are mainly French and altogether more prosperous.

Even though the improved shopping centre on the Ancienne Monnaie is clearly making a good impact (not least because of a convivial 'dry' bar/restaurant patronised by the North African tenants), it was clear that the obviously enthusiastic and open local management office is bound to have a perpetual uphill struggle in coping with two such different communities living so close to one another and in such contrasting housing conditions.

Marseilles could be the subject of a book in itself. Most of the estates visited were in the 13th, 14th, and 15th districts (arrondissements) of the city. The Frais Vallon estate of about 2,000 dwellings differed from the others, as the physical work there had been done in 1975, before the introduction of conventionnement, and so was more dated as well as less ambitious than what we saw elsewhere. The social problems seemed to cause special management difficulties, with a particularly high turnover of tenants, and three out of five on housing benefit. Management is quite intensive, with a staff of 25, plus a repairs team, of which three members are constantly engaged on lift maintenance.

Indeed, the social conditions on the estates in Marseilles generally seemed more acute than most. Migrants were the most striking feature, as at the Petit Séminaire estate, the Font Vert estate, and in one of the few remaining shanty town settlements which ironically is situated just below the virtually empty La Bricarde estate overlooking the Mediterranean. This is a clear example of the reluctance of HLM landlords to accept 'problem families', especially those who are likely to fall into rent arrears.

The HLM organisations are responding with different levels of intensive management, and some imaginative environmental measures, as for example on the picturesquely named Les Lilas and Les Oliviers estates in the priority planning zone 'ZUP No 1'. However, perhaps the most promising project in Marseilles is on another estate in ZUP No 1, Les Flamants, consisting of about 900 dwellings owned by the local OPAC. It not only has a local management office, but also is the subject of an ambitious tenant involvement programme run by an outside consultant. The emphasis on the need for the tenants to be the driving force in determining the fortunes of the estate is very similar to the PEP approach in England.

There is also great emphasis on young people on the estate. The programme involves the local schools. Leisure activities are organised for the evenings, weekends and holidays. Some young people have been recruited for the security teams which patrol the estate.

A typical range of physical and environmental improvements is in progress. However, the most innovative feature of this project is a major conversion of some of the housing into a college for infant teachers, social workers and nurses, which - like the Bioforce initiative at Les Minguettes - is intended to add a new social and economic dimension to the life of the estate. Despite the obvious success of the project so far, and the enthusiasm of those who are carrying it out, there was a real sense of its vulnerability to local political vicissitudes.

Valence, Le Haut is an estate of about 3,000 dwellings owned by the local OP on the outskirts of the medium-sized town of Valence south of Lyons. It has some bleak open spaces, for which development proposals are under consideration. The blocks themselves are rather more attractive than the general run, although some of them are said to be suffering from structural defects. One in five households on the estate is foreign. Rent arrears are high, and petty vandalism is more than usually noticeable. Although the estate still has a persistent problem with high numbers of empty dwellings, the local office is getting to grips with the management in a realistic and imaginative way. There is a local (uniformed) repairs and maintenance team, but tenants are responsible for cleaning their landings and staircases - which are well kept. There is a police presence on the estate, and more emphasis than is typical of French regeneration projects is given to physical security measures with the introduction of entryphones and locking entrance doors. With the creation of individual cellar storage areas, the total cost amounts to FF 3,000 (£230) per dwelling. Little is being spent on insulation and cosmetic improvements, mainly because of the rent increases which such improvements would cause. As at Les Minguettes, there are some encouraging new small shop ventures, and a new restaurant project. As at Les Flamants in Marseilles, there are proposals (as yet tentative in this case) to convert some unused housing into educational facilities, but here they would be for tenants as well as students from outside. A further comparison with Les Flamants is the obviously active involvement of elected members in the affairs of the estate.

At **Mantes-la-Jolie**, the Val Fourré estate is comparable in size with Les Minguettes, and is run by about as many HLM organisations. It consists of about 8,300 dwellings on a 320-acre site on the fringe of this industrial town of some 50,000 inhabitants in the Seine valley, 30 miles from Paris. About 28,000 people live on the estate itself. The population is young, with an average age of 37, and almost half are of foreign origin. The estate is in a priority planning zone (ZUP), whose economic hopes have not been realised, and there is substantial unemployment and poverty. It is characterised by its particularly drab design, high density, poor construction, and unattractive open space, although the setting on the Seine itself is a redeeming feature.

The scheme to revitalise the estate was launched in 1983, with work to rehabilitate the buildings as the starting-point. Although substantial sums have been spent on this physical rehabilitation work at an average cost of over FF 60,000 (£4,800) per unit, by all accounts, the consultation with the residents was less effective than it might have been, and some obvious mistakes were made. The condition of the open spaces and refuse chutes also indicates that coordination between the HLM landlord organisations and the municipality on service delivery still has some way to go.

There has been a growing emphasis, however, on social development. Like the project at Les Flamants in Marseilles, the Val Fourré has a consultant who concentrates on tenant consultation and involvement, with young people as an important part of her brief. Here too, a bar/restaurant has become a major social focus, especially with the immigrant community which forms half the population on the estate. Thorough procedures for tenant consultation have been developed and implemented.

Le Val Fourré is however a prime example of an estate beset by the structural economic weakness of the surrounding area. The municipality and central government have embarked on an ambitious venture to promote more jobs on the estate itself, by helping local companies to increase their capacity, and to promote tourism. The success or failure of this venture to bring some economic hope to the estate is particularly critical in this case to the wider social aims of the Commission's project.

Evaluation

In December 1987, a committee chaired by Mr Francois Lévy produced a report evaluating the impact of the National Commission's work so far. Although the committee appears to have done little detailed analysis of the costs and benefits of Commission schemes individually or as a whole, it is satisfied that they provide good value for money, and that rent arrears and numbers of empty dwellings have been reduced. It is impressed by the less tangible social effects, such as the improved image of estates, the constructive involvement of young people, and the development of local job opportunities. It also welcomes the way in which Commission schemes succeed in actively involving local authorities and the local community, putting much of the credit on the formal agreements between the various parties which underpin all Commission schemes.

On the debit side, the committee was concerned by the lack of clear criteria for selecting projects for Commission support, and by the absence of effective monitoring arrangements. In a comment which may well reflect a wider uncertainty about the emerging roles of the various tiers of local government following the radical moves towards decentralisation over the last decade, it criticises what it describes as the inadequate involvement of the intermediate levels - Région and Département - in Commission schemes. Also, and not surprisingly given the varied sources of potential public financial support for Commission schemes, it believes that the funding mechanisms are too complex and top-heavy.

The Committee notes three main question-marks over the Commission's activity. First, it points to the dilemma about trying to solve far-reaching economic and social problems affecting French society as a whole within the limited area (and society) of a housing estate, and wonders how far this is possible. Second, it refers to the questions raised by the reform of the housing benefit system, although it could just as well have voiced concern generally about any major government initiative which particularly affects the fortunes of problem housing estates and those who live on them. Third, it expresses doubts about the extent to which the benefits of Commission schemes will be long-term, although without citing any evidence for these doubts.

Nonetheless, the Committee is conscious of the broad support for the Commission's work at the local level, and ends with a ringing declaration of support for an initiative which it sees as a matter of national priority and a model for other national initiatives across the spectrum of government.

NOTES

1. *Construction* No 6, October 1987. A summary of information from the 1984 Housing Survey (Enquête logement), by L'Institut National de la Statistique et des Etudes Économiques (INSEE)
2. *Données sociales* 1987 p316, fig 1
3. *Recensement populaire* 1982, table 110
4. *Il était une fois l'habitat* by Guinchat, Chaulet and Gaillardot (Editions du Moniteur, 1981) p105
5. *Données sociales* 1987 p316, fig 1
6. 'Premiers résultats No 70', August 1986 (INSEE), table 2
7. *Données sociales* 1987 p318
8. Digest No 84/233 by Ministère de l'urbanisme et du logement, p4, derived from Recensement populaire data
9. 'Premiers résultats No 70', August 1986 (INSEE), p3
10. *Recensement populaire* 1982, table 301
11. 'Premiers résultats No 70', August 1986 (INSEE), derived from table 3
12. 'Aide-mémoire statistique' for 48e Congrès national HLM 1987, table 3.2
13. 'Premiers résultats No 70', August 1986 (INSEE), table 3
14. *Données sociales* 1987 p316
15. *Données sociales* 1987 p316
16. 'Premiers résultats No 89' April 1987 (INSEE), p1
17. 'Premiers résultats No 70', August 1986 (INSEE), p1
18. 'Aide-mémoire statistique' for 48e Congrès national HLM 1987, table 3.2
19. 'Rapport du Comité Directeur' for 48e Congrès national HLM 1987, p10
20. 'Rapport du Collège des dirigeants du dispositif d'autocontrôle' for 48e Congrès national HLM 1987, pp1 and 6 (second series)
21. 'Rapport du Collège des dirigeants du dispositif d'autocontrôle' for 48e Congrès national HLM 1987, p11 (second series)
22. *Annuaire* HLM 1982 p11
23. 'Rapport du Collège des dirigeants du dispositif d'autocontrôle' for 48e Congrès national HLM 1987, p13 (second series)
24. 'Rapport du Collège des dirigeants du dispositif d'autocontrôle' for 48e Congrès national HLM 1987, pp1 and 6 (second series)
25. 'Aide-mémoire statistique' for 48e Congrès national HLM 1987, table 2.6.2
26. Example provided by Commission Nationale pour le Développement Social des Quartiers
27. *Données sociales* 1987 p320
28. 'Rapport de la Commission sur les aides à la personne en matière de logement' (The Laxan Report, March 1987) p24
29. 'Aide-mémoire statistique' for 48e Congrès national HLM 1987, derived from tables 6.3 and 6.4
30. 'Aide-mémoire statistique' for 48e Congrès national HLM 1987, table 6.3

31. Digest No 84/233 by Ministère de l'urbanisme et du logement, p1, derived from Recensement populaire data

32. Digest No 84/233 by Ministère de l'urbanisme et du logement, p1, derived from Recensement populaire data

33. 'Premiers résultats No 89' April 1987 (INSEE), p1

34. 'Premiers résultats No 89' April 1987 (INSEE), p4

35. 'Premiers résultats No 89' April 1987 (INSEE), p4

three

THE FEDERAL REPUBLIC OF GERMANY

I   The general background

Population and housing stock

According to the Federal Statistical Office (Statistisches Bundesamt), the population of the Federal Republic of Germany and West Berlin was 61 million in 1985, having peaked at nearly 62 million in 1975 from 43 million on the same territory in 1939. The decline is officially expected to continue, to well below 50 million in 2030, but with a steady and significant increase both in the proportion and in the number of older people.

The average household size has gone down in the post-war years, from 2.99 in 1950 to 2.43 in 1982, by which time single-person households had become the largest group. Demographic trends therefore promise to continue to make some radical shifts in housing demand in Germany over the remainder of this century and beyond. Table 3.1 gives a more detailed breakdown of trends in population and household size in the area of the Federal Republic and West Berlin between 1950 and 1982.

Different sources put the total number of dwellings in 1985 at about 26 million[1] or 27 million[2] (accurate figures will be available when the results of the 1987 census - delayed since 1980 - have been analysed). Two dwellings out of every three (18.5 million) in the Federal Republic have been built since 1949, and one in five since 1972.[3]

Table 3.1:   Population and households

	Private household population	All	(thousands) Households Multi-person	One-person
1950	49,850	16,650	13,421	3,229
1957	53,860	18,318	14,945	3,353
1961	54,733	19,399	15,273	4,126
1970	60,176	21,991	16,464	5,527
1975	61,563	23,722	17,168	6,554
1980	61,431	24,811	17,318	7,493
1982	61,560	25,336	17,410	7,926
1985	61,006	26,367	17,504	8,863

Source: Information provided by BMBau; 'Statistiches Bundesblatt,Haushalte und Familien 1985', Table 2

Table 3.2 gives the best available estimates of the total housing stock in the area of the Federal Republic and West Berlin between 1950 and 1985.

Table 3.2:   Housing stock

(thousands)			(thousands)
1950	10,082	1978	24,708
1961	16,002	1980	25,406
1968	19,640	1982	26,076
1970	20,807	1985	27,081
1974	23,212		

Note: 1950 figure excludes the Saarland

Sources: United Nations Economic Commission for Europe, 'The Housing Situation in ECE Countries around 1970'; 'Bestand an Wohnungen', December 1982; Deutsches Institut für Urbanistik

Post-war history

The reasons for this huge post-war construction programme are twofold, and not far to seek. First, in 1945, the newly defeated and occupied country was facing war damage on a scale unseen in France, the Netherlands or the United Kingdom. In Germany 2.5 million dwellings had been destroyed during the Second World War, and many more had been seriously damaged.[4] In the area of what is now the state of North Rhine-Westphalia, out of 3,353,000 dwellings in 1939, one in five was totally destroyed during the war, and only two in five survived undamaged.

Second, the post-war housing market in Germany had to cope with an immediate and much more varied and dramatic pattern of immigration from outside the country than did France. In the five years following the end of the Second World War, no less than 8 million refugees - most of them of German origin - moved in, mainly from eastern Europe. By 1950, they formed 16% of the population of the newly established Federal Republic. A second wave from East Germany quickly followed. Their numbers had reached some 6 million by the time the Berlin Wall was built in 1961.[5] However, the immigrants who made the greatest social impact were the 'Gastarbeiter', workers from southern Europe and Turkey who flooded to the numerous unskilled factory jobs which were created by the 'economic miracle' of the late 1950s and the 1960s. From about 500,000 in 1955, this group had swollen to 4.38 million by 1985.

By all accounts, Germany has assimilated its large post-war immigrant population without great difficulty. Certainly, there have been no riots as there have been in France and the United Kingdom. Although information is not available by tenure, it is generally believed that they are concentrated in poorer private rented accommodation. However, there are also sizeable numbers in the social rented sector, especially in Berlin, where there is some anecdotal evidence of spasmodic minor friction, usually in the case of Turks with their unfamiliar lifestyle, to which landlords and German neighbours alike sometimes find it difficult to adjust.

Although numbers are past their peak, there were still almost 4.4 million foreigners in the Federal Republic at the end of 1985, nearly a third of them (1.4 million) from Turkey, and the majority of these were long-term immigrants of over 10 years' standing.[6]

Significantly, they are concentrated in the age groups in which their employment prospects are particularly weak. Nearly 100,000

Turks, or 7% of the Turkish population in Germany, are in the 18-21 age group, compared with 5.3% of the population as a whole, though the proportions are roughly comparable for the 21-35 age group.[7] Large numbers live in the areas of economic decline. Table 3.3 gives the numbers of foreigners and of Turks in particular for each state. Berlin is a special case, but the extraordinarily high concentration of Turks and other foreigners there is no less serious for that. On the other hand, high proportions of foreigners in the towns and cities are probably diluted by the rural parts of states such as Lower Saxony and North Rhine-Westphalia.

Table 3.3:   Foreign (and Turkish) population by state (1985)

State	Total population (thousands)	Foreigners Number (thousands)	% of total	Including Turks Number (thousands)	% of total
Schleswig-Holstein	2,614	85.1	3.3	31.2	1.2
Hamburg	1,586	170.8	10.8	54.5	3.4
Lower Saxony	7,205	274.9	3.8	90.5	1.3
Bremen	663	46.9	7.1	23.6	3.6
North Rhine-Westphalia	16,686	1,319.8	7.9	486.9	2.9
Hesse	5,532	512.3	9.3	131.2	2.4
Rhineland Palatinate	3,619	161.7	4.5	48.7	1.4
Baden Württemberg	9,254	840.0	9.1	236.5	2.6
Bavaria	10,963	667.8	6.1	189.1	1.7
Saar	1,048	45.4	4.3	7.1	0.7
West Berlin	1,853	254.3	13.7	102.7	5.5
Total	61,024	4,378.9	7.2	1,401.9	2.3

Source: *Statistisches Jahrbuch 1986*, Table 3.2

Immigration has continued into the late 1980s from various sources including people from the Indian sub-continent, the Middle East, 'boat people', and most recently a new wave of people of German origin from East Germany, Poland, and the Soviet Union (with a particularly dramatic influx in late 1989 and 1990).

On the other hand, internal migration was a less significant influence on housing development in Germany than it was in France in the post-war period. While much of the French housing boom in the 1950s and 1960s was due to the sudden migration from the countryside to the towns, in Germany, most of this migration had been earlier and more gradual. In 1870, two-thirds of the population of what is now the territory of the Federal Republic lived on the land; by 1939, this proportion had fallen to one-third. However, overall the urbanisation of Germany has gone further than in France. Only 16% of the German population now live in predominantly rural areas, while 55% live in the areas of big cities with a population of more than 300,000. Many of these cities - for example, Hamburg, the towns of the Ruhr, and Cologne - are in parts of the North and West of the country which are in structural industrial and economic decline.

In the immediate post-war years, with a decimated administrative machine and a ruined economy, the first priority was to use all available agencies to put up homes to meet the overwhelming needs. It is therefore hardly surprising that demarcation lines between different classes of housing provider were more blurred than elsewhere. Significantly, statistical records from the 1960s do not differentiate between the numbers of subsidised dwellings built for rent and for owner-occupation. In all, about 7.7 million of the 18.5 million dwellings built since the war have been supported with direct government subsidies, while a large proportion of the rest have been helped through tax breaks to owner-occupiers and private landlords.

Tenure

The owner-occupied sector represents 42% of the stock or some 11 million dwellings.[8] The trend over the last two decades has clearly been towards home ownership, particularly in newly built housing. Despite a sharp downturn in housing production overall, with completions dropping from 359,000 in 1984 to 225,000 in 1986, demand for family houses - which are the favoured form of housing for owner-occupation - has remained relatively strong (see Table 3.6 below). The government's stated policy is to increase owner-occupation to 50%, but the legislative and financial measures, such as the Home Ownership Assistance Act (Section 10(a) of the Einkommensteuergesetz), which have been introduced since the right-wing government of Chancellor Kohl came to power in 1982

appear in practice to have added little new impetus in that direction.
The only significant one is an offset against the annual tax bill (as
distinct from taxable income) of DM 600 (about £135 in actual
purchasing power) for each child, and perhaps the abolition of tax
on notional rent (an arrangement similar to the old Schedule A
taxation of owner-occupied property in the United Kingdom).

As in the other countries covered in this study, owner-
occupation is much higher in rural areas and small towns than in
larger towns and cities where most of the post-war building has
taken place. According to the 1978 *1% Sample Survey*, more than
one in two homes is owner-occupied in towns with less than 50,000
inhabitants, while the figure for cities with more than 200,000
inhabitants is only one in six. Table 3.4 gives the split between
owner-occupation and all forms of renting in 1982 according to the
size of communities.

Table 3.4: Tenure according to size of communities in 1982

Size of community	Owner-occupied (thousands)	Rented (thousands)	Total (thousands)	Proportion of owner-occupied (%)
>500,000	821	3,985	4,806	17
50,000-500,000	1,172	3,125	4,297	27
20,000-50,000	3,162	4,196	7,358	42
Smaller centres	2,612	1,571	4,483	58
Other	1,555	734	2,289	68
Total	9,322	13,911	23,233	40

Source: 'Wohnungsversorgung und Mieten der Haushalte 1978
und 1982', page 26

The social rented sector in the broadest sense of subsidised
rented housing subject to rent control (see below) amounts to about
4 million.[9] As will be seen in Section III, social rented housing is
not provided directly by local authorities. The landlords fall into
two main groups. First, there are non-profit bodies roughly
analagous to the HLM organisations in France, the
'woningcorporaties' in the Netherlands, and housing associations in
the United Kingdom. Of the 4 million total of social rented

dwellings under this broad definition, rather more than 2.4 million are owned by social (non-profit) landlord organisations as such.

Second, private landlords, both individuals and firms, in Germany can also provide subsidised social rented housing. They may engage a non-profit landlord organisation to manage their subsidised (and even their privately financed) housing on their behalf, and the management of about 400,000 dwellings is subcontracted to non-profit landlord organisations in this way. Furthermore, the non-profit landlord organisations can provide unsubsidised housing for rent. About 1 million of their 3.4 million total stock comes under this head. Non-profit landlord organisations can also build housing for sale to owner-occupiers. Between 1950 and 1986, they built 2.8 million homes for subsidised rent and over 900,000 for sale.[10]

At about 11 million dwellings, the private rented sector in the sense of landlords of housing for rent which does not attract direct government subsidies (although they enjoy considerable tax breaks) is nearly three times larger than the social - that is directly subsidised - sector.[11] It is subject to tight statutory regulation on security of tenure and rents. Although the rents for new tenancies are determined solely by market forces, rent increases for existing tenants must be justified by reference to other comparable rents in the locality. Genuine improvements to the property can attract rent increases up to 11% of the cost of the work.

Individual landlords and commercial organisations are active providers of privately rented housing. In the view of the Federal Housing Ministry, the main factors encouraging private individuals and firms to become and remain landlords are first, their confidence in property as a hedge against inflation, and second, the absence of any political threat to private landlords. However, the tax treatment of private landlords is widely considered to be at least as important as financial and political stability in encouraging the private rented sector. Traditionally, private landlords have always enjoyed better tax breaks than have owner-occupiers, and that is still the case. Landlords benefit from generous depreciation allowances and tax offsets which in effect amount to major subsidies. Indeed, with virtually no rent increases in many areas in recent years, it is probable that these fiscal incentives are now the main inducement to the private landlord to stay in business.

The position of the private landlord has been reinforced by the 1983 Act to Increase the Supply of Rented Housing (Gesetz zur Erhöhung des Angebots an Mietwohnungen), which, among other benefits for landlords (and also some for tenants), provided for a progressive but gradual adjustment towards market rents. The maximum allowable increase is 30% over three years. In practice, private sector rents are increasing as fast as the rules allow in the more prosperous areas of the south where it is often difficult for the typical household to find affordable housing, while rent rises are slight or even non-existent in the more depressed areas of the north and west where private rents are sometimes competitive with those in the social sector.

As will be clear from the foregoing, although the overall split between owner-occupied and rented housing is reasonably clear, the split between private renting and social non-profit renting is blurred. There is therefore a problem of definition between the two sectors, which is pursued in the next section. Table 3.5 gives the breakdown of tenures which can be drawn from statistics available from government sources and the Gesamtverband Gemeinnütziger Wohnungsunternehmen (GGW), the umbrella organisation for landlords in the social non-profit rented sector.

Table 3.5:   Tenure (1985)

	Number of dwellings (million)		%	
Owner-occupation	11		42	
Private (unsubsidised) renting	11		42	
of which, non-profit				
(GGW) landlords		1.0		4
Social (subsidised) renting	4		15	
of which, non-profit				
(GGW) landlords		2.4		9

Source: Constructed from data provided by BMBau and GGW

The one million unsubsidised dwellings owned by the non-profit landlord organisations represent a sector growing in size and importance, which will be considered in greater detail in Section IV. These are the dwellings on which no subsidy entitlement exists, either because they antedate the present subsidy arrangements, or because the subsidised loans have been repaid. Under the current legislation these dwellings remain under the same rent regime as social rented dwellings, but cease to be subject to local authority nomination rights. The landlord organisations can therefore be more selective in allocating these dwellings.

The housing market

Overall, the housing market is considered by many to have achieved equilibrium or even a slight surplus, though a reliable assessment will have to await full data from the 1987 census. The GGW puts the 1985 figures at 27.1 million dwellings and 25.7 million households. This compares with a housing shortage which was still real as late as 1970, when there were 20.8 million dwellings for 22.0 million households. However, as has been seen, there are considerable regional variations in all sectors. Moreover, several warning voices predict that the market will again be in deficit as early as 1990. The recent migration from East Germany adds force to this view.

The fortunes of the social rented sector in Germany are usually closely linked with those of the private rented sector. Where demand for rented housing is slackest - as has been seen, principally in the north and west - the lower differentials between private and social rents do at least enable private landlords to pick and choose their tenants, and so increase pressure on the social rented sector to take problem families. It is often said that these social pressures on the social rented sector are compounded by the requirement (which, however, is variable in its application) for tenants with incomes above the qualifying threshold to pay a rent supplement, which some commentators believe may encourage these more prosperous tenants to transfer to the private sector. Moreso than in the other countries covered by this study, there is therefore a fairly free market within the rented sector as a whole.

As in France, although government policies have traditionally favoured the construction of flats as the usual form of housing for urban wage-earners, there is a clear trend towards houses and maisonettes, with new-build numbers split roughly evenly in the stock as a whole between flats on the one hand, and houses and maisonettes on the other. Table 3.6 gives figures for approvals and completions of buildings containing one or two dwellings, and buildings containing three or more dwellings between 1977 and 1986.

Table 3.6:   House-building in Germany 1977-1986

	(thousands)			
	Approvals		Completions	
	1 or 2 dwellings	3 or more dwellings	1 or 2 dwellings	3 or more dwellings
1977	230	94	227	152
1978	271	124	240	100
1979	250	109	236	97
1980	229	122	249	114
1981	195	130	220	118
1982	151	149	189	126
1983	185	192	167	140
1984	152	149	176	183
1985	132	89	152	128
1986	132	61	141	84

Source: 'Ausgewählte Strukturdaten für die Bauwirtschaft',
           August 1987

Conditions

Space standards are high, at an average of about 82 square metres
per dwelling, but with owner-occupied dwellings considerably
larger (about 105 square metres) than rented dwellings (about 67
square metres). Per capita floor space rose from 15 square metres
in 1950 to 34 square metres in 1985. Levels of amenity are also
high, again with owner-occupiers at an advantage. Seven dwellings
in ten have central heating, with a clear shift towards the use of gas
in recent years, and about nine in ten have a bath or shower.

II   History of the social rented sector

As in France, the Netherlands and the United Kingdom, social
rented housing in Germany has its roots in the reactions of 19th
century idealists to the housing conditions which were brought
about by the industrial revolution. The original concept of German
social housing is generally credited to Victor Aimé Huber, a
university professor who was inspired by the housing conditions

which he saw on a visit to London to set up the first German social housing company in Berlin as early as 1848. The first Cooperative Act was passed in the 1860s. However, progress on the ground remained slow, mainly because of the reluctance of the traditional lending institutions to invest in these new enterprises. Towards the end of the 19th century, firmer foundations were laid, first with the 1889 Second Cooperative Act, which provided limited liability protection for cooperatives, and second, with the introduction of old age and invalidity pensions' insurance in the same year. This latter scheme - especially when it was extended to employees in 1911 - put substantial funds into the hands of public financial institutions, which were empowered to make cheap loans available to housing cooperatives. From this period date a variety of social housing projects, including the first garden city developments, and some still popular estates originally built by employers for their workers.

Although the First World War intervened before the new movement could make much progress on the ground, it took off in earnest in the inter-war period, helped not least by the fiscal measures to promote house-building which were introduced in 1924. By the mid-1920s, no less than 4,000 small building cooperatives and non-profit housing associations had been formed, under the sponsorship of trade unions, employers, churches, charities, political parties, and local authorities. This was the period of innovative garden city developments spearheaded by Bruno von Taut (see Section VII) and taken up by the Bauhaus school of Walter Gropius, by Mies van der Rohe and many others. Most of what remains of this period is subject to preservation orders.

The Great Depression and the subsequent National Socialist takeover took a serious toll on the further progress of the cooperative movement, with the number of cooperatives declining to something over 2,000 in 1939. Nonetheless, the still extant law which gave non-profit landlord organisations their statutory basis (das Wohnungsgemeinnützigkeitsgesetz) dates from 1940. At the outbreak of the Second World War, the total stock of the non-profit sector amounted to about 560,000 dwellings which was less than half the social rented stock in the United Kingdom at that time, but three times that in France.

In the early post-war years, work concentrated first of all on the immediate task of repairing war damaged buildings. The vast new-build programme took off after 1952. There were now roughly

2,400 non-profit housing organisations (Gemeinnützige Wohnungsunternehmen) whose contribution to this new-build programme amounted to nearly 40% of all dwellings built for sale and for rent in the early 1950s. In some of the large cities such as Hamburg and Berlin, the non-profit housing organisations were for a time contributing up to 80% of the new dwellings. This share steadily but gradually declined over the next three decades, falling to rather more than 10% in 1985. However, altogether in the great post-war house-building boom, the non-profit housing organisations built more than a quarter of the overall total of new homes built between 1950 and 1985.

Much of their post-war building was once again highly innovative, but also more contentious. The scope for grandiose new ideas was increased by the freedom offered in the vast housing developments built in the 1960s and 1970s on green field sites on the fringes of towns and cities. However, notorious as some of them have since become, post-war housing estates in Germany do not seem to have gained quite the national ill-repute which bedevils the 'grands ensembles' in France. They are considered in greater detail in later sections.

Coinciding with the massive expansion of the stock owned and managed by the non-profit housing organisations, the post-war period has also seen a steady reduction in their numbers, mainly through rationalisation of their operations and mergers. From over 2,400 landlord organisations in 1950, their numbers fell to about 1,800 in 1985, bringing their average stock from under 350 units to nearly 1,900 units. Section III looks at the various kinds of non-profit landlord organisation in detail, and at the great range in the size of stock which they own and manage. Table 3.7 gives the progression for the total stock of the non-profit housing organisations, and of the number of organisations over this period.

The peak in the post-war German social building programme was rather earlier than in France. Taking into account the social rented housing built by other landlords (outside the non-profit sector) it reached about 170,000 completions a year between 1950 and 1955, after which the annual average fell gradually to about 110,000 between 1970 and 1975. From then on, output in Germany reduced more sharply than in France and the United Kingdom, and much more sharply than in the Netherlands, going down to under 40,000 in 1985.[12] Table 3.8 gives figures for completions in the social sector - that is, all subsidised housing for rent or for sale -

between 1949 and 1981, showing also the number of subsidised dwellings built each year for every 10,000 of the population.

Table 3.7: Number of non-profit housing organisations and their total stock 1950-1985 (units)

	Number of organisations	Total stock
1950	2,430	813,810
1955	2,389	1,596,941
1960	2,285	2,113,776
1965	2,189	2,592,697
1970	2,055	2,926,699
1975	1,918	3,223,775
1980	1,849	3,326,692
1985	1,803	3,374,385

Source: 'Der Lange Weg', p 44 (GGW)

Table 3.8: All completions in the social sector 1949-1981 (including housing for owner-occupation)

	Total completions	Number per 10,000 of population		Total completions	Number per 10,000 of population
1949	153,340	31	1965	228,606	39
1950	254,990	51	1966	203,510	34
1951	295,580	58	1967	192,690	33
1952	317,500	62	1968	177,686	30
1953	304,240	59	1969	183,217	31
1954	309,502	60	1970	137,095	23
1955	288,988	55	1971	148,715	24
1956	305,740	58	1972	153,214	25
1957	293,260	55	1973	169,336	27
1958	269,234	50	1974	148,121	24
1959	301,187	55	1975	126,660	21
1960	263,205	47	1976	127,776	21
1961	241,899	43	1977	139,630	23
1962	242,464	43	1978	104,900	17
1963	228,757	40	1979	105,600	17
1964	248,543	43	1980	103,700	17
			1981	90/100,000	15/16

Source: 'Bundesbaublatt', December 1982, Table 6, page 833

Meanwhile, Germany saw the first indications that the large-scale housing estates so favoured by the planners in the 1960s and early 1970s were beginning to pose problems. Rising numbers of empty dwellings, and increasing difficulties in letting housing in some areas, were already giving concern to landlords and government as early as 1973. However, as is explained in the previous section, in Germany the problems of the social rented sector tend to go in cycles led by changing patterns of supply and demand in the private rented sector. This is less the case in the other countries covered by this study.

The more recent problems will be considered in greater detail in Section VII. In summary, in the early 1980s, many non-profit landlords again found themselves with substantial numbers of dwellings which were empty because there were simply no applicants for them. The tenants on the large estates in particular were becoming increasingly disadvantaged both socially and economically. In some areas, competition from the private rented sector was providing a viable alternative for many tenants. Rising rent arrears added to landlords' problems. Those who could move did so, adding to turnover rates and to numbers of empty dwellings.

III   The landlord organisations

As is explained in Section I, there is a considerable overlap between private (commercial) landlords and social (non-profit) landlords in Germany. Private landlords can provide housing for rent on a commercial and on a subsidised basis, and the main condition attached to their receipt of subsidy is that the controlled 'Kostenmiete' rent regime described in Section IV applies to their subsidised stock until the subsidised loans have been paid off. Private landlords own over 1.5 million out of the total of 4 million subsidised dwellings, and over a million - or two out of three - of the social rented dwellings owned privately belong to small landlords, that is individuals or couples. The arrangements are closely regulated, and among other rules, the profits which can be distributed are restricted to 4% on the (limited) invested capital.

Of the 11 million privately financed dwellings for rent, about 1 million belong to non-profit social landlords. As was explained in Section I, these dwellings are either stock which pre-dates the present subsidy system, or on which the subsidised loans have been paid off. The rents remain controlled under the 'Kostenmiete' rules, but the dwellings cease to be subject to local authority nominations.

Non-profit landlord organisations

There are about 1,800 organisations which are predominantly social, non-profit landlords as such. These organisations belong to the GGW, the umbrella organisation based in Cologne which acts as a lobby and information centre for the movement. It operates through a regional network of offices which have the key executive function of monitoring and supervising the financial performance of the individual landlord organisations (see below).

The total rented stock belonging to GGW member organisations amounted to nearly 3.4 million dwellings in 1985, 2.4 million of them were the object of public subsidies and therefore in the social rented sector proper. Table 3.9 gives the overall breakdown of GGW members by size at the end of 1985.

Table 3.9: **Breakdown of GGW members by size of rented stock (Dec 1985)**

Number of dwellings	Organisations Number	% of landlords	Dwellings Number	% of dwellings
<100	303	16.2	12,332	0.4
101-500	562	31.5	149,820	4.4
501-1,000	308	17.2	224,586	6.7
1,001-2,000	280	15.6	404,448	12.0
2,001-3,000	103	5.8	250,590	7.4
3,001-5,000	103	5.8	405,955	12.0
5,001-10,000	93	5.2	644,373	19.1
10,001-15,000	17	0.9	211,895	6.3
15,001-25,000	20	1.1	397,043	11.8
25,001-50,000	11	0.6	416,074	12.4
>50,000	3	0.2	257,269	7.6
Total	1,803	100.0	3,374,385	100.0

Source: **'Der Lange Weg', p 44 (GGW)**

The average stock of under 1,900 dwellings is roughly the same
as that of social landlord organisations in the Netherlands. On the
other hand, it is less than half that of HLM organisations in France,
and less than a sixth of the average local authority stock in
England. However, as will be seen, some of the German landlord
organisations are very big indeed.

Non-profit housing organisations have further roles as builders
and developers of housing for owner-occupation and as managers
of housing for third parties. Given the need for management
arrangements for privately owned flats, the two roles overlap to
some extent. In 1985, GGW members were managing over
425,000 dwellings for third parties, nearly 190,000 of them owner-
occupied.[13]

It will by now be abundantly plain that the blurred demarcation
lines between tenures make it nearly impossible to provide
aggregate data for the social rented sector as such. When we come
to look at the tenants in Section VI, the limited available
information applies entirely to the rented sector as a whole. In this
section and in Section V which considers the buildings, the best
available information is regarding the total rented stock of
3,374,385 dwellings owned and managed by the 1,803 GGW
members (figures at the end of 1985). However, it should be kept
in mind that not all these dwellings are in the social rented sector,
still less are they or their landlords necessarily representative of the
social rented sector as a whole.

Over the years, the non-profit landlord organisations have
distinguished themselves as active builders of new housing, and
more recently - as will be seen in Section IV - they have been
increasingly active in work to refurbish their stock. For the most
part, they run efficient management operations in terms of effective
repairs and rent collection services, but few of them as yet have
done much to develop forms of intensive social management.
However, the management challenges of the 1980s, particularly the
high vacancy rates which affected several landlord organisations,
have focussed attention on the need for a more conscious social
management input. Examples of some of the social management
initiatives which are being developed are considered in Section VII.

Cooperatives

Of the 1,803 GGW landlord members, 1,183 or nearly two-thirds
are cooperatives (Genossenschaften). These are the descendants of

the organisations which pioneered social housing in Germ.
Traditionally they are private organisations backed for example
trade unions, the churches, and charities. In 1985, they owned ju.
over a million dwellings, an average of 862 each. A typical size is
about 500. However, despite much rationalisation over the last
three decades, they still vary greatly in size. In 1985, over 200
cooperatives had a stock of less than 100 dwellings, while less than
30 had more than 5,000.
They tend to have strong local links. They are often said to be
highly selective in their choice of tenants, letting housing only to
their members, who in 1985 totalled over 1.6 million nationally, or
an average of nearly 1,400 for each cooperative. The difference
between the number of dwellings and the number of individual
members is due in part to those who are on the waiting-lists for
homes, but some tenant households may contain more than one
member, and some members may have no immediate intention of
applying for a home.

Despite the name, cooperatives vary greatly in the extent of their
active tenant involvement, though the tenants are represented as of
right on their supervisory boards. The average individual stake of
members is hardly significant at DM 1,450 at the end of 1986
(about £330 in actual purchasing power), on which the maximum
return permitted by law is 4%. However, members who are
actively seeking a dwelling will normally have a much higher
investment, in order to pay the initial (refundable) charge of up to
5% of the cost of providing the dwelling, which may be as high as
DM 60 per square metre (the purchasing power equivalent of about
£1,100 for a typical flat). Tenants of cooperatives must therefore
have some resources behind them. Thus it is hardly surprising that
cooperatives are largely free of management problems.

Although with a large and flexible rented sector, there is little
need in present conditions for formal mobility arrangements in
Germany, the cooperative movement makes some additional
contribution to mobility through the 'Ring' to which belong nearly
300 organisations owning about 500,000 dwellings. Individual
members of these organisations can carry their seniority with them
when they move to other parts of the country.

Companies

The other major providers of non-profit social rented housing are
the limited liability companies (Gesellschaften mit beschränkter

Haftung and Aktiengesellschaften) which at the end of 1986 numbered 587 or less than a third of GGW members. Although there are far fewer companies than there are cooperatives, they own in total more than twice as much stock - over 2.3 million dwellings compared with less than a million belonging to cooperatives. Their average size approaches 4,000 dwellings, but the range is even greater than with cooperatives. A third of all companies fall in the bracket between 500 and 2,000 dwellings. At the extremes, about a quarter of companies in 1986 had less than 500 dwellings, while 50 had more than 10,000 and 3 companies had more than 50,000. Of these, by far the largest was Neue Heimat, the trade union landlord company with about 300,000 dwellings, whose current misfortunes are considered in greater detail below.

The companies are sponsored mainly by employers, trade unions, the churches, and perhaps most significantly in view of their role in allocations (see below), by municipalities. In 1986, municipalities had a controlling interest in over half of them, owning in all about a third of the stock belonging to the companies, that is over 750,000 dwellings. With the exception of Neue Heimat, and some of the companies which are sponsored by national employers such as the railway and the post office, they are locally based. The biggest, such as the municipal landlord company SAGA in Hamburg with about 100,000 dwellings, are to be found in the major cities and industrial areas.

Relationships

As in France, landlords in the social rented sector have a complex web of institutional relationships. The Federal government in Bonn is responsible for setting the statutory framework, including the periodic fixing of factors affecting subsidy (see Section IV). On policy issues, it deals with the GGW as the voice of the individual non-profit landlord organisations.

Any funds which may be made available at this level are channelled through the governments of the 10 Länder (states) and West Berlin. The Länder fix the actual levels of subsidy for their areas, and distribute the necessary resources - including any special help which they may decide to make available - through the municipalities to the individual organisations. With the current withdrawal of central government funding for social housing, the financial burden now falls virtually entirely on the Länder, hitting the poorer ones particularly hard.

The municipalities, of which there are about 1,800 in the Federal Republic, are therefore the landlord organisations' main point of contact with government on matters to do with resources. In this respect, the smaller cooperatives and companies sometimes allege that they do less well than their larger brethren, especially the municipal companies although, as has been seen, they do tend to have the easier tenants, and their stock is said to be in relatively good condition.

Even more significant is the municipalities' role on allocations and lettings. All applicants for social housing have to go through the municipal housing office (Wohnungsamt) which alone is responsible for checking whether the applicant's income comes below the qualifying limit (see Section VI), and if so, for issuing the 'Wohnberechtigungsschein' or certificate of entitlement which acts as the passport to a flat of the requisite size. In maintaining their waiting-lists and in making allocations, the municipal housing offices have their own individual points systems. The applicant may already be a member of a cooperative waiting for a vacancy, or have another landlord in mind, in which case, the subsequent allocation is a matter for direct negotiation. However, in other cases, the municipality has considerable powers of direction over both applicants and landlords.

Insensitive use of these powers over the years is often said to be a major cause of the social problems on some estates, to which we return in Section VII. However, it is worth noting at this point that according to a Federal Research Institute study (see pages 143-144 below), the municipalities had nomination rights to 59% of all dwellings on the 154 large estates for which information was provided on allocations and lettings, and to no less than 64% on the very largest estates of over 5,000 dwellings. As will be seen, the arrangements for coordination of allocation policies between the municipalities and the landlord organisations vary greatly from one area to another.

The municipally sponsored companies see themselves at the greatest disadvantage, as they tend to be the landlords of last resort, taking the tenants whom the cooperatives and privately sponsored companies prefer to avoid. However, it should be remembered that traditionally, the poorest tenants tend to be housed at the lower end of the private rented sector rather than in the social sector. With the growing trend towards modernisation in both sectors, and the consequent increases in rents, the poorest tenants are often said to be facing growing difficulty in finding housing which they can afford.

As suggested above, the problems of these tenants are inevitably exacerbated by the reduction in the social rented stock as subsidised loans are paid off. According to GGW estimates, 1.73 million dwellings built between 1950 and 1965 which are now in the social sector will have transferred to private status by the late 1990s. Section IV explains the financial effects of this trend, both for tenants in terms of higher rents, and for landlords in terms of potentially higher returns, at least in areas of strong demand. However, there is also a major management implication, in that the municipalities lose their nomination rights to dwellings as soon as the public financial stake in them disappears.[14] According to one estimate by the Federal Research Institute, by the year 2000, municipal nomination rights will apply to less than 1 million of the present 4 million dwellings in the social rented sector, with the likely result that the poor and disadvantaged will find housing opportunities increasingly curtailed as landlords become free to let their property to better-off tenants without being limited by the statutory income ceiling which applies to dwellings in the subsidised social rented sector.

Particularly in areas where landlords have met difficulty in letting their dwellings or in getting a balanced social mix among their tenants, there is a growing tendency towards rivalry - not all of it constructive - between social landlords about resources and about potentially difficult tenants. However, more than seems to be the case in France, landlords claim to compete with one another in terms of the quality of their service, and to offer their tenants value for money. This is particularly evident on the large estates where, as in France, several landlords may be involved.

As in France and the Netherlands, municipalities are responsible for services such as refuse removal, street lighting on estates, and the provision of communal facilities. However, landlords in Germany often have a greater responsibility for maintaining open space. They also often provide the communal laundry facilities which are a standard requirement, and which in many cases are a wasting asset with the growth in ownership of domestic washing machines. The landlord organisations are responsible for keeping lifts clean and in good order, but tenants are normally responsible for their parts of staircases and pavements (although landlords may take on these responsibilties). Minor repairs and repairs reporting are normally done by the resident block caretaker, and although some landlord organisations have their own in-house repairs teams for major jobs, this work is usually contracted out to private firms. Audit of the non-profit landlords is the responsibility of the GGW through its regional federation of ten offices. Every landlord organisation has to belong to a 'Prüfungsverband' or audit association based at one of these offices. The GGW prides itself that out of over a thousand insolvencies among landlords in the decade from 1976 to 1985, only seven involved GGW members.

The collapse of Neue Heimat

There is, however, great concern that the good name of the movement will be seriously affected by the more recent financial collapse of Germany's largest social landlord, the trade union company Neue Heimat.

The collapse of Neue Heimat was due to a series of financial and management misjudgements. Considerable losses were incurred through speculation in central America by the private development side of the organisation, and by unsuccessful 'build for sale' projects from which the proceeds had been intended to subsidise the non-profit landlord activities of the Neue Heimat organisation. The problems were compounded by false assumptions about the scope for future social housing developments, with expensive land purchases - on values which later collapsed - financed on the security of the organisations management and maintenance reserves.

Early efforts to restore financial viability through sales to tenants were unsuccessful, and in 1988, Neue Heimat was forced to divest itself of its landlord role altogether. In nine of the Länder, and West Berlin, arrangements have been made to transfer the housing and the tenants to existing state government landlord companies on a basis which will enable them to break even, taking into account the need for higher than average expenditure on repairs, management, and maintenance, but without undue rent increases. For example, in North Rhine-Westphalia, the 38,000 Neue Heimat dwellings have been transferred to the state government landlord company at a nominal price of DM 1.00, and the state government has pumped in DM 180 million additional capital (or the equivalent of over £1,000 in actual purchasing power per dwelling) to make the operation viable.[15] Untypical though this story is of the general relationship between social landlords and government, it does illustrate that in

134 Federal Republic of Germany

the last resort, social landlords and their tenants in Germany have
no statutory or moral claim on the community at large.

Education and training

The GGW provides professional education and training in the same
way as its counterparts in France and the Netherlands. It has its
own training centre near Dusseldorf, where most of the activity is
in the form of short courses on specific issues for operational staff,
although it and other organisations also lay on recognised three-
year part-time general housing courses leading to a qualification at
roughly the equivalent of technician level in the United Kingdom.
About 1,500 people from non-profit landlord organisations were
enrolled on such courses in 1985. The GGW is now developing a
more advanced qualification in housing management to respond to
acknowledged needs. The ten regional federation offices of the
GGW provide advice to their member organisations on demand, but
neither the GGW nor government has espoused any ongoing role as
a national clearing-house of good practice on housing management
issues.

IV Finance

As has been shown, the borderline between the private and social
rented sector in Germany is more blurred than elsewhere. In order
to understand the financing of the social sector it is therefore
necessary to show how the various forms of landlord are subject to
different financial regimes. As has been shown in Section I, the
thriving 'free market' private sector is in reality closely regulated,
giving tenants the protection of controlled, comparative rents and
security of tenure, while landlords enjoy substantial tax advantages.
    Private landlords who provide social housing for rent enjoy the
same tax advantages, and also - under the terms of the Dwellings
Regulation Act (Wohnungsbindungsgesetz) - receive building
subsidy, providing first, that they charge the controlled social rent
(Kostenmiete), and second, that they accept only tenants whose
incomes are low enough to make them eligible for social housing.
    Non-profit (GGW) landlord organisations receive building
subsidy on the same terms as private landlords, but without their
tax advantages. However, as has been shown, some of them also
own unsubsidised housing, usually dating from before the Second

World War and the 1950s. As will be seen later, this category is increasing as loans are paid off. Such property remains subject to rent control, but not to the income ceilings which apply to subsidised housing. Nor, most importantly, do the municipalities have allocation rights to it.

As in France and the Netherlands, social landlords in Germany operate as independent cost centres. Their subsidised and privately financed stock is naturally subject to separate accounting arrangements. However, with pooling or cross-subsidisation between different parts of their subsidised stock virtually unknown at least so far, their individual holdings of social housing - and indeed individual blocks of housing - are usually treated as separate accounting entities.

Bricks and mortar subsidies

Under the First Housebuilding Act (I. Wohnungsbaugesetz) of 24 April 1950, which provided the original statutory framework for public support for housebuilding and renovation across the board in the post-war years, social landlords received bricks and mortar subsidies in the first instance by means of long-term interest-free or low-interest loans. As financial pressures increased, these subsidies were replaced - under provisions introduced by the Second Housing Act (II. Wohnungsbaugesetz) of 1956 - with a system of decreasing support on outgoings (known as 'degressive subsidies'), which reached their peak in the years between 1969 and 1974.

The new arrangements involve loans on which the initially low interest rates taper over time towards money-market rates. The amount of rent subsidy per square metre would also go down by preset amounts over the years. This system was based on the assumption that rising incomes would enable tenants to meet the increased costs through higher rents. This expectation has not been met, with the consequence that special forms of additional support have been needed, not least in some areas to prevent rents in the subsidised sector overtaking private sector rents.

The payment of subsidy, and the consequent determination of actual controlled rent levels, is the responsibility of the Länder governments, but on the basis of key inputs to the calculation which are fixed by the federal (central) government. These are standard levels of management and maintenance expenditure, with a set allowance for rent income lost on empty housing. In 1987, the annual management allowance was set at DM 240 per dwelling, the maintenance allowance at between DM 8.00 and DM 12.50 per square metre, depending on the age of the property, and the rent loss factor at 2% of the collectable rent. Thus, on an average sized flat of 60 square metres with a typical monthly rent of DM 6.00 per square metre and on the top maintenance allowance, the annual management and maintenance allowance for the purposes of subsidy calculation amounts to about DM 1,075, or the purchasing power equivalent of some £250. The breakdown is shown in Table 3.10.

Table 3.10: Calculation of typical management and maintenance allowance (1987)

	DM
Standard management allowance	240.00
Maintenance 60m^2 @ DM 12.00	720.00
Rent loss factor: 2% of annual rent of DM 4,320 (60m^2 @ DM 6.00 x 12)	86.40
Total	1,046.40

Source: Constructed from figures provided by BMBau

To an English housing manager, this level of management and maintenance allowances will seem remarkably low, although it should be noted that the German landlord organisations do not have the substantial transfer payments which are made from English local authority housing revenue accounts to other departments. On the other hand, German rents do include the costs of water, refuse removal, and staircase lighting, but not heating or costs of other ancillary services.

Nonetheless, management and maintenance allowances are a matter of heated debate between the Federal government and the GGW which argues that the levels are quite unrealistic. According to the GGW, actual expenditure on maintenance in 1986 averaged DM 15.76 per square metre, while independent sources claim that a management allowance of DM 350.00 is justified. In part, the problem lies with a system of standard management and maintenance allowances across the country which fails to provide the flexibility needed to cope with varying conditions. For example, cooperatives, which as we have seen in Section III are generally well run and trouble free, may need less than landlord companies with large amounts of problem housing in the big cities, and the management problems which go with it. The revised levels which were introduced for 1988 give an across the board increase in the management allowance to DM 320.00, and tapered increases in the maintenance allowance to DM 16.50 per square metre for property built before 1970, to DM 12.00 for property built between 1970 and 1979, and to DM 9.00 for property built since then.

The interest on the debt (which is based on the original sum rather than the outstanding debt) is a much larger element in the calculation of the basic unsubsidised rent (Kostenmiete). This, and the amount of debt repayment vary greatly, according to the age of the dwelling and the interest rate currently applying to it.

For a newly built flat, the total unsubsidised monthly rent is currently in the region of DM 20.00 to DM 25.00. To bring this down to the typical approved (controlled) level of about DM 6.00 therefore means subsidy levels of 70% or more in the later 1980s. This compares with some 40% in the early 1970s. Table 3.11 gives the average rent calculation for the Federal Republic for a dwelling in the social rented sector in 1983. It shows that a monthly subsidy of nearly DM 14.00 per square metre was needed to reduce the average basic rent of some DM 20.00 to an average approved rent of just over DM 6.00.

Table 3.11: Calculation of basic rent (Kostenmiete) (Average for the Federal Republic, 1983)

Costs per square metre	DM
Interest	16.27
Debt repayment	2.20
Management	0.29
Maintenance	0.75
Rent loss factor	0.10
Other administrative costs	0.42
Total	20.03

Source: Ulbrich and Wullkopf, 'Nachsubventionierung - Fass ohne Boden?' in Stadtbauwelt 86

The state (Land) government sets its own level of subsidy to bring this basic rent (Kostenmiete) down to the approved rent which is what the tenant actually pays. Although the monthly average is about DM 6.00 per square metre, in practice, rents can vary widely between similar dwellings, largely because of the vagaries of the interest tapering arrangements described above. This depends largely on when they were built, and can therefore contribute significantly to the unpopularity of newer dwellings.

According to the Federal Research Institute study of large estates described below, 4% of dwellings across the sample - which, it should be emphasised consists of problem housing and is therefore not representative of the stock as a whole - were empty because of lack of demand, and four out of ten of these were empty specifically because the rents were said to be too high. Some states, for example North Rhine-Westphalia, have therefore introduced special levels of subsidy for unpopular and expensive housing. Thus, while a typical approved rent in 1987 was in the region of DM 6.00 per square metre, the rents on some unpopular estates under the normal rules would have been over DM 8.00. The effect of the special subsidy has been bring them down to near the typical level.

Although the landlord organisations can subsidise rents or provide an enhanced standard of service, and indeed do so not infrequently where there are management difficulties, they are limited by strict rules on cross-subsidisation, and all such proposals have to be approved by the Länder (state) authorities. These subsidies or improved levels of service therefore usually have to be financed from the organisation's private resources.

The shift from new-build to maintenance and renovation

The reduction in new-build activity from the middle of the 1970s was accompanied by a major increase in the proportion of effort going into the maintenance and upgrading of the stock. Figures for the early 1980s show modernisation going ahead at well over 200,000 units a year, which means that one in fifteen social rented dwellings is being brought up to modern standards annually. According to an analysis by the GGW of their members' 1981 improvement programmes, a high proportion of the older, pre-1956 stock is being modernised - about one in ten in 1981. However, the post-1956 stock is also quite heavily represented in improvement programmes, with one in twenty of this more recent stock being modernised in 1981. Table 3.12 gives the overall trends in expenditure on new-build, maintenance and modernisation between 1962 and 1985.

Table 3.12: Expenditure by non-profit housing organisations on new-build, maintenance and modernisation 1962-1985 (in current and constant prices)

	Total DM(million)		New-build %	Mainten-ance %	Modern-isation %
	Actual out-turn	Constant prices (1976)			
1962	4,629	9,700	93.2	6.2	0.6
1963	5,323	10,600	93.4	6.0	0.6
1964	6,589	12,600	93.9	5.6	0.5
1965	7,345	13,500	93.9	5.6	0.5
1966	7,479	13,300	93.1	6.3	0.6
1967	7,424	13,500	92.2	7.1	0.7
1968	6,889	12,100	88.2	9.6	2.2
1969	7,328	12,100	87.3	10.0	2.7
1970	6,255	8,800	83.0	12.9	4.1
1971	7,994	10,200	85.0	10.8	4.2
1972	10,482	12,500	87.0	8.7	4.3
1973	12,199	13,600	87.4	7.8	4.8
1974	11,628	12,200	84.9	9.9	5.2
1975	9,329	9,600	77.9	13.6	8.5
1976	8,398	8,400	69.4	17.4	13.2
1977	9,258	8,800	68.6	18.0	13.4
1978	7,845	7,000	57.2	23.0	19.8
1979	9,046	7,400	57.5	21.3	21.2
1980	10,658	8,000	59.4	19.8	20.8
1981	11,932	8,500	62.9	19.3	17.8
1982	11,714	8,100	63.2	20.4	16.4
1983	11,828	8,000	61.1	21.6	17.3
1984	11,354	7,400	59.8	24.2	16.0
1985	9,788	6,300	52.5	30.7	16.8

Source: 'Der Lange Weg', p 46 (GGW)

Unit costs averaged DM 8,700 in 1981 (the equivalent of about £2,150 at 1985 UK prices). However, costs varied widely, ranging as low as DM 2,000 (£500) for minor improvements, and as high as DM 50,000 (£12,500) in extreme cases. As is to be expected, the oldest buildings were the most costly and the post-1956 stock the cheapest to improve. Dwellings built in the inter-war period cost rather less than those built in the early post-war period.

Replacement of windows is by far the most frequent element of modernisation programmes, followed by the replacement of heating systems and thermal and sound insulation measures. Updating of electrical installations and rewiring is more frequent than work on bathrooms, while kitchens do not rate a separate mention.

Day-to-day management and maintenance expenditure totalled DM 3,008 million in 1985,[16] or about DM 890 (£205) per unit. To a growing extent, the rise in expenditure on maintenance and modernisation is having to be financed from rent rises. Before 1982, the federal government had a special programme to support improvement and energy saving work in the social rented sector. This money was usually combined with additional support from the state governments and municipalities. Since then, federal support for housing as such has been on the decline, and from 1986, it has been targetted exclusively on the promotion of home-ownership. Capital support for improvement work is therefore now available only from the states and municipalities, though some states such as North Rhine-Westphalia have been using urban aid (Städtebau) funds from central government to support work on housing estates.

As improvements usually lead to rent rises, even though the extent of the increase is limited by law to 11%, tenants are actively concerned to limit such expenditure. As we shall see below, this is in no small part because housing benefits cover only part of the increased costs. Significantly, the GGW handbook which instructs landlords on tenant involvement in improvement proposals goes into considerable detail about the rent implications of different levels of work and terms of borrowing.

Housing benefits

All households are eligible to apply for housing benefit (Wohngeld), which is calculated on household income and size, and outgoings on housing. It is heavily biased towards tenants. About 1% of owner-occupiers draw benefit, compared with 13% of tenants. The average level of benefit to the households which claimed it in 1986 was DM 144, or a purchasing power equivalent of about £33 a month. The total national bill in 1987 is estimated at DM 3,500 million (£800 million) compared with DM 2,469 million in 1985 and DM 1,835 million in 1980. At an estimated 1.8 million in 1986, the number of households receiving housing benefit more than doubled the 1970 figure of 0.9 million.[17] About 15% of tenants in the social rented sector were receiving housing benefit in 1987.[18] Apart from increasing unemployment (see Section VI), a likely reason for the increase in the number of recipients is that more of those who are eligible for housing benefit are now claiming it. There has also been a sharp increase in the number of recipients of social security in the 1980s, from 2.1 million in 1981 to 2.6 million in 1984.

Housing benefit keeps the outgoings (excluding heating costs) of recipient households down to a little below 20%, which is the typical proportion of disposable income which a household in the social rented sector spends on rent. The main reason for the sharply increasing national total in housing benefit payments since 1980 is the even more sharply increasing levels of rents, particularly in the social rented sector. Between 1980 and 1985 the average monthly rent per square metre charged by GGW landlords rose from DM 4.50 to DM 5.84, or just under 27%, rather more than the 24% rise in the rented sector as a whole, and than the 21% rise in the cost of living.[19]

Although access to housing in the social rented sector is means-tested (see Section VII), about a quarter of the tenants already in the sector have incomes which have risen above the qualifying limits since they moved in (although this proportion is often said to be substantially over stated because of the workings of the reporting system). In four of the ten states, such tenants pay a rent supplement (Fehlbelegungsabgabe) towards the subsidy on their dwellings. In 1983, the total claw back through these rent supplements amounted to about DM 25.7 million (or the purchasing power equivalent of £5.6 million), and the proportion of social sector tenants subject to the supplement varied between 17% in North Rhine-Westphalia to 30.7% in Bavaria.[20]

An emerging trend of crucial importance for the social rented sector is the transfer of dwellings from social rented to privately financed status as the publicly supported loans on them are repaid. The management effects of this transfer are discussed in Section III. In financial terms, non-profit (GGW) landlords lose, because they are not liable to tax and therefore lack the taxation advantages enjoyed by private landlords.

A new political impetus in this direction was provided by the proposal made in October 1987 by Finance Minister Stoltenberg to remove the non-profit status of companies but not cooperatives. After a period of consultation and debate, the federal government decided to put this proposal into effect from 1 January 1990. This move could have far-reaching implications at the local level, as one effect might be to increase pressure for municipalities to support local social landlord organisations, with a consequent increase in their direct involvement in local housing provision.

V   The buildings

As in France, the stock in the German non-profit social rented sector is characterised by its newness and the overwhelming proportion of flats. About four out of five dwellings in the stock of the non-profit landlord organisations in 1986 had been built since 1948, compared with about two out of three dwellings in the stock as a whole (see Table 3.13).

Table 3.13: Age of the social rented stock in relation to the stock as a whole

	Social rented %	Overall %
Before 1919	3.1	7.9
1919-1948	15.8	28.6
1948 and after	81.1	63.5

Source: 1978 Housing Survey/GGW *Wohnungswirtschaftliches Jahrbuch 1987/88*, p 138

Over half (55%) of the non-profit social rented stock was built in the quarter century from 1957 to 1982. As has been shown in Section II, the social housing programme peaked earlier in Germany than in France, the Netherlands, and the United Kingdom, and also tailed off earlier than in France and the United Kingdom, and much earlier than in the Netherlands. Table 3.14 shows the age of rented stock owned by non-profit landlords.

Table 3.14: Age of the rented stock owned by non-profit landlords

Period of construction	Number of dwellings	%
Before 1950	813,810	24.1
1950-1965	1,778,887	52.7
1966-1970	334,002	9.9
1971-1975	297,076	8.8
1976-1980	102,917	3.0
1981-1985	47,693	1.4
Total	3,374,385	100.0

Source: Constructed from 'Der Lange Weg', p 44 (GGW)

At 2.9% in 1982, the proportion of houses containing one or two dwellings was much smaller even than the proportion of houses in the French social rented sector. The proportion of houses in the stock overall is rather lower than in France. Of the 3.25 million dwellings built between 1953 and 1979, 41.5% were houses containing one or two dwellings.[21]

As with the social rented stock elsewhere, no comprehensive information is available about the distribution of the flatted stock among estates of different sizes and by numbers of storeys. Some useful, if selective, information is available, however, from the study of large estates undertaken in 1986 for the Federal Ministry of Housing by the Federal Research Institute for Planning (Bundesforschungsanstalt für Landeskunde und Raumordnung). This study took as its definition of large estates those consisting of more than 500 dwellings, and dating from the 1960s and 1970s. These high density estates are to be found mainly on the fringes of large towns and cities in densely populated regions. The study was not concerned with the many smaller estates of between 200 and 500 dwellings which are usually more closely integrated within the areas which they serve.

On the basis of information which was obtained on 233 estates, the Federal Research Institute estimates that there are between 500,000 and 600,000 dwellings on large estates in Germany, between 400,000 and 450,000 of them in the social rented sector, with the rest privately rented or owner-occupied. Social rented housing on large estates therefore represents about a tenth of the social rented stock as a whole, and 16% of the social rented stock owned by non-profit (GGW) landlord organisations. However, about half of all the social rented stock built between the mid-1960s and mid-1970s is to be found on these large estates.

Table 3.15 shows the distribution of the estates by size of those for which responses were received. Over 160 of the estates consisted of between 500 and 2,000 dwellings and accounted for about a third of the dwellings. A middle band of some 50 estates of between 2,000 and 5,000 dwellings accounted for a further third or so. The remainder was in 14 estates all of more than 5,000 dwellings. Thus, up to 400,000 homes in Germany are to be found on estates of over 2,000 dwellings, and up to 200,000 are on 14 estates of over 5,000 dwellings. It is this group of estates which attracts most of the attention of the media.

Table 3.15: Distribution of large estates by size

Number of dwellings per estate	Estates Number	%	Dwellings Number	%
< 1,000	110	48.3	64,576	14.8
1,000-2,000	53	23.2	78,108	17.9
2,000-5,000	51	22.4	165,767	38.1
> 5,000	14	6.1	127,183	29.2
Total	228*	100.0	435,634	100.0

Note: * No response on size of 5 estates

Source: Bundesforschungsanstalt für Landeskunde und Raumordnung

The 14 huge estates are also significant because they include virtually all the high-rise blocks of thirteen and more storeys found by the study, and which contain one in ten of dwellings on all the estates covered . One in four dwellings was in blocks of between eight and ten storeys. About two-thirds were in blocks of seven storeys or less. This information is not inconsistent with GGW estimates that about half a million dwellings belonging to the non-profit housing organisations are in blocks of five or more storeys. Housing specialists are firmly convinced that this is where the real problems are to be found. Problems with lifts in particular are often cited.

There are considerable similarities between the built form of German and French estates, stemming as so many of them do in both countries from the geometric patterns pioneered by such architects as Gropius and Le Corbusier. Access in high-rise and medium-rise blocks in Germany as in France is usually by lifts and staircases leading to a small number of flats on each floor, and with limited use of balcony or deck access. However, entryphones and locking main doors are much more common than in France.

In the non-profit social rented stock overall, the dwellings - at an average size of about 59 square metres in 1986 including kitchen, bathroom and entrance-hall[22] - are smaller than in the rented sector as a whole (67 square metres), and considerably smaller than dwellings in the owner-occupied sector where the average is 105 square metres.[23] Table 3.16 gives the distribution of dwellings in the social rented sector by size in 1986.

Table 3.16: Distribution of dwellings in the social rented sector by size (area)

Size in square metres	%	Size in square metres	%
<40	11.1	80-100	10.1
40-60	41.3	>100	1.5
60-80	36.0		

Source: GGW *Wohnungswirtschaftliches Jahrbuch 1987/88*, p 140

The main difference between the social rented sector and the rented sector overall is in the proportion of medium sized dwellings. According to a survey carried out by the GGW of the situation at the end of 1977, 78% of the social rented stock at that time was in the 40 to 80 square metre range, compared with 62% for the rented sector as a whole (according to the 1978 *1% Sample Survey*).

Information giving size comparisons by numbers of rooms is less clear cut than in France, the Netherlands, and the United Kingdom. Tables 3.17 and 3.18 give respectively the findings of a GGW survey of the stock of all its members in 1977, and the Federal Research Institute survey of large estates in 1985. It should be noted that the German definition includes the room used as a kitchen. The findings show considerable differences between the size-pattern in the stock as a whole and that on the large estates, though the latter may be distorted by the incompleteness of the returns.

Table 3.17: **Distribution of dwellings by size (number of rooms) overall in non-profit rented sector 1977**

Number of rooms per dwelling	(%)
1-2	13.2
3-4	74.9
5+	11.9

Source: GGW

Table 3.18: **Distribution of dwellings by size (number of rooms) on large estates in 1985**

Number of dwellings per estate	Total number of dwellings	Number of rooms per dwelling (%)			
		1-2	3-4	5+	No response
< 1,000	53,741	24.6	57.9	1.0	16.5
1,000-2,000	58,191	33.1	54.9	3.1	8.9
2,000-5,000	78,088	26.2	52.7	1.9	19.2
>5,000	78,410	38.3	53.4	1.8	6.5
Total	268,430	30.9	54.4	2.0	12.7

Source: Bundesforschungsanstalt für Landeskunde und Raumordnung

The findings are consistent, however, with the GGW's view that in the period immediately after 1948, small dwellings of one or two rooms predominated in the rented sector overall, but from 1957, four-room dwellings gain sway. With the marked trend towards smaller households, this pattern points to a growing mismatch between dwelling size and household size. On the other hand, the 1985 survey found a high proportion of one and two-room flats, a very small proportion with five rooms or more, and the majority in the three and four-room bracket.

Mainly because of their age profile in comparison with the stock as a whole, the social rented sector fares well on basic amenities. Table 3.19 gives comparative proportions of dwellings with internal WC, bath or shower, and central heating in 1981.

Table 3.19: Amenities

	% Social rented	Overall
Inside WC	100	94
Bath/shower	91	88
Central heating	62	62

Source: 1978 Housing Survey/GGW *Wohnungswirtschaftliches Jahrbuch 1981/82*, p 36

The 91% average of social rented dwellings equipped with bath or shower masks some significant variations. Although the position has no doubt since changed, in 1978 29.4% of the dwellings constructed before mid-1948 still lacked a bath or shower, although cooperatives with three-quarters of their dwellings so equipped, were doing better than companies where only two-thirds of dwellings had a bath or shower. There were also major regional variations. More than nine out of ten older dwellings in Berlin had a bath or shower, compared with just over six out of ten in Bavaria.[24]

According to the GGW, social rented dwellings reach only the overall average on central heating because it could not be afforded in the early post-war years, while in some areas, tenants are again asking for individual stove heating in improvement schemes.[25]

VI The tenants

It is a long-standing feature of subsidised housing in Germany that access to it should be reserved for those who need it most, although the net has traditionally been cast widely. Table 3.20 gives samples qualifying annual income limits in 1986. There are further adjustments for special categories, such as pensioner households. However, the typical income threshold for single person households is the equivalent of less than about £6,400, while for four-person households it is about £14,500. On these criteria, about 40% of households are eligible for social rented housing, including about 30% of those in employment.

Table 3.20: Qualifying gross income limits for social rented housing (1986)

Single person	DM 21,600
two-person household	DM 31,800
three-person household	DM 39,800
four-person household	DM 47,800

Source: 'Modernisierung und Mieter' (GGW)

There is also a second but small category of subsidised housing (2. Förderungsweg) at higher rents for more prosperous tenants with incomes up to 40% above these qualifying limits.

Partly because of data-protection legislation, landlords have limited economic and social information about their tenants. Better aggregate information will be available when the results of the 1987 census have been processed and published. The most recent reliable detailed information about tenants in the social rented sector is to be found in the *1% Sample Survey* of 1978. This showed that four and five-person households were more heavily represented in the social rented sector than among private sector tenants (19% as against 17%). More were aged 60 or over (36% as against 34%). And among the economically active, 53% were in manual occupations, as against 43%.

The median net monthly income of tenants in the social sector was lower than that in the private rented sector, at DM 1,610 compared with DM 1,660. Table 3.21 gives a fuller range of comparisons between households in the social rented sector and in the population as a whole. Currently, although accurate data are not available, it is generally thought that entrants to the social rented sector are relatively poorer, with virtually all entrants with incomes well under the qualifying threshold in areas of high demand.

Table 3.21: Household incomes (1978)

Monthly net income (DM)	Social sector main tenants Number (thousands)	%	All households Number (thousands)	%
<800	351	8.6	2,183	9.2
800-1,200	677	16.7	3,350	14.1
1,200-1,600	834	20.6	4,124	17.4
1,600-2,000	681	16.7	3,352	14.1
2,000-2,500	666	16.4	3,605	15.2
2,500-3,000	353	8.7	2,175	9.2
3,000-4,000	301	7.4	2,322	9.8
4,000-5,000	64	1.6	784	3.3
>5,000	26	0.6	576	2.4
Not stated	112	2.7	1,229	5.2
Total	4,065	100.0	23,700	100.0

Source: *Wohnungsstichprobe 1978*, Vol. 5, Table 1

Not surprisingly, Table 3.21 shows that except at the very bottom of the scale, lower income households are over-represented in the social rented sector. However, at the upper end of the range, perhaps a quarter of households are above the income limits for social housing, and so liable to repay subsidy under the 'Fehlbelegung' rules. It is often suggested that the increasingly competing rents in the private sector are encouraging such tenants to move out of social housing, and so intensifying the trend towards social residualisation. The income-related rent levels operated in some of the states are said to have a similar effect.

At the other end of the range, it is unofficially estimated that 15% of households in the social rented sector receive housing benefit (Wohngeld), although it is generally accepted that a much greater number are eligible to claim. The income limits for housing benefit are typically 80% of the qualifying thresholds for social rented housing (see Table 3.20). Although there is little statistical information about tenants in the social rented sector as such until the results of the 1987 census have been analysed, some useful information is available about the lower income groups generally, from which - by definition - its tenants come.

Work by the German Institute for Economic Research (Deutsches Institut für Wirtschaftsforschung) shows that tenants are doing considerably worse than owner-occupiers in the income stakes, and so gives some general support to the thesis that they are becoming increasingly disadvantaged. However, with the growing trend in Germany as elsewhere towards owner-occupation among those who can afford it - which is encouraged in Germany by the front-loading of the fiscal benefits - this trend is hardly surprising.

Although unemployment remained low, and even decreased through the late 1970s, the proportion of unemployed began to rise sharply at the start of the 1980s, from 3.8% in 1980 to 9.3% in 1985. Foreigners were particularly hard hit. Although they formed only 7.2% of the population, they formed 11.4% of the unemployed.[26] Young people too were heavily represented. Over a quarter of the unemployed at the end of 1985 were under 25.[27] Just under half were without any job qualification, and nearly a third of these were without any academic qualification either.[28]

According to the official *Yearbook of Statistics* (*Statistisches Jahrbuch 1986*) which is the nearest German counterpart to *Social Trends*, lower income households spent 19.5% of their disposable incomes on direct housing costs in 1981. By 1985, this proportion had risen to 21.9%, increasing the share of the household income going on housing by slightly over one-eighth. However, this increase was less than for the middle and higher income households, both of which saw the slice which direct housing costs took out of their disposable incomes rise by nearly a fifth in the same period.

As is explained in Section IV, housing benefit enables the households which qualify for it to keep the proportion of their incomes which goes on direct housing costs down to just under 20%. Again according to the *Yearbook of Statistics*, in 1984, about 1.35 million main tenants, or between 12% and 13% of households across the rented sector as a whole were drawing housing benefit, (and as mentioned above and in Section IV, unofficial estimates put the proportion of social sector tenants receiving housing benefit at 15%). More than 85% of the recipients had monthly incomes of under DM 2,000. This supports the view quoted above that many social sector tenants are probably well below the income threshold for social rented housing. The monthly rents for these households ranged predominantly between DM 150 and DM 500, depending largely on income. Over two-thirds were in accommodation with central heating and bath or shower. None of this is inconsistent with the limited available data about tenants, rents and conditions specifically in the social rented sector.

However, the *Yearbook of Statistics* provides two pieces of information of greater note about tenant recipients of housing benefit. First, as Table 3.22 shows, more than half the recipients - which here include about 100,000 owner-occupiers and a similar number of sub-tenants, as well as the 1.35 million main tenants - are single person households. Their average monthly outgoings on housing (rent or repayments) amount to DM 367, or the equivalent of roughly £85, on which the average housing benefit payment in 1984 was DM 118.

Table 3.22: Housing benefit recipients (all tenures) by household size and outgoings on housing

Household size	Number (thousands)	%	Average monthly housing outgoings (DM)
Single person	845.5	54.6	272
two-person	263.6	17.0	371
three-person	150.5	9.7	455
four-person	156.8	10.1	565
five-person	77.0	5.0	626
six-person and over	55.2	3.6	645
Total/Average	1,548.5	100.0	367

Source: *Statistisches Jahrbuch 1986*, Table 18.14.3

Second, Table 3.23 shows that in the 15 million strong rented stock overall, nearly one in ten housing benefit claimants lives in a post-1978 dwelling, although dwellings of this age constitute less than 2% of the 4 million total of social rented dwellings as a whole. This figure is supported by Table 3.13 in Section V which shows that only 1.4% of GGW members' 3.4 million stock was built between 1981 and 1985. The Federal Research Institute study of large estates which is quoted in other sections of this report also shows that the proportion of housing benefit claimants in recently built accommodation is much higher, with about one in four in housing built in the 1970s and after.

The view that the worse-off families live in the newer housing gains further weight from the apparent under-representation of

housing benefit recipients in dwellings built during the boom years
of the social rented sector.   Some 60.8% of housing benefit
recipients live in housing built before 1965, but 76.8% of the stock
owned by GGW landlords was built in that period (see Section V,
Table 3.13).

**Table 3.23: Average rents and ages of housing occupied by tenants
receiving housing benefit**

Age of housing	Tenants Number (thousands)	%	Average rents (DM)
Up to 20 June 1948	308.0	22.8	5.13
21 June 1948-1965	514.9	38.1	5.57
1966-1971	202.3	14.9	6.41
1972-1977	200.4	14.8	6.76
1978 and later	127.3	9.4	6.76
Total/Average	1,352.8	100.0	5.91

Source: *Statistisches Jahrbuch 1986*, **Table 18.14.4**

In part the distortion in allocations is due to the higher rents for
such housing, but housing managers also frequently allege that the
municipalities are using their nomination rights to steer poorer (and
by implication, difficult) families towards such housing. On the
other hand, some of the municipalities can and do argue that they
are under such pressure from homeless families - whom in practice
they have to house, though they are not statutorily bound to do so -
that they have to place these families where there is room, and
where they have allocation rights. As has been shown, this is
predominantly in the 1970s stock.

More generally, the allocation arrangements between
municipalities (who as we saw in Section III, are the initial link
between aspiring tenants and their landlords-to-be) and non-profit
housing companies are often alleged to be ineffective. However, as
was also shown in Section III, municipalities have increasingly
introduced arrangements to improve coordination of allocation
arrangements. For example, Cologne has had, for over ten years, a
formal structure of meetings with local social landlord

organisations, while Bremen has developed similar arrangements within its 'Bremer Modell' initiative (see Section VII).

VII Management problems and solutions

As we saw in Section II, concern about problems in the social rented sector began in Germany as elsewhere in the early to mid-1970s. In Germany (and in the Netherlands), this concern has tended to focus on the high and rising numbers of empty dwellings on some estates, and on the financial problems that this implied for landlords and, ultimately, for tenants. As in the Netherlands, although some landlord organisations have been concerned about the social implications, these have generally had a lower priority than in France and the United Kingdom.

In Germany, the really serious problems are concentrated on a small number of very large estates, especially those with high-rise blocks, and usually - as in France in particular - on the periphery of large towns and cities. The problems are also largely confined to the big landlord companies, and have hardly affected the smaller companies, still less cooperatives.

Mainly in response to the rising numbers of empty dwellings in the late 1970s and early 1980s, there was a growing fear among landlord organisations that the management problems which some of them were facing on a few estates could rapidly spread. Thus although Germany certainly has its share of problem estates, it will be seen that there has been an emphasis on prevention as well as on cure, as landlord organisations saw the image of the social rented sector deteriorating under two major historic influences.

Physical problems

First, although flats on the post-war estates were usually pleasant enough internally, physical problems were beginning to show or assume greater importance as expectations changed in a social housing market which was beginning to shift from its historic state of under-supply to one of over-supply in some regions.

The pioneering building techniques of the 1960s played their part. At best, the appearance of the buildings suffered prematurely, while at worst, the residents began to suffer the effects of technical defects, particularly in reinforced concrete and flat roofs. Although the problems have not been quantified nationally, the GGW talks of mounting anxiety about how the remedial costs can be met. Nevertheless, the condition of the stock appears to be less of an issue than in the United Kingdom.

The oil crisis of the early 1970s hit Germany particularly hard, and more than most, the residents on the new estates with their largely oil-fired district heating systems faced not only sharply increased costs, but also emerging difficulties with cold-bridging, condensation, and water and wind penetration.

The shape and size of the buildings were often found to set up wind flows which increased the spread of litter. This was not infrequently exacerbated by inadequate maintenance by landlord organisations and municipalities in their not always clearly defined spheres of responsibility, which in turn encouraged vandalism and other signs of hostility among the residents.

Above all, landlord organisations perceived the anonymity of the environment and the starkness of the facades as the major physical contributor to the off-putting image of problem estates. The unsympathetic design of many estates, especially the larger and more modernistic examples, not only made it difficult for their residents to develop a sense of belonging, but also increased the sense of alienation between those who lived there and the world at large which saw the estates as intrusive eyesores at the borderline between the cities and the countryside. Moreover, the media increasingly presented a deteriorating image of social housing, which added to the residents' sense of rejection and isolation.

Management, social and economic issues

Second, by the end of the 1970s, a growing number of landlord organisations were beginning to appreciate the need for more sensitive management approaches. Not only were they facing greater difficulty in finding tenants as the market reached equilibrium, but also they felt that they were having to accept more of the poorer tenants who had traditionally gone into the private rented sector.

While the overall vacancy rate in the social rented sector remained low at under 1% (although the German practice of not counting dwellings as empty for the first three months makes this figure difficult to compare with those elsewhere) on some of the large estates, it has temporarily reached well over 10% or 15%. In 1985, the Federal Research Institute study which is cited at various points in earlier sections of this chapter found an average vacancy rate of 3.2% on the large estates which it sampled.

Although firm information is not available, Germany appears to suffer less than the other countries covered by this study judging by the standard indicators of management difficulties, such as rent arrears, which the Federal Research Institute study put at 1.9% on the large estates. High turnover rates were mentioned on specific estates, rather than as a general issue. Vandalism came low on the list of problems reported by landlords, and crime or even the fear of crime were hardly mentioned except as a youth issue.

As Section IV has shown, the rents for recently built housing are higher than in the older stock, and have been rising more sharply than in the social rented sector generally, not least because the newer dwellings are usually larger. Even more important, they are uncompetitive with private sector rents in some areas, and so exacerbating the drift of the better-off tenants in particular from the estates. As will be seen in the examples described below, landlord organisations have set great store by measures to provide specially subsidised rent structures to maintain as broad as possible a social spectrum on the estates which they believe to be at risk.

Allocation policies and practices have long since been seen as the critical management issue. The arrangements between landlord organisations and the municipalities - which as we have seen, are the initial link between aspiring tenants and the landlord organisations - have often been ineffective, especially on the large estates. These estates have often suffered problems from the outset because they were let indiscriminately, with high concentrations of families depending on social security, of large families and (on some estates) of immigrant families, in the rush to get them tenanted.[29] Subsequent lettings have also frequently been unsuitable, especially of families with young children in high-rise flats, or of elderly people in areas far from shops and leisure facilities.

Some of the larger housing companies have traditionally had highly centralised management structures, often with a rigid separation between the development and management sides of the organisation, and with considerable departmentalism within the management side. There is increasing recognition that a less remote and more human relationship with the tenants is needed, although as will be seen, where local offices have been introduced, their functions and opening times are limited.

To the extent that many of the problem estates were and are in areas of structural economic decline, landlords can only operate on the margin. Above all, they face mismatches between the number of potential tenants and the number of dwellings as the expected population growth and job prospects have failed to be realised in many areas. A GGW sample survey of its member organisations in 1983 provided clear evidence of a north-south divide in Germany, with empty dwellings and difficulties in letting largely in the traditional industrial areas such as the Ruhr, the lower Rhine and the north, while the prosperous south of the country was relatively free of these problems.[30] However, it will be seen that there have been some local economic initiatives to break the dormitory image by promoting shopping centres and by bringing in employment opportunities, if only through extensive use of the ABM scheme, the German equivalent of the Community Programme.

As elsewhere, German landlords increasingly recognised that the emerging problems were in no small part due to the failure of various ancillary services on estates to materialise when they should, or at all. Health care, communal facilities and shops depended on other agencies in the public and private sectors, which did not necessarily share the housing providers' perceptions of priority. Although the Federal Research Institute study indicates that most of the large estates are now reasonably well served by public transport, progress in this direction has been slow and patchy. While schools may have been generally appropriate to the numbers and ages of the children on the estates in the early days, they have not always adapted to the inevitably changing needs as the children grew older. Still less were suitable youth and leisure facilities brought in for the growing numbers of teenagers. The examples include measures to improve or fill in gaps in the social and economic infrastructure on some estates.

Although, as is explained in Section VI, landlords rarely have detailed information about the incidence of social problems on their estates, such as numbers of unemployed tenants and young people, single parent families, and immigrant households, several are taking steps to provide special support where it is clearly needed.

In some cases, landlords have recognised the need for community development measures, and have introduced schemes to promote greater tenant participation in the fortunes of their problem estates. More than 80 tenants' councils have been set up, although almost all are limited to advisory and social activities, and tenants have rarely been quick to participate in these ventures, with numbers voting in elections ranging typically from 15% to 20%, and from 5% to 50% at the extremes.[31] On the other hand, more intensive nurturing has produced some impressive examples of tenant participation, especially in the development of improvement schemes.

Government programmes

Thus, by the early 1980s, several landlord organisations felt that if they were to arrest the physical and social decline on a few estates, which they saw as leading to potentially overwhelming management and financial problems on a wide scale, they would need additional targetted government resources to make some major physical changes and to reduce rent levels on some estates.

Landlord organisations were able to draw on support from a variety of sources at the federal, state, and municipal levels, but in particular from two main, alternative sources. First, in response to the pressing calls for help from some prominent landlord organisations, in 1983, the federal government launched a research progamme of experimental projects in conjunction with the relevant state and municipal authorities to develop measures for improving living conditions on post-war estates. This programme has supported experimental projects on 18 estates at a total cost to the federal government over five years of DM 23.8 million. The estates range in size from small ones of about 200 dwellings to vast complexes of 17,000, with a total of some 45,000 dwellings. The programme is currently being evaluated by two private research firms, GEWOS, and ARGE Kirchhoff/Jacobs/Mezler.

Second, in some cases, the state governments have funded physical renewal schemes out of Städtebauförderung resources (the German equivalent of the English Urban Programme, which is partly supported by the federal government), sometimes with additional revenue support to reduce rents below the normal approved - or controlled - rent (see Section IV).

The examples considered below include projects funded from both these sources. However, it should be noted that the initiatives have come mostly piecemeal from the landlord organisations themselves, and that in most cases not only have they contributed funds from their own resources, but also they have supplemented the physical and rent support measures with a variety of steps to improve their management of the estates.

Chorweiler estate, Cologne

The Chorweiler estate on the northern outskirts of Cologne consists of about 5,000 dwellings altogether, though according to the original plan in the mid-1960s, it was to have been more than twice as large. It was built in two stages, the first in the early 1970s and the second in the early 1980s, in blocks of various heights ranging from 4 to 23 storeys.

Although there is about 10% owner-occupation, most of the estate consists of social rented housing owned and managed by 14 landlord organisations. The two largest are the former Neue Heimat organisation (see Section III) with 1,870 dwellings, and the Aachener Gemeinnützige Siedlungs- und Wohnungsgesellschaft which of its total stock of some 10,000 dwellings has about 1,400 on Chorweiler. The landlord organisations have a good working relationship with the Cologne city housing office which has extensive nomination rights on the estate, and since 1976 they have jointly funded an advice office with two part-time staff on the estate itself. However, there is by no means universal confidence that such a large number of landlord organisations leads to an efficiently managed estate.

Despite its peripheral location, the estate has excellent transport links with the city centre. The infrastructure is good, with a comprehensive range of communal and recreational facilities, and a large and attractive covered shopping centre with about 70 shops.

Although at the outset the dwellings were quite easy to let, the estate soon became unpopular, with a vacancy rate at its peak of 15%. This unpopularity was increasingly compounded by pressure to let the dwellings to anyone who would take them, which led to concentrations of socially disadvantaged families. Unusually, the estate has a high proportion of immigrant tenants, reaching levels of up to 40% in some central areas. Car ownership is low, leading to large numbers of empty garage spaces. Social security recipients rose by nearly a half between 1981 and 1985. Turnover in the central (Neue Heimat) area rose from an already high 31% in 1981 to a rate of 45% in the first quarter of 1985.

Some of the landlord organisations have made limited improvements to the environment and the entrances to the blocks, but the approach at Chorweiler has concentrated on management measures which is unusual for problem estates in Germany. The first was the introduction in 1985 of a special rent subsidy by the state government of North Rhine-Westphalia, which brought the rents down from about DM 8.00 per square metre to near the national average of about DM 6.00. It is a matter of continuing debate whether the credit is due to the reduction in rents or to the growth in local demand which occurred about the same time, but the vacant dwellings on the estate were soon filled, and empties are no longer a problem. Turnover is also down.

However, the success was felt by some to be double-edged. The low rents are said to have attracted mainly poorer tenants and so reinforced the image of Chorweiler as a sink estate. In 1985, the city of Cologne therefore also agreed to remove the qualifying income threshold to enable more prosperous families to move into Chorweiler. In the first year, 40% of new tenants were above the income limit, and 15% were above the limit in the second year.

The landlord oganisations had already come to the conclusion in 1985 that more fundamental steps to involve the tenants were necessary if the estate were to be turned round in a long lasting way. The merits of Chorweiler were marketed widely in the Cologne area, and brought in about 200 new tenants. An estate news-sheet 'Leben in Chorweiler' (Life in Chorweiler) was started as a first step in promoting greater tenant identity. The resident caretaker arrangements were strengthened to provide for better workloads for the caretakers, and to make them more accessible to the tenants. Tenants who did the caretaking around their own dwelling when no caretaker was available became eligible for a monthly bonus of DM 50.00.

Then, in 1987, the landlord organisations appointed a consultant to work on the estate and develop a strategy for active tenant participation in the improvement programme for the estate. The strategy published in the summer of 1987 after extensive and intensive consultation with the tenants and other interests envisages a range of practical mechanisms for bringing residents on the estate together. These include an estate office, a poster workshop, courses and activities for old people, children and the handicapped, reopening the cinema, individual tenants' gardens, and a monthly discussion forum chaired by a TV personality.

Apart from the communal development of proposals and priorities for improving the estate, the strategy includes ideas for developing self-help advice with the problems which commonly beset individuals in poor communities, such as ways of balancing the household budget.

Roderbruch estate, Hannover

Roderbruch is an early 1970s estate of about 3,000 dwellings on the northern outskirts of Hannover. It is owned and managed by several landlord organisations of which the largest is the Gemeinnützige Baugesellschaft Hannover (GBH), a company owned jointly by the city council and the city savings bank. It has about 600 high-rise flats at Roderbruch. In 1985, one in ten of them was empty.

Partly as a result of pressure from the landlord organisations, the estate has good transport links with the city centre, and is well provided with shops and communal facilities. The GBH is building private houses for owner-occupation in the area. At DM 250,000 for a house with a floor area of about 100 square metres, they are apparently selling well.

Because of its municipal sponsorship, the GBH accepts a high proportion of socially and economically disadvantaged tenants, including people from East Germany, Poland, and especially from Turkey. The estate suffers from a variety of management problems including high turnover and rent arrears.

Out of its own resources, GBH has improved the entrance halls of its multi-storey blocks on the estate. Caretaking services have been stepped up, and a social worker appointed with her own office, to provide instruction courses and counselling for tenants in difficulty, in particular single parent families.

Another major social landlord organisation on the Roderbruch estate is the Firma Gundlach. Unlike the other landlord organisations described in this chapter which belong to the 'non-profit' sector, Gundlach is a private company which owns nearly 700 dwellings on the estate, most of them in high density eight-storey blocks. They include sheltered accommodation for older people, and specially adapted flats for the physically and mentally handicapped, which are staffed by the city which also nominates the tenants.

Like GBH, the Gundlach company responded to the growing buyers' market which developed in the late 1970s with physical and management measures to improve the competitiveness of the housing and the service, but more so than GBH, the Gundlach company has sought to develop tenant involvement.

The physical improvement work has concentrated on the approaches to the blocks. In keeping with the 'green' trend in Germany, pergolas have been erected around the entrances, with shrubberies along the front of the blocks and on top of the underground garages.

With a large proportion of poor tenants, especially single parent families and immigrants, the garage accommodation (which state planning law requires to be at set levels) is under-used. The Gundlach company has therefore transformed 170 square metres of garage space into social and communal facilities, including a meeting room and a multi-purpose room. On their own initiative, the tenants have set up a cafe. The company has appointed a social worker to generate a wide range of activities, including practical courses for parents, play groups, gymnastics, a youth group, jumble-sales, and excursions, as well as discussion groups and individual counselling. The costs of the improvement work and the social worker are met from the company's own resources.

Bremen

Bremen and its sister-city Bremerhaven about 40 miles to the north together constitute the smallest of the German states. It has a strong tradition as a city-state - one of the ancient northern Hanseatic League, like Hamburg - with a large and generally advantageous overlap between the functions of city and state, not least in matters of housing.

The housing stock of the city of Bremen is unusual for a major German city in that about 100,000 of the total of around 250,000 or so dwellings are houses, mostly terraced. About a third of the stock is in buildings containing one or two dwellings. High and even medium-rise housing is therefore much less common than in other cities, and is still regarded by many as an alien post-war innovation.

The social rented sector in the city currently comprises about 70,000 dwellings, or more than a quarter of the total stock, and two out of three dwellings in the social rented sector are owned and managed by three municipal landlord companies, the largest of which is GEWOBA with about 35,000 units which previously belonged to the now defunct Neue Heimat organisation.

GEWOBA as the successor to Neue Heimat Bremen is most conspicuously involved on the **Osterholz-Tenever** estate which with its zigurat of white high-rise blocks provides all traffic approaching by the motorway from the south with its first impression of Bremen. Conversely, the motorway with its noise and fumes is a dominant feature in the life of the residents of Osterholz-Tenever. Originally part of a planners' dream to increase the population of Bremen to a million by the year 2000, plans for this green-fields peripheral estate were drawn up in 1964, with most of the construction taking place in the 1970s. As a demonstration project for new directions in public sector housing design with its underground garages and separation of vehicle and pedestrian traffic on different levels (and consequently entry to many blocks at three levels), the estate attracted special funding from the federal government in Bonn.

Although it was soon realised that the original scheme was over-ambitious and building virtually ceased when 2,600 flats had been completed, the price of curtailing the development has been large tracts of empty land, a shopping centre near the edge of the estate, and poor public transport links with the city centre. On the other hand, it is well equipped with schools and facilities for young people.

From the outset, the estate proved difficult to let, and its competitive position worsened with its relatively high rents in an area where housing supply and demand were increasingly in balance.   With municipal nomination rights at a high level, Osterholz-Tenever has always had relatively more socially disadvantaged and poor tenants than, for example, neighbouring Hahnenkamp (see below). At the worst point, in 1985, vacancies were approaching 20%, and turnover was 37%. The rent arrears of former tenants amount to over 3% of the collectable rent.

The immediate reaction of the city council and the landlord organisation was the usual one in Germany. The city provided special subsidies to reduce rents, while the landlord organisation increased its subsidies for the rents of the shops in the shopping centre and elsewhere on the estate. The landlord organisation also embarked on an improvement scheme which so far has cost some DM 5 million, or the equivalent of about £450 a dwelling. Some facades have been given colour treatment, individual gardens have been provided, entrances have been improved, with some of the work done by unemployed young people from the estate. Security work includes better lighting, and complex three-way entryphone systems to cope with the three entry levels.

Residents of Osterholz-Tenever are fortunate in having the landlord organisation's district office for the 18,000 dwellings which it manages in the south of Bremen based on the estate. Clearly, considerable effort has gone into making it accessible and responsive.   It is responsible for providing the block caretaker service, for lettings, rent collection, tenant advice, and repairs -

which are now carried out by independent contractors who have replaced the earlier unwieldy and more expensive direct labour organisation. The results have been gratifying. Turnover had gone down from the peak of 37% to 12%, or about the Bremen average by the end of 1987. Vacancies had halved in the same period, although as in the Netherlands and in Germany generally, much of this improvement is put down to rising demand for social rented accommodation as households decrease in size, and to the cut-back in new-build in the subsidised sector. The influx from East Germany has also been significant. The rent arrears of tenants in 1988 were about 1% of the collectable rent.

Nevertheless, major social and management problems remain. There is obvious scope for better coordination of service delivery between the landlord organisation and the various municipal departments. Although landscape maintenance is satisfactory in the areas for which the landlord is reponsible - which again are maintained by a private contractor - a variety of municipal departments provide a mixed quality of service in other areas such as school grounds, youth facilities, and street cleansing.

A further notable gap has been the apparently ingrained lack of interest on the part of the landlord organisation in involving the tenants in the extensive and costly work which has been done to improve conditions on the estate, despite - or perhaps because of - experience with some quite vocal tenants groups which have formed spontaneously in some blocks to air their grievances.

This gap is being filled as the city council and GEWOBA begin to feel their way towards a more intensive partnership to provide the mix of physical and management measures which both parties feel is necessary if the estate is to be turned round fundamentally. This is the initiative known as the **'Bremer Modell'**, which is exciting interest among social housing organisations elsewhere in Germany. It begins with the appointment of a consultant (or in this case two consultants) paid by the city council to work closely with the tenants to explore their housing needs and aspirations. The consultants report to a committee representing the interests of the landlord organisation, the city council, and the tenants, but with the local authority as the ultimate paymaster for the special measures which may be approved and the landlord as the owner, having a right of veto.

The Bremer Modell approach was evolved in the mid-1980s on the Varreler Baeke estate nearer the centre of Bremen by the same team whose members are now beginning work at Osterholz-Tenever, and are already working at Grohner Düne (see below). Essentially, it involves extensive tenant consultation in the development of a package of measures to improve conditions, but with the emphasis on physical work to improve the environment, security, and access arrangements, with the cost being shared between the landlord organisation and the city. However, the team is increasingly looking for ways of enhancing employment opportunities.

The initial objectives of the scheme for Osterholz-Tenever are to improve communication and relationships within the blocks themselves, within the estate, and with the rest of the city. In the first instance, the ideas canvassed at large and small meetings are intended mainly to minimise the effect of physical barriers such as breakdown-prone lifts, unsympathetic entrances and staircases, and the fences, wasteland and motorway which separate the estate from the world at large. As in other projects in Germany, the consultants' approach is to put proposals to the tenants rather than to seek their ideas, though this is in part due to the ubiquitous difficulty in opening a consultative process without any certainty of whether the scheme will go ahead at all, or what level of resources might be available for it. At the time of the visit, the tentative proposals for the pilot 22-storey block involved lift improvements, remodelling of the entrance hall, appointment of a concierge, better facilities for refuse disposal, and garage improvements

The neighbouring but better placed **Hahnenkamp** estate provides a sharp contrast. Built in the second half of the 1960s, this small estate of 272 dwellings in eight four-storey blocks is typical of many in Germany which now need extensive modernisation and rectification of technical defects. Although about one in three tenant households receives some form of social security payments, the population is relatively stable and more prosperous than the Bremen average. The management problems have been a mismatch between the preponderance of large flats and the declining size of households, and high heating costs because the insulation has been made ineffective by damp penetration into the wall cavities. As a result, by 1984, the estate was suffering from a rising vacancy level which reached 4.5% the following year.

From a British (or French) viewpoint, it is surprising that such an estate should figure among those selected for the Federal Housing Ministry's experimental scheme, as the problems involved are predominantly matters of housekeeping and maintenance commonly faced by landlords. The apparent justification for federal help is the value of the project as a demonstration of an economical and effective package of physical measures in close consultation with the tenants to provide comprehensive new heating and insulation arrangements, extensive remodelling including conversion of some of the larger flats into smaller units, and external and environmental improvements, including the roads, shopping centre and a tram stop.

The total cost of the work on the buildings and the environment is some DM 14 million, which is equivalent to about £11,000 a unit. This is two-thirds of equivalent new-build costs. Part of the cost has been met from the landlord organisation's own resources, but DM 6 million is being contributed in roughly equal proportions by federal and local government, with the possibility of further support of up to DM 1 million for the environmental work. Local government is also providing an annual revenue subsidy of DM 1.5 million. As a result, the rents have not had to be increased, while heating costs have been halved.

The **Grohner Düne** estate at the other end of Bremen is to British eyes a much more likely recipient of central government support. It consists of about 570 dwellings altogether, in system-built blocks of between 7 and 15 storeys built in the early 1970s in an industrial area close to the river Weser. The whole area was originally scheduled for clearance. With the subsequent shift in emphasis towards rehabilitation of the existing stock, the clearance programme was not carried through, and the Grohner Düne estate stands incongruously beside a sensitively restored and traditionally redeveloped residential area.

Despite the negative image which it inevitably has from this unfortunate juxtaposition, the Grohner Düne does benefit from good transport links with the city centre by the suburban railway which terminates beside the estate, and from a good shopping centre and other social and communal facilities in the immediate neighbourhood. The flats are also spacious and well-equipped internally. On the other hand, the bleak aspect of the buildings is exacerbated by a stark and windswept environment, and maintenance had been seriously neglected from the outset.

It is generally accepted that the blame lies with the unusual form of ownership. Grohner Düne is owned by two real estate companies which now have little interest in the property even as a capital asset, and would apparently like to get rid of it altogether. Expenditure on maintenance has therefore always been low.

The estate has been managed by a series of separate companies. The bulk of it (420 dwellings) was managed by a social landlord company Nordwestdeutsche Siedlungsgesellschaft (NWDS) from 1977. From 1986, this part of the estate was managed by the Neue Heimat landlord organisation until responsibility was taken over by GEWOBA (see above) when Neue Heimat got into its national difficulties. The other 150 or so dwellings were originally managed by a local management company, which handed over this responsibility in 1987 to a private landlord company.

There were letting difficulties from the outset, which over time were compounded by indiscriminate allocation policies, for example to short-term foreign tenants, and in particular to locally based United States forces personnel and their families who tended to form an internal ghetto in the already stigmatised estate. Turnover in the Neue Heimat property reached 28%, and there has been a persistently high vacancy rate in the larger flats. As late as 1988, despite efforts towards a more balanced lettings policy and the departure of the Americans, one in three tenants were still foreigners, mostly Turks.

Nonetheless, the estate had always had the advantage of a core of stable and strong-minded tenants, who - unusually - voiced strong opposition to the then landlord organisation's proposals for improving the estate in 1985. The result has been an exercise in active tenant participation in partnership with the new landlord organisation and the city council under the Bremer Modell arrangements described above.

Following various initiatives to improve the estate's environment, the estate was selected for special funding under the federal experimental programme described above, and over two years, a total of DM 2.2 million (equivalent to about £900 per dwelling) split equally between central and local government was spent on measures such as landscaping to reduce wind nuisance, tree planting, the construction of a pavilion for social activities and other communal facilities, the installation of more secure mail-boxes, better lighting, and fenced off garden areas.

With the help of the consultant assigned to the project by the city council, the tenants have participated in the formulation of these measures, and are being drawn into more active involvement in the running of the estate. The balance in the relationship between the tenants, the (expanded) staff of two caretakers, and the consultant is bound to be delicate, with the consultant often at risk of sacrificing his all-important independent status to his role in practice as a proxy for management interests.

Nonetheless, the achievements in social development and tenant animation on the estate are already considerable. At the management level, efforts are being made to promote the role of the caretakers by having them show round potential new tenants. There are proposals for tenants to replace the spasmodic entrance and staircase cleansing service provided by an outside contractor. Most significantly, the annual maintenance budget of DM 300,000 has been opened up to the tenants so that they can influence priorities and reduce costs by taking on some of the routine repairs and maintenance work themselves. Both with cleansing and repairs, all concerned hope not only to save money, but also to encourage a more positive attitude among the tenants towards the upkeep of their estate.

On the wider social front, while government is funding the capital costs of the new communal facilities such as the laundry room, the tenants are responsible for their upkeep, sometimes with the help of other government programmes. For example, the ABM scheme for the long-term unemployed is funding teachers for the afternoon classes for children with special learning problems. These are far from rare with the high foreign population on the estate.

There is widespread confidence that the estate is beginning to turn the corner, and the number of vacant flats has gone down significantly though in part this is due, as elsewhere, to the general increase in demand. However, as has been shown, the ethnic balance is still heavily weighted towards foreigners, and turnover is high.

Hamburg

Hamburg, with Bremen 60 miles to the southwest, is the other Federal Republic's city-state and a former member of the ancient Hanseatic League. It has a population of about 1.6 million - about three times that of Bremen - and a total housing stock of 760,000, about 280,000 or 37% of which is subsidised social rented housing.

Half of this social rented housing is owned and/or managed by two companies. The now defunct trade union sponsored company Neue Heimat formerly owned about 40,000 dwellings, now transferred to the city. The municipal housing company, generally known by its acronym SAGA, owns or manages about 100,000 dwellings, and the estates considered below all belong in part to SAGA.

As the only municipal landlord organisation in Hamburg, SAGA has close administrative and political links with the city-state. The senator (or minister) for housing matters is ex officio chairman of SAGA's board of management, and the various municipal departments with housing interests are also represented. Elected members are often closely involved in the company's affairs, including new-build and renewal projects, and individual lettings cases, in which they have a local interest. Although the city in its overall role in the allocation of social rented housing is seeking to reach agreements with all the non-profit landlord organisations in Hamburg to take their share of disadvantaged families (with financial guarantees from the city), it is commonly accepted that SAGA in practice accepts the majority of problem cases.

With a cutback in its new-build programme from over 5,000 dwellings a year at its peak to a couple of hundred in the foreseeable future, combined with up to 8,000 priority homeless cases a year and a growing number of socially disadvantaged families, the city feels under increasing pressure in coping with those in need. At the same time, the ready availability of competitively priced housing in the private rented sector provides a real alternative for the rather better-off people who might otherwise want social rented accommodation.

SAGA and Neue Heimat are therefore major political and economic forces in Hamburg's social housing. The financial problems of Neue Heimat on the national scene have been described elsewhere in this chapter. At the local level, the financial crisis of SAGA is just as serious, and although the reasons are structural rather than the mismanagement which caused the downfall of Neue Heimat, the political and financial dilemma facing the city government is no less great.

It is also an unpromising basis on which to begin the decentralisation of SAGA's housing management structure which is widely acknowledged as needed if the organisation is to cope effectively with one of the largest stocks of housing in West Germany. Nonetheless, with support from the city, and in two cases from the federal experimental programme, SAGA has embarked on some interesting physical and social renewal schemes.

Dannerallee in the north-eastern suburb of Jenfeld involves the greatest tenant participation, mainly because of a fortunate mix of dynamic personalities from among the tenants with the consultant assigned by SAGA to the project. The estate of 576 flats in four 15-storey blocks built in the late 1960s is adjacent to an estate of 4-storey walk-up blocks which are generally successful. The four Dannerallee blocks soon acquired the reputation of a dumping-ground for problem families, and in the early 1980s, they and their surroundings began to show the classic symptoms of an estate caught in a spiral of decline.

A group of tenants concerned primarily with the difficulties which this decline was causing for old people living in the blocks, decided on a self-help approach. Their initiative coincided with the start of the federal government's experimental programme, and they received support in the form of the SAGA consultant and a total of DM 1.5 million (or rather less than the equivalent of £900 per dwelling) from the federal government, the city and SAGA for capital expenditure. By drawing also on the ABM programme for the long-term unemployed, the tenants have been able to provide and staff a wide range of communal facilities, including a community hall with a stage and catering facilities, a youth club in disused cellar accommodation, a sauna, and children's play areas. A more recent initiative has been the establishment of an advisory centre.

The environment has also been transformed, much of it through the efforts of the tenants individually and in groups, by the creation of private gardens around the blocks, by the planting and training of climbing plants up the blocks, by landscaping work including the digging and planting of an ornamental pond, and the creation and planting of artificial hills between the blocks to reduce wind nuisance.

In all these activities, the tenants have shown remarkable resourcefulness in obtaining materials and equipment such as the sauna, and the rubble, soil and trees for the artificial hills at little or no cost. They have also been remarkably successful in marshalling the support and cooperation of SAGA staff and of the tenant body as a whole, in part through a cheerful estate newspaper which they publish every two months to promote social activities and greater communal awareness.

Kirchdorf-Süd on the southern edge of Hamburg is a much larger estate, consisting of about 2,300 flats in massive 11 to 14-storey blocks built in the early 1970s. Two of the blocks, containing about 1,000 flats in all, belong to SAGA, and the remainder to a variety of cooperatives and private companies.

Despite the frequent claims that non-municipal landlords can be more selective than companies such as SAGA, by all accounts most of the landlord organisations at Kirchdorf-Süd accept more than the average number of disadvantaged tenants. Although there are few empty flats, about 30% of the tenants are in arrear with their rent, and the turnover rate is 13% (which with change of tenancy costs, said to be in the region of DM 10,000 (over £2,300), is a matter of serious financial concern to the landlord organisations). About 30% of the tenants are foreigners. The population is said to be ageing, largely because young people are put off by the lack of entertainment facilities. Rents are high, although heating costs are low.

The aspect is bleak, and the entrances to the blocks and the lifts are litter-strewn and smell. Although the balcony access arrangements between the lifts and the flats involve quite short walks, they are particularly windswept in this exposed environment. Communication within the estate itself is hampered by drainage canals, which also attract an array of tyres, shopping-trolleys and other debris. Although it has a good bus service, the estate is remote from the city centre, and it is also cut off from the neighbouring owner-occupied housing by an (unnecessary) four-lane feeder-road.

The federal government and the city have agreed on a DM 10 million project within the experimental programme. This is the equivalent of nearly £1,500 per dwelling. A broadly based steering group including representatives of the landlord organisations, the tenants, the various municipal departments with an interest, and the political parties has been set up under local authority chairmanship, but there is widespread feeling that it is too cumbersome to provide much drive. Support to the tenants is provided by an architectural team, and here too there is some disappointment about the extent of real tenant involvement, particularly in the determination of priorities.

In the first three years of the project, the emphasis has been on environmental improvements and on the provision of communal facilities. Some entrances have been improved, at a cost of about DM 80,000 (some £27,000) each. An empty flat has been converted into a cafe at a similar cost, but in the absence of plans for running it, it opens for only two afternoons a week. An ambitious workshop costing DM 200,000 (nearly £70,000) has been built for young people to work on their mopeds, but this too appears to be under-used - not least because of protests from residents in the neighbouring blocks. Other social measures include advice and training sessions for mothers of young children, and advice to tenants generally. Some of the landlord organisations have set up offices on the estate, but as is normal practice in Germany, most contact between landlord and tenant is through block caretakers.

Steilshoop, like Osterholz-Tenever in Bremen, was one of the pioneering departures in new social housing design which received special federal government support when it was built in the early 1970s. In comparison with the other two estates described above, it is quite fortunately situated on former allotment land to the north of the city centre, but with only passable public transport links until it is connected to the underground system some time in the 1990s. The estate is well provided with other amenities; schools, health care, shops, and communal facilities.

The estate consists in all of less than 7,000 dwellings, nearly all of them in 20 open-ended ring-shaped blocks of varying heights, ranging between 6 and 13 storeys. The blocks are situated in two parallel V-shaped rows in an extensive landscaped area.

The estate is owned by 55 landlord organisations, most of them non-profit companies and cooperatives, but some private companies and individuals. SAGA owns three of the ring-blocks in the central part of the estate, comprising about 800 flats.

From the outset, the SAGA blocks have been recognised as a problem zone in an otherwise successful estate. The other landlord organisations have been able to select their tenants and therefore have a relatively stable population which keeps management and maintenance costs down, the SAGA flats housed high proportions of foreigners, social security recipients, families with large numbers of children, and single parent families.[32] In the early 1980s, the social problems in this area of Steilshoop attracted the attention of the media, and the stigma spread to other parts of the estate, where even some of the cooperatives began to experience difficulty in letting their flats. By the beginning of 1985, about 100 SAGA flats were empty, mostly in the central area.

With support from the city, which in turn drew on the urban aid (Städtebauförderung) programme funded by the federal government, SAGA adopted a broad based approach to rescue its part of the estate which was generally regarded as a canker poisoning the rest. The rescue package was developed in consultation with the tenants, and a key feature was the appointment of a social worker as consultant and catalyst between the parties.

The physical work has involved extensive landscaping and improvements to the outside of the blocks, such as attractive entrances, fenced off gardens and climbing plants.   Security measures include effective entryphones and better lighting. Bicycle and pram stores have been built to save wear and tear in the entrance halls and staircases.

Socially based measures include a kindergarten, an area where young people can let off steam and a workshop where they can repair their mopeds, as at Kirchdorf-Süd. Another similarity with Kirchdorf-Süd is the cafe costing DM 500,000, which SAGA nursed along until it became viable in its own right.

SAGA has set up an estate based office with a staff of 15 including the block caretakers. Apart from the normal management functions, the office acts as a social focus, and provides advice and support to the tenants, for example on how to deal with actual or potential rent arrears.

The rents themselves have been specially subsidised by the city to make them competitive with rents elsewhere in Hamburg. Although the vacancy rate - which is now negligible - might well have fallen anyway with the increased pressure on the housing market, estates such as Steilshoop are the most vulnerable to distortions in the local rent structure. It is therefore arguable that the special rent subsidies are necessary to ensure a stable demand for housing on such estates.

At a cost of DM 16 million or the equivalent of over £3,500 per dwelling owned by SAGA, the project is vastly more expensive than the other two considered above.   In particular, Dannerallee shows how the right - though fortuitous - combination of tenants and management can achieve more physical and social transformation at a fraction of the cost. On the other hand, the high cost of the Steilshoop project may arguably be justified by its effect in preventing the whole estate of nearly 7,000 dwellings from entering a probably irreversible vortex of decline.

Berlin

With a population of about two million, West Berlin was the largest city in Germany.   Although (until reunification) it was constitutionally not fully a part of the Federal Republic, to all intents and purposes it was a city-state similar to Bremen and

Hamburg. Berlin as a whole is now the capital of the reunited Germany, but the remainder of this chapter is concerned with the former West Berlin with its total housing stock of about 1.1 million dwellings, most of them built or rebuilt since the Second World War.

The social rented sector totals more than 420,000 dwellings, or 38% of the stock, and is therefore a much larger proportion than the average in Germany, even in the larger cities. It is owned and managed by a large number of landlord organisations, but dominated by eight non-profit companies with individual holdings of over 10,000 dwellings, and which between them account for about 200,000 dwellings, or nearly half the social rented stock.[33] Much of this housing is in the inner city areas of Berlin, and consists of typical modern estates, as well as major rehabilitation schemes on older property acquired from private landlords in the artisan and working class districts, for example, by the DEGEWO and GESOBAU landlord organisations in Wedding, GEHAG in Schöneberg, and other companies elsewhere in the inner city areas.

It is in areas such as this that the main concentrations of foreigners - especially Turks, who as has been shown in Section I are particularly numerous in Berlin - and other socially and economically disadvantaged people have traditionally sought housing, because of the low rents. There are therefore problems of adjustment in the areas where old private rented housing has recently been replaced or refurbished, with consequent progressive rent increases, and these difficulties are expected to intensify as the supply of cheap housing for such groups diminishes.

However, in the older inner city purpose-built estates, there remain some major sources of cheap housing. One example is the **Sozialpalast**, a complex of high density high-rise blocks (with some structural problems) incorporating a wartime bunker and bridging a main traffic artery. This is subsidised housing owned by a private landlord organisation which apparently willingly accepts low-income tenants in receipt of social security and housing benefit support, until such time as it moves into the private sector on completion of repayment of the subsidised loans. This estate looks shabby and neglected, with a depressingly obvious concentration of poor tenants.

Wassertorplatz is a typical inner city purpose-built estate owned by a non-profit landlord organisation, GEWOBAG. It consists of about 1,750 flats (including 126 for old people) in high and medium-rise blocks near the site of the Berlin Wall, which completely changed the character of the locality from a bustling part of the city centre to a lifeless fringe area. Thus, like some other inner city estates in Berlin, it also shares some of the disadvantages of a peripheral estate. The gaunt structure of the overhead suburban railway dominates another side of the estate, and is a constant source of noise and vibration. The facades of the buildings have recently been brightened up, and the environment is well maintained though cheerless. However, the poor standard of street-cleansing points to inadequate coordination between the landlord organisation and the municipal services, while the unkempt condition of some of the gloomy entrance halls to the blocks underlines the management and maintenance problems of the landlord organisation itself.

As is typical of housing in the social rented sector in Berlin, empty flats are rare. Turnover is low too, with only 90 flats changing hands in 1987. Although it was built to house people moved out of clearance areas in Kreuzberg, and is widely regarded as a dumping-ground, there are strong communal bonds which reduce the urge to move elsewhere. More significant indicators of social malaise are the high number of rent arrears cases which go to court, and the higher than standard cost of dealing with vandalism and other abuse of the property, which amounted to the equivalent of about £200 per dwelling in 1987. A local office is open to the public for one session of two hours per week to deal with management enquiries, and for four two-hour sessions to deal with maintenance enquiries. This in itself represents a higher level of maintenance activity than is normal.

While Berlin, moreso than other large cities in Germany, has inner city problem estates, it also has its fair share of peripheral estates, some of which were built to provide homes for families from the inner city clearance areas. Almost by definition in the peculiar conditions of West Berlin, these peripheral estates are situated near the Berlin Wall which divided the city from East Berlin, or the Iron Curtain which divides it from East Germany, and so accentuate their isolated situation.

The best-known of these estates in the outside world is the **Märkisches Viertel**, which is situated on land which was formerly allotments with some small-scale private housing (some of which remains) near the former Berlin Wall, about six miles to the north of the city centre. It was built in the mid-1960s and early 1970s on the initiative of the city architects and planners as part of a grandiose planning project to rehouse people from clearance areas in the city centre as well as newcomers and those who were already living in the locality.

The estate consists of about 16,000 flats, virtually all in the subsidised social rented sector, and except for one block, all owned and managed by the municipal non-profit landlord company, GESOBAU, which has its main office beside the shopping centre on the main road which forms the axis to the estate. (GESOBAU also owns about 9,000 dwellings elsewhere in Berlin, most notably in the inner city district of Wedding, where it has a branch office). Internally, the flats are well equipped and well laid out, but their design has exacerbated the poor access arrangements. Inadequate thermal and sound insulation are particular problems for people who were previously unaccustomed to living in flats.

The suburban railway line is inconveniently placed at one side of the estate, and most of the residents therefore need to travel by at least two forms of transport to reach the city centre, or to get to the industrial districts in the northern part of Berlin where 60% of them work. There are few job opportunities in the vicinity. Apart from these inadequacies in transport and employment, the Märkisches Viertel has gradually gained a comprehensive range of social and economic infrastructure facilities. The estate is also near some attractive countryside. Nonetheless, partly because people from outside the Märkisches Viertel have traditionally had little cause or inclination to visit the estate, it has long since suffered from a negative image among the population of Berlin as a whole, and the need to combat this image among outsiders was one of the main starting-points for the initiative described below.

Surprisingly, the Märkisches Viertel has little in the way of social problems. The proportions of tenants who are recipients of social security, who are Turks and foreigners from other Mediterranean countries, or who are socially or economically disadvantaged in other ways are significantly below the Berlin averages. Conversely, 36% of the tenants have incomes above the eligibility threshold for social rented housing. There is little crime. Comprehensive studies by the Freie Planungsgruppe Berlin in 1984 and by the Institut für Markt- und Medienforschung in 1985 showed that 69% of the residents had lived there for more than ten years, and the great majority were satisfied with the estate, with only 15% saying that they would prefer to live elsewhere.

When there have been social and management problems, they have been short-lived. In the mid-1970s, there were some early signals of trouble, but they eased of their own accord as people unaccustomed to high-rise living adapted themselves to it, as the social and economic infrastructure developed, and as the earlier concentrations of very young children grew older. Later, in the early 1980s, the same ageing process brought problems with teenagers. Combined with a slackening in demand, and an increase in physical disrepair, turnover doubled to about 8% - although this was still below the Berlin average, and the number of empty dwellings remained low, as did rent arrears.

With clear warning signals coming from the mounting vacancy rate in the Federal Republic, and with increasing concern about technical defects in many of the buildings, particularly the deterioration of the concrete panels in blocks in the southern part of the estate, which is more conspicuous than the northern part, in that it contains the shopping centre and lies along the main axis road through the estate.

Negotiations with the city government and the federal government produced a DM 26.4 million (about £6 million) package for a large-scale physical improvement programme for the roughly 1,330 flats in this area, known as Gages and Leo. DM 6 million of of the cost came from the city, and DM 6 million from the federal government's experimental programme, with the remainder coming from GESOBAU's own resources, from reserves and the disposal of assets. The work was planned and begun in 1984, and completed in 1987. The unit cost for the housing which is benefitting directly from the programme comes to about DM 20,000 (or the equivalent of about £4,500). To encourage a greater individual commitment to the estate, the landlord company gives tenants here and elsewhere on the Märkisches Viertel the option of a contribution of up to DM 4,000 towards the cost of improvement work to bathrooms and kitchens.

The work has been concentrated in the area of the road along the axis of the estate. The aim is to give the road itself the character of a boulevard with trees, secondary access, car spaces and landscaping in the stretches between the roadway and the blocks of flats, although there has been conflict with the city authorities about proposals to remove some existing trees in order to improve the layout. A major scheme is underway to provide underground car-parking facilities. The exteriors of the blocks have been repaired and the thermal insulation improved, with a finishing bold colour treatment to give the blocks an individual identity in an area where their anonymity was previously so great that the fire brigade complained about the difficulty in finding its way. The entrance halls have been extended with strikingly designed wooden porches and improved entryphone facilities. Inside, the lifts have been refurbished, with better lighting and mirrors to reduce vandalism. The entrance halls have potted plants and benches, which appear to be surviving well.

The project appears to be led mainly by architects, and measures to develop the economic, social and management base play a minor part. The main change is in the shopping centre which has been given an effective facelift, and is now said to attract customers from outside the Märkisches Viertel. However, it and the improvement of the open market area have caused substantial difficulties for the secondary shopping areas elsewhere on the estate itself. There are also some reports of problems in securing the cooperation of the property company which owns the main shopping centre. The only social measure has been the conversion of a redundant school into an arts centre.

As shown above, most of the Märkisches Viertel is managed from the GESOBAU headquarters on the estate itself, and day-to-day repairs are said to be effectively done by outside contractors. Proposals to broaden the role of the resident block caretakers have run into job description problems, and there is little sign that their resolution is a high management priority. The small amount of the stock which is managed by another municipal landlord organisation DEGEWO (see description of Gropiusstadt below) has the same level of rents as similar GESOBAU housing, and there is no sense of competion between the two organisations in the standard of service which they offer.

The project has been developed under the patronage of a steering committee of about 20 people, with representatives from local and central government, and the three political parties, as well as GESOBAU and the planners and architects responsible for the work. As part of the price of its financial support, the federal government insisted on tenant representation, and three tenants were selected - allegedly on their reputation as protestors - to the committee which met five times in 1984, its year of activity. Although there are mixed views about the extent to which the tenants were able to influence the project - and their contribution seems at best to have been reactive - it is generally agreed that they were positive and realistic, and five active tenants organisations still exist within the estate.

With hindsight, the huge additional investment in the renovation of the Märkisches Viertel seems difficult to justify on management grounds at least. At the time the project was launched there was little sign of trouble, and the main arguments for it were the need to deal with the structural defects coupled with a feeling that slackening demand in Berlin could lead to the severe and costly management problems which were then already afflicting many estates in the Federal Republic. The project was therefore a preventative measure, and generally acknowledged as such at the time.

It is also arguable whether there was enough active tenant participation in the project. GESOBAU ascribe the admittedly low involvement of the tenants to apathy on the tenants' part, which lends weight to the view that the tenants were not seriously dissatisfied with their lot, and so casts additional doubt on the need for the project, at least as a social measure. However, if housing demand had not rallied unexpectedly, as it did after the scheme was launched, it is possible that the estate would have entered a spiral of decline.

Although **Gropiusstadt** is less widely known internationally than the Märkisches Viertel, it is on a similar - indeed larger - scale, and presents some revealing similarities and differences. Although the planning process began in 1955, its construction too dates from the late 1960s and early 1970s.

The estate consists of some 19,000 dwellings built on a green field site south of Berlin close to the Iron Curtain. The leader of the 1930s Bauhaus movement, Walter Gropius was responsible for much of the original concept - although many of his ideas, in particular his plan for the estate to be a low-rise development, were later modified in the interest of economy. Its inspiration was the nearby 1920s Hufeisensiedlung (Horseshoe estate), and with its roughly 4,000 low-rise houses and flats laid out in a horseshoe pattern around a lake and attractive landscaping, is still a successful model of the garden city developments of its era. The Hufeisensiedlung is owned by the GEHAG landlord company which was founded in the 1920s, and was the originator of Gropiusstadt where it has the largest holding of over 8,000 dwellings.

Gropiusstadt bears little resemblance to its illustrious forerunner. Although it pays lip-service to it in the form of one horseshoe complex (instead of the 12 originally planned), it dominates the landscape with its densely built mixture of high, medium and low-rise flats and maisonettes spread out along a spine road and underground railway line which were constructed specially to serve it. It therefore has good transport connections with the city centre. The social infrastructure is also well developed, with a hospital, schools, churches, and four shopping centres each beside one of the underground railway stations. The shopping centres and associated multi-storey car-parks in particular were victims of the economies which were made during the construction of the estate. Access is cramped and difficult, and the pedestrianised shopping areas are windswept and unattractive.

Unlike the Märkisches Viertel, Gropiusstadt is managed by a plethora of different landlord companies and cooperatives, many of them small, three of them medium-sized, and two of them large municipal landlord companies. One of these is DEGEWO, which owns over 4,000 dwellings, or about a quarter of the total on the estate. (DEGEWO also owns and/or manages about 27,000 dwellings elsewhere in Berlin.) There are said to be few demarcation problems between the different landlord organisations and the city authorities on service delivery.

Although as elsewhere, there is no apparent sense of competition between the landlord organisations, it is generally accepted that DEGEWO as a municipal company takes more than its fair share of socially disadvantaged tenants, including ex-prisoners and alcoholics - who are allocated to DEGEWO housing by the city, or are attracted to it by the low rents which it enjoys because of its period of construction. Unusually for an estate in Germany, petty crime is rife. Thus, unlike the Märkisches Viertel where there is at most only a marginal social variation between different parts of the estate, the area of Gropiusstadt which is owned and managed by DEGEWO has the reputation of a sink area in an estate which otherwise has a favourable image not only among its residents but also in Berlin as a whole.

As on the Märkisches Viertel, part of the DEGEWO response has been to make physical improvements to the dwellings and their environment. A problematic multi-storey block with internal corridor access has been reduced in height, with improvements to the security, entrance halls, lifts, corridor lighting, and thermal insulation at a cost of DM 4.5 million (or the equivalent of about £17,000 for each resulting unit). Plans are being developed for major improvements to the shopping centre and the associated multi-storey car-park. The company has also taken over responsibility for subsidising the well-used fully equipped laundry room, and has fitted out a room on the top floor of a 24-storey block for social functions.

Management and maintenance are also comparatively intensive, with an estate based office (though it is open to the public only once a week for management enquiries and twice a week for maintenance matters) and an estate based repairs team to do all but major repairs.

A more broadly based initiative is, however, getting underway. Faced with a perceptible shift in the age-profile of the tenants from the early over-representation of families with young children towards over-representation of older tenants, as well as some evidence of growing or possible management problems, in the early 1980s some of the landlord organisations were beginning to think that preventative measures were necessary. There were also emerging technical problems with the concrete. In part, they took their cue from the federal government support for the Märkisches Viertel initiative, as did the Berlin senate, which in 1985 earmarked DM 2 million towards work in Gropiusstadt. An architectural and planning firm, Martin und Pächter was commissioned to prepare an analysis of the physical and social problems and to develop proposals under the patronage of a steering committee similar to the one at the Märkisches Viertel.

As on the Märkisches Viertel, the measures which have been proposed and which began to be implemented in 1987 consist almost entirely of physical work to rectify design and technical defects, to improve landscaping, and to bring the shopping centres up to standard. Considerable emphasis was placed on the development of a green axis through the estate, and to creating a network of walkways.

Despite the existence of some tenants' groups, the initiative has achieved little active tenant participation in developing the proposals, and what involvement there has been is confined to commenting on plans put forward by Martin und Pächter. A major further inhibition on all the parties, and especially on the scope for tenant consultation, is the long-term financial uncertainty surrounding the project. So far, a total of DM 6 million has been committed by the city, the landlord organisations, and the commercial participants, but the total expenditure could be ten times this amount, spread over as many years. The Gropiusstadt project therefore suffers so far from the risk of raising false hopes among the tenants.

The **Hildburghauser Strasse** estate in Marienfelde is another peripheral estate isolated beside the former Iron Curtain to the south of Berlin. It consists of about 5,500 high-rise dwellings, some 4,000 of which are owned and managed by DEGEWO, which has set up an estate based office with similar arrangements to the others described above. The infrastructure is fair rather than good, with passable shopping facilities, although there is a school and youth club, and the bus service to the centre of Berlin has recently been improved. The blocks are well maintained, and work is in progress to improve the gloomy entrance halls and provide better security.

The measures which have already been taken have cut down vandalism and problems with alcoholics, but graffitti and other abuse testify to quite serious social problems, especially in one daunting 25-storey tower block. However, here as elsewhere, the tenants are happy with their flats once they get to them. The age-profile of the tenants is dominated by high numbers of elderly and young people, some of whom find it difficult to get along together. On the other hand, as is general in Berlin, the number of empty dwellings is negligible, and rent arrears are low.

As has been shown above, DEGEWO has already taken steps to improve security and the environment, and to intensify the management of its part of the estate. As at Gropiusstadt, it also subsidises a well-used laundry room. Future plans include fencing in garden areas around some blocks, which will then be allocated to tenants to maintain, and the planting of climbing plants against the starker blocks.

The **Thermometersiedlung** and **Woltmannweg** are adjacent estates divided by a main but under-used road in the same general area to the south of Berlin and close to the former Iron Curtain. They both belong to the Gemeinnützige Siedlungs- und Wohnungs-baugesellschaft Berlin mbH (GSW) - which with about 52,000 dwellings is the largest non-profit landlord organisation in Berlin. About 10,000 GSW dwellings are on large estates. Management is decentralised to 13 local offices. The city has nomination rights in some GSW blocks, which can have the effect of concentrating disadvantaged tenants in certain areas.

Despite their proximity to one another, the Thermo-metersiedlung and Woltmannweg present a sharp contrast. The Thermometersiedlung is a typical high-density 1960s estate of nearly 2,900 flats (1,150 belonging to the GSW) in blocks of up to 21 storeys. The remaining flats belong to a variety of landlord organisations. They are system-built, with drab grey asbestos cement panels. The backdrop of old factory buildings and chimneys adds to the depressing effect.

GSW has taken a number of individual initiatives over the years to improve the estate, and is now preparing a comprehensive improvement scheme. Using funds provided by the city of Berlin, GSW has commissioned consultants to develop proposals for the layout, architectural design and colour scheme. The scheme is the subject of detailed consultation with the tenants. An opinion survey has been conducted, and the elected tenants committee is closely involved in the development of the scheme.

Woltmannweg is a new estate of about 900 dwellings built mostly in the 1980s to replace the notorious Lichterfelde estate, commonly known as the 'Mau Mau estate'. This consisted of about 460 cramped, damp and insanitary dwellings built in the early 1950s to house about 2,000 people who were homeless refugees or from clearance areas, supposedly on a temporary basis, with many families sharing facilities. Although the project is less one of turning round an estate as a whole and more one of solving the social and housing problems of what became a particularly difficult community by providing most of them (and twice as many other people who moved into the new Woltmannweg from elsewhere) with decent accommodation, it is included here as a remarkable example of long-term tenant consultation and participation.

Despite the substandard living conditions and social tensions in the Mau Mau estate, good internal social support and self-help mechanisms developed over the two decades during which so many families lived in very close proximity. By the early 1970s, the local municipal authorities were beginning to make plans for rehousing the inhabitants in accommodation similar to the Thermo-metersiedlung which had in the meantime been built the other side of the road.

As a result of the discussions which took place, however, the latent communal strength in the Mau Mau estate began to find expression in a tenants group which formed spontaneously as early as 1973, and which soon attracted support from the local church authorities who funded outside advisers. The tenant based initiative gathered momentum with the decision of the Berlin Senate the following year to commission the Deutsches Institut für Urbanistik (German Institute for Urban Studies) to prepare a report and proposals for rehousing the community.

In 1977, the Berlin Senate decided to go ahead with a new-build scheme, and the following year, a social support team was set up to develop proposals in close consultation with the tenants. Over the next nine years, the joint planning group met more than 50 times, and was instrumental in bringing the tenants' influence to bear on all aspects of the design of the new estate. Tenants visited other estates in busloads to learn from their experience. They were thus directly involved in the design of the buildings and layout with its arrangements for segregating cars and pedestrians, the landscaping (reminiscent of the Hufeisensiedlung), ecological and environmental principles, the range of social facilities (shared with the Thermometersiedlung), shops and commercial facilities, public transport needs, and provision for children and older people who together form over a third of the population.

It is generally agreed that much of the credit for the successful collaborative way of working which characterised the development of the Woltmannweg estate goes to GSW and the city, which between them have also had to bear high rent subsidy costs. The capital costs of the project were some DM 2,700 per square metre (or the equivalent of about £43,000 per unit). In order to make the housing affordable to the existing community, and to attract new tenants from outside, the 'economic rent' (Kostenmiete - see Section IV) of DM 25.35 per square metre has been reduced to an actual rent of about DM 3.00 (plus heating and service costs) for tenants from the original estate, as compensation for what they had been through. This is less than half the rent which would normally be payable by tenants in the social rented sector.

Woltmannweg is a rare and possibly unique example in Germany of intensive cooperation between the tenants and the various providing agencies. The result is an impressive estate visually, and although it is not without its social tensions, the management structure is designed to cope with them, and as is shown by the 14% proportion of foreigners among the tenants, there is no attempt to exclude the socially disadvantaged. Indeed, its main achievement has been to show the way in which socially stigmatised families can successfully integrate themselves with the wider community.

Conclusions

In Germany, the evident problems of the social rented sector are less acute than in the other countries covered by this study. Where there are problems, it is widely - but not universally - thought that they are confined to high-rise accommodation, mainly in large peripheral estates. Although the built form of these estates is claimed to account for some of their management problems, they are also - because of the comparatively large size of the dwellings and the date of their construction - more expensive to rent, and so less popular.

In part, the relative lack of management problems in Germany may be due to the continuing existence of a large and active private rented sector which has traditionally housed the poorest tenants at its downmarket end. However, with the contraction in the supply of this cheap accommodation, and the simultaneous contraction in the number of social rented dwellings to which local authorities have nomination rights, many housing experts predict increasing residualisation in the remaining social rented sector as it comes under greater pressure from the poorer families.

So far, these are largely problems on the horizon, although viewed with growing concern by some sections of the non-profit sector in particular. Meanwhile, with the virtual disappearance of the vacancy problems which so alarmed the social rented sector and government at all levels in the 1970s and early 1980s and not least with the huge increases in demand with the new influx from East Germany, it is widely felt by many onlookers in government and elsewhere that the management difficulties have receded. As has been seen, most of the special measures which have been taken with government support over the last five years have been concerned with environmental improvements and to rectify physical defects, or to reduce rents.

Some commentators and landlord organisations take the view, however, that the social rented sector still suffers from underlying and growing social problems of such magnitude that more radical management measures are needed if it is to cope with its changing clientele and the structural changes which it faces as the stock subject to local authority nomination rights contracts. As has been seen, several landlord organisations, often in partnership with the state and municipal authorities, have been developing new approaches to management. These have so far been home-grown developments in response to local conditions and initiatives, but as they have gained momentum, the GGW as the non-profit movement's umbrella organisation is taking an increasing interest in developing and promoting management innovations.

NOTES

1. 'Monograph on the Human Settlements Situation and Related Trends and Policies', presented by the Federal Ministry for Regional Planning, Building and Urban Development, and the Federal Ministry for Economics to the UN ECE Committee on Housing, Building and Planning (September 1987) p52

2. *Zahlen - Daten - Fakten 1960-1985* published by the Gesamtverband Gemeinnütziger Wohnungsunternehmen e.V. (GGW), line II 2.

3. 'Monograph on the Human Settlements Situation and Related Trends and Policies', presented by the Federal Ministry for Regional Planning, Building and Urban Development, and the Federal Ministry for Economics to the UN ECE Committee on Housing, Building and Planning (September 1987) p52

4. 'Wirtschaftliche, soziale und städtebauliche Probleme der Grossiedlungen des Sozialen Wohnungsbaus in der Bundesrepublik Deutschland', paper by Manfred Fuhrich and Hartmut Meuter of the Bundesforschungsanstalt für Landeskunde und Raumordnung, Bonn-Bad Godesberg (15 January 1987) p1

5. Information provided by Dr Eugen Dick, Federal Ministry for Regional Planning, Building and Urban Development

6. *Statistisches Jahrbuch 1986* table 3.17

7. *Statistisches Jahrbuch 1986* table 3.17

8. 'Monograph on the Human Settlements Situation and Related Trends and Policies', presented by the Federal Ministry for Regional Planning, Building and Urban Development, and the Federal Ministry for Economics to the UN ECE Committee on Housing, Building and Planning (September 1987) p52

9. 'Monograph on the Human Settlements Situation and Related Trends and Policies', presented by the Federal Ministry for Regional Planning, Building and Urban Development, and the Federal Ministry for Economics to the UN ECE Committee on Housing, Building and Planning (September 1987) p52

10. Constructed from GGW *Wohnungswirtschaftliches Jahrbuch 1981/82* p148, and GGW *Wohnungswirtschaftliches Jahrbuch 1987/88* p162

11. Constructed from 'Monograph on the Human Settlements Situation and Related Trends and Policies', presented by the Federal Ministry for Regional Planning, Building and Urban Development, and the Federal Ministry for Economics to the UN ECE Committee on Housing, Building and Planning (September 1987) p52

12. *Zahlen - Daten - Fakten 1960-1985* published by the Gesamtverband Gemeinnütziger Wohnungsunternehmen e.V. (GGW), line I.12.

13. *Zahlen - Daten - Fakten 1960-1985* published by the Gesamtverband Gemeinnütziger Wohnungsunternehmen e.V. (GGW), line I.11.

14. 'Wirtschaftliche, soziale und städtebauliche Probleme der Grossiedlungen des Sozialen Wohnungsbaus in der Bundesrepublik Deutschland', paper by Manfred Fuhrich and Hartmut Meuter of the Bundesforschungsanstalt fur Landeskunde und Raumordnung, Bonn-Bad Godesberg (15 January 1987) p28

15. Announcement on 16 December 1987 by NRW Minister for Urban Development, Housing and Transport

16. *Zahlen - Daten - Fakten 1960-1985* published by the Gesamtverband Gemeinnütziger Wohnungsunternehmen e.V. (GGW), line I.14.2

17. *Wohngeld- und Mietenbericht 1987* published by the Federal Ministry for Regional Planning, Building and Urban Development, p16

18. Information provided by Dr Eugen Dick, Federal Ministry for Regional Planning, Building and Urban Development

19. *Zahlen - Daten - Fakten 1960-1985* published by the Gesamtverband Gemeinnütziger Wohnungsunternehmen e.v. (GGW), lines I 9, II 9, and III 4

20. Parliamentary Answer of 9 April 1984

21. Constructed from data given in paper 'Housing Policy and the Development of the Housing Market in the Federal Republic of Germany' by Dr Eugen Dick, Federal Ministry for Regional Planning, Building and Urban Development (27 June 1986), table 1

22. GGW *Wohnungswirtschaftliches Jahrbuch 1987/88* p140

23. Constructed from 'Monograph on the Human Settlements Situation and Related Trends and Policies', presented by the Federal Ministry for Regional Planning, Building and Urban Development, and the Federal Ministry for Economics to the UN ECE Committee on Housing, Building and Planning (September 1987) p53

24. GGW *Wohnungswirtschaftliches Jahrbuch 1987/88* p139

25. GGW *Wohnungswirtschaftliches Jahrbuch 1987/88* p140

26. *Statistisches Jahrbuch 1986* table 2.1

27. *Statistisches Jahrbuch 1986* table 6.11

28. *Statistisches Jahrbuch 1986* table 6.11

29. 'Wirtschaftliche, soziale und städtebauliche Probleme der Grossiedlungen des Sozialen Wohnungsbaus in der Bundesrepublik Deutschland', paper by Manfred Fuhrich and Hartmut Meuter of the Bundesforschungsanstalt für Landeskunde und Raumordnung, Bonn-Bad Godesberg (15 January 1987) pp12-13

30. *Wohnungsteilmärkte zwischen Angebot und Nachfrage* Materialien 8, published by GGW July 1983

31. Unpublished report 'Städtebaulicher Bericht: Probleme hochverdichteter Neubausiedlungen der 60er und 70er Jahre' by the Bundesforschungsanstalt für Landeskunde und Raumordnung, Bonn-Bad Godesberg (draft of 15 July 1987) section I 3.3.4

32. 'Hamburg-Steilshoop: 15 Jahre Erfahrung mit einer Grossiedlung' report no 01.074 in series Modellvorhaben, Versuchs- und Vergleichsbauvorhaben, published by the Federal Ministry for Regional Planning, Building and Urban Development, 1985 p12

33. GGW *Wohnungswirtschaftliches Jahrbuch 1987/88* pp206

four

THE NETHERLANDS

I The general background

Population and housing stock

According to the Dutch Ministry of Housing, Physical Planning and Environment, the population of the Netherlands in 1985 was 14.5 million, having risen from under 13 million in 1970.[1] It is expected to rise to nearly 15 million by the end of the century. The average household size was 2.6 in 1985, compared with 3.2 in 1971.[2] Two-thirds of households consist of two, three or four people.[3]

As will be seen, figures about the stock vary slightly from one source to another. According to the *Statistical Yearbook of the Netherlands* 1986, the housing stock totalled 5.35 million dwellings in 1985, having risen from 4.85 million in 1980, and 4.39 million in 1975. Some 70% of the stock (3.7 million dwellings) have been built since 1945. As in France and Germany, the post-war new-build programme started more slowly than in the United Kingdom. Although it steadily gained momentum, it was not until the mid-1960s that production first topped 100,000 dwellings a year. It reached its peak of about 150,000 dwellings in the early 1970s, and since then dipped below 100,000 only in 1979 and 1985. The overall house-building programme - and, as will be seen later, the social programme too - have therefore continued at a high level for much longer than in France, Germany and the United Kingdom.

As in France and Germany, slum clearance has played a smaller role than in the United Kingdom, with the number of dwellings cleared remaining on average below 10,000 a year between 1961 and 1986. Although over 120,000 dwellings were destroyed or seriously damaged in the war, and there was a large backlog of neglect and disrepair, the main political impetus behind the post-war housing programme in the Netherlands was one of overall national economic reconstruction. Governments followed a low rent policy with a view to keeping down labour costs and so increasing the competitiveness of Dutch products in world markets.

The main demographic factor was the need to provide for a rapidly growing population, as the birth-rate rose and immigration increased. Between 1945 and 1980, the population rose by about five million.[4] This increase, coupled with the decline in household size noted above, has been a dominant factor in the demand for housing in the post-war era.

Migration from the countryside to the towns also played a major part. In 1850, seven people out of ten in the Netherlands lived on the land, and one in two still lived on the land a century later, in 1950. However, by 1975, three-quarters of the population lived in urban areas. Urbanisation in the Netherlands, as in France, was therefore largely a post-war phenomenon, in contrast with Germany and the United Kingdom where the major shift from the land to the towns took place before the Second World War.

Some two million of the population live in Amsterdam, Rotterdam, the Hague and Utrecht and some smaller towns. Together these form the 'Randstad', a series of towns and cities forming a ring about 40 miles in diameter around an area of agricultural land. This is the industrial, commercial and administrative core of the Netherlands, and its housing differs in some major ways from that in the rest of the country.

In the country as a whole, 43% of dwellings are owner-occupied and 57% are rented, but in the four main Randstad cities, only 17% of dwellings are owner-occupied compared with 83% in the rented sector. The differences in age profile and type of dwelling are even more dramatic. Overall, 30% of dwellings were built before the Second World War, and 70% in the post-war period, but in the four Randstad cities, this ratio is almost reversed, with 66% of dwellings built before the Second World War. Table 4.1 gives the age profile for the stock as a whole, using figures from a survey undertaken in 1985/86 by the Ministry of Housing, Physical Planning and the Environment (VROM).

Table 4.1:   Housing stock by period of construction (1985/86)

	Number (thousands)	%
Before 1906	347.3	6.6
1906-1930	509.9	9.7
1931-1944	438.4	8.3
1945-1959	747.2	14.1
1960-1969	964.2	18.2
1970 and later	1,868.7	35.4
Unknown	407.9	7.7
Total	5,283.5	100.0

Source: *Woningbehoeftenonderzoek 1985/86*, Table 1, (Central Bureau of Statistics, 1987)

While nearly 70% of dwellings in the Netherlands overall are houses, and just over 30% flats, the ratio of houses to flats in the four Randstad cities is more than reversed, where flats represent between 60% and 80% of the stock.[5]

Standards of amenity

Although standards of amenity are generally good, with 82% of dwellings having a bath or shower in 1977, and 95% with an internal WC, the condition of the stock is causing concern.[6] One in five dwellings is in need of repair, and already in 1983, Parliament therefore adopted the first 'Multi-year Programme for Urban Renewal', with the aim of improving about 60,000 dwellings a year. The programme is presented to Parliament each September with the annual Budget statement.

Space standards are going down, partly because of the need for economy in the subsidised sector, and partly because of greater demand for smaller accommodation as household sizes have come down and energy costs have increased. The average number of rooms declined steadily from 4.7 in 1975 to 4.2 in 1981, while the average area peaked at 74 square metres in 1976, and then fell to 63 square metres in 1981.

The poor quality of older inner city property has long since been seen as a major contributory cause of the drift from the biggest cities. Amsterdam lost 16.1% of its population between 1960 and 1978, while Rotterdam lost 19.1% and the Hague 23.3%.[7] The strategy for dealing with the growing urban housing problems was developed in the 1972 *Report on Housing* and the 1976 *Third Report on Physical Planning*. The plan adopted by Parliament was to expand four 'Growth Cities' and to build 13 'Growth Centres' as large new dormitory housing developments within easy reach of existing or new major employment centres. Thus the Growth Cities were grafted on to major regional centres in the south and north of the country, and were essentially local government initiatives. The Growth Centres were central government initiatives, developed on green field sites on the outer fringes of the Randstad area, some of them, such as Lelystad, on the vast tracts of land reclaimed from the sea - the 'polders'.

Tenure

According to the plan adopted by Parliament in 1979, the total number of dwellings to be built in the Growth Cities and Growth Centres in the 1980s was in the region of 200,000, with a mix of tenures including 40% to 50% social housing for rent. Although this programme has since been curtailed, it is still going ahead in a modified form. It is partly in developments such as these - especially those where transport facilities, social amenities and employment opportunities have been slower to materialise than was planned - that serious problems have emerged in the social rented sector. These are taken up again in later sections. Table 4.2 gives the breakdown of the stock by tenure in 1986.

The owner-occupied sector rose from 28% of the stock in 1947 to 43% in 1979, a level which it has held quite consistently since then. In 1984, it had reached some 2.2 million dwellings. Market confidence was however shaken in the early 1980s when house prices which had risen sharply from a median figure of Hfl 110,000 in 1976 to a peak of Hfl 175,000 in 1978 fell back to Hfl 140,000 in 1982. Increased rates of interest and stagnation of personal income after the second oil crisis are seen as the main cause of the changed view of the market. As a result, completions dipped from a high of nearly 64,000 in 1980 to a low of just over 34,000 in 1982. The fall was particularly marked in the up-market unsubsidised sector.

Table 4.2:   Tenure (1985/86)

	Number of dwellings (thousands)		%
Owner-occupied	2,281.2		43.2
Private renting	730.0		13.8
of which,			
individual landlords		401.5	7.6
companies		328.5	6.2
Social renting	2,190.4		41.6
of which,			
housing associations		1,846.7	35.0
municipalities		343.7	6.6
Unknown	81.8		1.5
Total	5,283.5		100

Source: *Woningbehoeftenonderzoek 1985/86*, Table 1 (Central Bureau of Statistics, 1987)

It has long since been government policy to promote **home ownership**, and even more so, the health of the construction industry.   Various forms of special help are therefore made available to purchasers of new dwellings for owner-occupation. For example, from the 1950s until 1984, there was a system of tapered subsidies to purchasers of new dwellings during the first few years of ownership.   Following the collapse in the market, the annual subsidies, which can be substantial, ranging up to Hfl 5,500 (about £1,200) taxable, have since 1984 been at a fixed rate over a set number of years, depending mainly on the household income and on the price of the property.   This subsidy was reduced to Hfl 5,000 from 1 January 1988.   Municipalities can also guarantee loans to owner-occupiers, with support from central government. Interest payments are normally deductible without any limitation against income tax.   According to the Ministry of Housing's survey quoted above, the owner-occupied stock is in slightly better condition than the average.

The **private rented sector** amounted to about 20% of the stock, or 1.1 million dwellings in 1984, in comparison with 60% (or under 1.3 million dwellings) in 1947.   Although there is not much difference between the total figures over nearly 40 years, substantial changes have taken place within the private rented sector. Nearly half the present stock has been built since 1945, which means that some 700,000 dwellings which were in the private rented sector at that time have since been demolished or transferred to other tenures, principally into owner-occupation, but some to municipalities and housing associations under urban renewal schemes. This shift has been predominantly in the domain of individual landlords, who still dominate the sector (see Table 4.2 above), but who are being overtaken by companies operating at the more expensive end of the market. Significantly, unsubsidised housing for rent soared from just over 600 units in 1983 to over 4,000 in 1985.

Subsidies are, however, available to private landlord companies who charge the 'basic' - that is controlled - rents set by the government for housing built since 1975. Such private landlords therefore provide an extension to the social rented sector on a similar basis to many private landlords in Germany, and are categorised as 'other non-profit' as a subset of social renting in Table 4.2 above. The system is in effect the same as that which applies to the social rented sector, which is described in detail in Section V, and provides for tapered payments over up to 50 years to help bridge the gap between the controlled rent and actual costs. In 1984, Hfl 741 million of the Hfl 2,941 million subsidy programme for some 1.3 million rented dwellings was destined for privately rented dwellings. Other arrangements, similar to those applying in the social rented sector, are available to help private landlords to improve pre-war and post-war housing. Depending on the age of the property, these consist variously of loans and grants to subsidise the capital and revenue costs.

The housing owned by individual private landlords is in the worst condition, mainly because of the remaining 544,000 privately rented pre-war dwellings, although those built between 1945 and 1970 are also much worse than those built in the same period in other tenures. The strict rent controls are often cited as a cause of this disrepair, although individual landlords are sometimes accused of neglecting their property.

The **social rented sector** in the sense of dwellings built under the Housing Act grew from under 265,000 dwellings or 12% of the total stock in 1947, to 2,190,400 dwellings or 39% of the stock in 1986. The sector is dominated by housing associations (Woningcorporaties) who, in 1986 figures, own and manage

1,847,000 dwellings, or four out of five of those in the social rented sector. There are also about a third of a million subsidised dwellings owned by non-profit foundations without the non-profit status of housing associations. The remainder of the subsidised stock is owned by municipalities. According to the Ministry of Housing's survey, dwellings in the social rented sector are on average in nearly as good condition as those in the owner-occupied sector, although there are considerable variations around the average. The stock belonging to the housing associations is in relatively good condition, while that owned by the municipalities is in worse condition, partly because a substantial part of the municipally owned stock has been acquired from the private rented sector, but mostly because the municipalities' stock is older.

Household and dwelling balance

According to the Ministry of Housing's estimates of the household and dwelling balance, in 1986 there was still a shortfall of some 127,000 dwellings in the Netherlands as a whole, though with considerable regional variations. The shortage is concentrated in the Randstad area, while supply exceeds demand in some areas in the north and south west of the country. Elsewhere, the housing market is generally in equilibrium. Estimates of annual need for new dwellings in the 1980s range between 91,000 (by the Ministry in 1984) and 118,000 (by the Economic Institute for the Building Industry in 1983).[8] There is general agreement that the need for new dwellings will decline from the beginning of the 1990s as the number of entrants to the housing market goes down because of demographic trends, although there will be countervailing pressure from the other direction with the continuing decline in household sizes and the growing need to replace the older stock.

The wider macro-economic concerns of the Dutch government are, however, already forcing a major reassessment of housing policy with the main shift of emphasis towards a reduction in public sector investment in housing as a whole, in favour of greater private investment, and a greater share of individual household budgets being devoted to housing costs. Meanwhile, the annual budget of the Ministry of Housing was reduced from Hfl 16,661 million in 1987 to Hfl 15,008 million in 1988, with a reduction in the overall new-build programme from 98,000 to 94,500 units, and with as great as possible an emphasis on promoting owner-occupation and on renovation.[9]

II   History of the social rented sector

Social housing in the Netherlands originated in very much the same way and about the same time as its counterparts in France, Germany and the United Kingdom. From the middle of the 19th century, philanthropic organisations and individuals, the churches, and employers increasingly felt that living conditions in the towns not only were socially unacceptable, but also posed a threat to health and industrial prosperity. The second half of the 19th century therefore saw some privately funded initiatives to provide decent and affordable housing for industrial workers in the larger cities. However, numbers were small.

The turning-point came at the start of the 20th century when the 1901 Housing Act recognised the principle of public support for social rented housing, while also laying the initial ground-lines for a wider planning framework. This legislation opened the way for private bodies to build new housing and to undertake slum clearance projects, and received a ready response from the Roman Catholic and Protestant churches, from the growing trade union movement, and from employers. By the early 1920s, over 1,000 housing associations had been formed. From this period date the first large-scale housing developments, influenced by the new faith in mass housing and high-rise building as the economic answer to housing needs after the First World War. This came from the radical ideas of architects such as Gropius and Le Corbusier internationally, and the Amsterdam School nearer home, which fell on rather more fertile ground in continental Europe than they did in the United Kingdom.

The history of social housing in the Netherlands is also closer to that of France and West Germany in that its main development came later than in the United Kingdom. Although, as elsewhere, its foundations were firmly laid in the first half of the 20th century, its development as a major provider of housing came after the Second World War. Until 1970, municipalities were major providers, especially the larger cities. However, under the 1962 Housing Act, which with the Physical Planning Act of the same year together replaced the 1901 Housing Act when they were implemented in 1965, the municipalities now build and manage housing only when there is no practical possibility of its being provided by a housing association. By all accounts, this change was uncontentious politically, although not all municipalities were eager to relinquish their house-building activities, and it was necessary to issue a government circular in 1969 to remind them of their changed responsibilities. Some of the larger municipalities have remained partial providers; for example, Rotterdam's share varies annually between 15% and 25%.

Table 4.3 gives trends in housing completions by the various providers in the post-war period, showing the changing ratio between those financed with public loans, 'Housing Act dwellings', and those privately financed, and also the shift from municipal to housing association provision after 1965.

Table 4.3: Average number of completions by sector 1945-1982

	Housing Act dwellings Municipalities and central government	Housing associations	Private sector (rented and owner-occupied)	Total
1945	40	27	322	389
1950	18,493	12,280	16,527	47,300
1955	17,501	14,911	28,407	60,819
1960	19,768	21,929	42,118	83,815
1965	25,663	29,863	59,501	115,027
1970	19,139	30,993	61,155	117,284
1972	9,886	62,494	79,892	152,272
1975	5,188	40,685	74,901	120,774
1980	5,319	38,154	70,283	113,756
1982	8,056	66,256	48,998	123,310

Source: 'Some Data on House-building in the Netherlands 1986', Table B (VROM)

In addition to the Housing Act dwellings shown in Table 4.3, the social landlord organisations have built 'Premium Assisted' rented dwellings. These are subsidised dwellings financed by private borrowing, and at a rather higher standard and rent than Housing Act dwellings. They are intended for better-off tenants, on a similar basis to dwellings built under the 'Second Subsidy Stream' in Germany (see Section IV of Chapter 3).

The increase in activity by the municipalities in 1982 can be put down to the work which they are doing to acquire and rehabilitate rundown private sector stock in the inner cities. These dwellings are sometimes then transferred to housing associations. The figures for 1972 (the peak year for the social rented sector), 1975 and 1982 also show the close relationship between the social rented sector and the changing fortunes of the private market.

Although the government tends to use the new-build social housing programme as a regulator for the construction industry, there is growing concern about the condition of the older stock (see Section I). The social rented sector has two roles in the Multi-year Programme for Urban Renewal which Parliament adopted in 1983 to address the problems in the pre-1971 stock. First, as suggested above, the municipalities are acquiring and rehabilitating rundown private housing in the inner cities. The recent survey by the Ministry of Housing estimates that municipalities are holding 50,000 acquired dwellings, two-thirds of them in bad or very bad condition. Under the Multi-year Programme, 12,000 dwellings a year in this category were due to be modernised in 1987, 1988, and 1989. Central government subsidies are available for such work, providing that the rehabilitation costs do not exceed 80% of the replacement costs.

Second, the social rented sector already owns a substantial number of purpose-built Housing Act dwellings which are in need of modernisation. In 1983, 56,000 of these dwellings were classified as very bad, and 283,000 as moderate to bad.[10] The Multi-year Programme originally planned for 40,000 Housing Act dwellings to undergo major repair and improvement annually between 1984 and 1989, but actual numbers have exceeded the programme. There were 56,100 improved units in 1983, 71,400 in 1984, and 71,200 in 1985.

The Multi-year Programme has since been stepped up, to 46,075 in 1987, and 48,000 in 1988. However, in 1987, there were significant changes to the subsidy system (see Section IV below) in order to compensate the government for the reduction in its income as housing associations replaced their public sector loans with cheaper borrowing from the private sector. The number of improvements supported with state subsidy has in consequence been sharply reduced.

Apart from problems of disrepair, some of it in quite recently constructed stock, the social rented sector also began to suffer from serious management problems in some parts of the stock, such as high vacancy and turnover rates, and rising rent arrears since the end of the 1970s. At the same time, there has also been concern about increasing crime rates. As elsewhere, these problems coincided with the economic reversals following the oil crises of the early and late 1970s. In the 1970s, the Netherlands also saw a large influx of immigrants from the Mediterranean countries, and above all from the former Dutch colony of Surinam when it gained independence in 1975. Many of these immigrants were housed in the social rented sector, often creating large local concentrations living in conditions with which they were totally unfamiliar (see Section VI).

III   The landlord organisations

As has already been shown, the social rented sector in the Netherlands is dominated by housing associations. The Ministry of Housing puts the housing associations' total stock in 1984 at 1,538,000 and the municipalities' stock at 246,000. Although other sources provide slightly different totals, these figures are used in the following tables.

Housing associations

There were 874 housing associations in 1984. They are incorporated as non-profit associations or foundations. Housing ownership cooperatives as such do not exist in the Netherlands, mainly because the legal status of cooperatives as profit-making entities makes them ineligible for public financial support. However, there are signs of some localised grass roots interest in initiatives such as tenant management cooperatives or other forms of tenant management.

Two-thirds of the housing associations have a stock of under 1,800 dwellings, and less than one in nine has a stock of over 4,000 dwellings. The average size in 1987 was about 2,200 dwellings. Over a third of them are in North Holland and South Holland, the two provinces which include the densely populated Randstad area (see Section I). Table 4.4 gives a breakdown of housing associations by size.

Table 4.4:   Breakdown of housing association landlords by size of stock (1984)

Number of dwellings	Housing associations Number	%	Dwellings Number (thousands)	%
<600	216	25	75	5
600-1,799	346	39	335	21
1,800-3,999	209	24	564	35
>4,000	103	12	630	39
Totals	874	100	1,538	100

Source: Unpublished 'Memorandum on the Admission Policy' provided by VROM

Municipal landlords

The number of municipalities in the Netherlands has been going down over recent years. Of the roughly 710 which now exist, 332 were landlords of social rented housing in 1984, and 284 in 1988. The management staff are local government officers, unlike their equivalents in the French and German municipally sponsored social landlord organisations. Some of the municipal landlord organisations are independently incorporated companies, while others are departments of the local authorities themselves. More than two-thirds of them are very small, with under 600 dwellings. Only 20 municipalities have over 4,000 dwellings. These predominantly are the bigger cities with the greatest financial problems. Table 4.5 gives a breakdown of the municipal landlords by size of stock.

Table 4.5:   Breakdown of municipal landlords by size of stock (1984)

Number of dwellings	Municipalities Number	%	Dwellings Number (thousands)	%
<600	228	69	45	18
600-1,800	68	20	47	19
1,800-4,000	16	5	47	19
>4,000	20	6	107	44
Totals	332	100	246	100

Source: Unpublished 'Memorandum on the Admission Policy' provided by VROM

Relationships

In comparison with their counterparts in France and Germany, Dutch housing associations have a quite straightforward pattern of relationships with central and local government, and with their umbrella organisations. Central government is formally responsible for their initial registration as approved institutions, on which depends their entitlement to support from public funds. The essential qualifications are that the purposes and finances of the association should be confined to housing, that its constitution and scope of operation should provide for proper participation by tenants and other local interests, that the balance between private and public interests should be appropriate to the local conditions, and that the organisations should be soundly based financially. On the advice of the municipality and regional office, and of the Consultative Commission for the Registration of Housing Associations, the minister decides whether to recommend the issue of a Royal Decree. In practice, few new housing associations have been registered in the last two decades.

Central government is also ultimately responsible for monitoring the performance of registered housing associations. Associations are under a statutory obligation to make an annual report to the minister about their activities, and they are also subject to periodic audits by the ministry. In practice, the Ministry is interested only in proposals to change the constitutions of associations, and in their financial soundness. It has virtually no direct involvement in the management of the housing.

However, through a system of annual returns on the lines of the English Housing Investment Programme arrangements, central government determines the overall housing strategies of the municipalities. Central government is also responsible for setting general financial rules, in particular on the permitted (rather than recommended) level of annual rent increase, and it may from time to time set up general inquiries such as the recent stock condition survey, or issue general policy guidance, such as current advice to social landlords to concentrate on low income groups. This general policy function is carried out by the ministry's Inspectorate of Housing, with its out-stationed inspectors (roughly the equivalent of regional housing controllers in England) in each of the 12 provinces who act as the eyes and ears of central government on the ground. In formulating its housing policies, the government also draws on the advice of its National Advisory Council on Housing - normally known by its Dutch acronym, RAVO - a group representing a wide range of interests among housing specialists, producers, and consumers, appointed and serviced by the ministry.[11]

The housing interests of the 12 provincial governments have traditionally been limited to general planning matters, although with the current trend towards decentralisation, they may gain a limited role in the allocation of housing resources.

The real executive responsibility is in the hands of the roughly 710 municipalities, whose powers are currently being further enhanced by the government's decentralisation policy. It is the municipalities which in effect control and steer social housing activity within their areas, within annual budgets determined by the ministry on the basis of an allocated number of units multiplied by standard unit costs. They are therefore the channel for all central government subsidies and grants for social housing, (and for central government loans until they were abolished at the end of 1987). The municipalities lobby the central government through its regional Inspectors for these resources. They may also provide financial support and guarantees on their own account, and often provide land from their own land banks.

The municipalities also play an important role in the allocation of all dwellings in their areas - including the owner-occupied sector - especially in the western Randstad part of the country which is covered by the 1947 Housing Allocation Act and the 1984 Housing

Allocation Ordinance, although the difference between this part of the country and the rest is due to be removed. Although the rules, and their implementation, are subject to considerable local variation, in practice, the municipalities and the housing associations are usually able to agree on allocation policies, and in particular look after the interests of disadvantaged applicants. However, tensions between social landlords and municipalities about allocations are not unknown.

Thus, apart from matters connected with registration and financial audit which are the responsibility of central government, the key relationships for housing associations are at the local level, with the municipalities.

From the early days, the movement felt the need for a central source of advice and representation of its interests. Because of the traditional sectarian division of public bodies on religious lines, a number of organisations were set up, which eventually merged into the two existing umbrella organisations. The Nationale Woningraad (NWR), or National Housing Council, dates from 1913 and has about 700 member organisations among the housing associations and municipal landlord companies, mainly in the north, east, and densely populated west of the country. The NWR has traditionally represented the interests of the secular housing associations and the municipal landlord companies. Altogether, NWR member organisations manage some 1.2 million dwellings.

The Nederlands Christelijk Instituut voor Volkshuisvesting (NCIV), or Netherlands Christian Housing Institute, was formed in the 1970s through a merger of the two existing Roman Catholic and Protestant organisations. The NCIV has about 360 members, mostly in the south of the Netherlands. A few of them also belong to the NWR. NCIV members tend to be the smaller housing associations with a religious base. Altogether, they own and manage about 650,000 dwellings.

The umbrella organisations act as a national lobby for their members' interests, and are represented on the major consultative bodies such as the National Advisory Council on Housing, RAVO, (see above). They act as a source of consultancy advice for their members on specialist management issues - like their French equivalent, the UNFOHLM, and perhaps rather moreso than their German equivalent, the GGW - for example on business automation and on improvement methodology.

Like their French and German counterparts, they are also becoming increasingly involved in the training of housing managers and board members, both on specific issues and in developing a formal professional qualification. The NWR has recently started three two-year in-service courses for housing staff who attend the training centre at Nunspeet for two days a month. One of them is on housing management, the second on maintenance, and the third on administration and accounts. The costs are borne by the employing housing associations.

IV Finance

As in France and Germany, social landlord organisations in the Netherlands - both housing associations and municipal companies - are independent cost centres, and each block of dwellings is usually a separate accounting unit. Subsidies and rents are therefore directly linked to the historic cost of the property itself, and to the cost of work which is done to it subsequently.

As is explained in Section III, central government determines the annual programme of new-build and renovation activity through a system of annual bids by the municipalities, who then allocate the number of units to be built or renovated by the individual landlord organisations. Until 1988, work was largely financed by means of government loans at fixed market rates of interest, which were not necessarily advantageous in the long term. The resulting problems are considered below. From 1988, government loans have ceased to be available.

Bricks and mortar subsidies

Central government has hitherto been closely involved in new-build project control, mainly as this was seen as the only effective way of ensuring that bricks and mortar subsidies and rents were kept down to an acceptable level in dwellings for which the taxpayer at large is the main paymaster.

For Housing Act dwellings built under these arrangements, subsidy is in effect a form of deficit financing intended to bridge the gap between the real revenue cost of providing and running the dwelling on the one hand, and the controlled rent set by central government on the other.

Until the end of 1987, the level of annual subsidy was determined individually on the basis of the actual costs incurred under the system known as the 'dynamic cost rent', because of its built-in inflation assumptions. Under this system, the estimated real revenue cost of providing the dwelling is based on a calculation to amortise the likely costs over a 50-year period, and takes in interest at a rate projected over 10 years in the first instance, with additional factors for forecast management and maintenance, and other running costs. Typically, the 'dynamic cost rent' in the first year amounts to between 6% and 9% of the capital cost of the project.

Every year, central government sets the controlled, or 'basic', rents which are actually payable by the tenants. The formula for calculating this basic rent is simpler, being a percentage of the original construction cost, varying according to the size of the dwelling and according to the construction cost within that size bracket.

For example, at 1984 prices, the basic (actual) rent on a single-person dwelling costing Hfl 92,000 would have been calculated at 5.25% of that figure, that is an annual rent of Hfl 4,830 or Hfl 402.50 (about £90 at 1984 real purchasing power) a month. The rent on a dwelling of the same size, but costing Hfl 111,000 would have been calculated at 6.25%, that is Hfl 6,937.50 a year. At the other end of the size range, the rent on a six-person dwelling costing Hfl 120,000 would have been calculated at 5.75%, and on a dwelling the same size costing Hfl 129,000, it would have been calculated at 6.25%. Thus, not only was the actual rent directly linked to the cost of the dwelling, but there was also a gearing mechanism which inflated the rents of the more expensive dwellings.

The figures given in the preceding paragraphs to illustrate the difference between 'dynamic cost rents' and 'basic rents' demonstrate that the gap to be bridged by subsidy could be wide. In 1984, the overall subsidy budget amounted to Hfl 2,941 million (about £635 million) for a total of 1.3 million rented dwellings - most of them Housing Act dwellings - which were then eligible for subsidy. At that time, the subsidy bill was expected to continue to rise.

From 1 January 1988, however, this open-ended form of subsidy has been stopped in favour of a fixed annual rate of subsidy which is deducted from the cost of providing the dwelling. The rent level therefore now represents the difference between this subsidy and the cost of provision. This change is in line with the present government's concern not only to contain costs but also to reduce bureaucracy. Thus, central government has also delegated much of its responsibility for setting rent levels to the local level. Social landlord organisations will now individually propose their rent levels for the coming year to the municipality. From the beginning of 1988 the municipalities have also had a greater share of the responsibility for achieving economy in new-build projects. Individual project control has to a great extent been replaced by a system of nationally standardised and subsidisable building costs per square metre (with refinements to allow for buildings of different sizes).

Annual subsidies on new projects are therefore now based on these standard costs. However, the new system also provides for individually assessed capital subsidies on items which do not lend themselves to standardisation, such as inaccessible sites, difficult foundations, and regional variations. There is also a 5% tolerance level, which as well as providing a buffer against cost variations, can be used to provide limited permutations of numbers and dwelling quality.

Thus, with the exception of the capital subsidies for special items (see previous paragraph), subsidy is no longer related to actual costs but to the standard costs. Only rarely under the new system, does the government subsidise expenditure which exceeds the standard cost levels. Higher costs therefore become a matter for the landlord, the municipality, and the tenant, with the most probable outcome being higher rent levels than would otherwise have been the case. This system is intended not only to reduce central government involvement in local housing issues, but also to encourage housing associations and municipalities to make all possible economies.

Section II described the growing importance of renovation work under the Multi-year Programme for Urban Renewal which sets the overall number of Housing Act and other dwellings to be renovated each year. The number of dwellings to be renovated in each municipality by the individual landlord organisations is determined through the normal allocation process.

New arrangements for financing renovation work were introduced at the beginning of 1987. The municipalities are responsible for project control and monitoring, and for paying out subsidies from a budget provided by central government. They also have some discretion to top up from local funds. The amount of subsidy payable depends on the age of the dwelling and on the relationship between the renovation cost and the cost of an equivalent new-build dwelling (according to scales laid down by central government).

The permitted level of rent increase is also determined by the relationship between the renovation cost and the cost of an equivalent new-build dwelling, and it too enters into the subsidy calculation. The arrangement for determining this rent increase is known as the '1,2,3 system', because of the sliding scale of percentage points which encourages the widest possible difference between renovation and new-build costs. Thus, the rent increase amounts to 1% of improvement costs which are less than a fifth of the equivalent new-build costs, but rises to 3% of improvement costs which are more than half the equivalent new-build costs. Table 4.6 provides a worked example.

Table 4.6: The 1,2,3 system

Example:	Improvement cost		Hfl 50,000	
	Equivalent new-build cost		Hfl 80,000	
		Hfl	Rate of rent increase	Amount of rent increase
Portion of improvement cost which is <20% of new-build cost (Hfl 80,000)		16,000	1%	Hfl 160
Portion between 20% and 50%		24,000	2%	Hfl 480
Portion >50%		10,000	3%	Hfl 300
Total improvement cost/ annual rent increase		50,000		Hfl 940

Source: Constructed from 'The Financing of Housing and Housing Subsidies in the Netherlands' pp 26 and 27 (VROM, 1985)

The level of subsidy can vary between nothing and four-fifths of the total improvement cost, according to the age of the dwelling, the relationship between the improvement cost and equivalent new-build cost, and the permissible rent increase under the '1,2,3 system'. Table 4.7 gives the Ministry of Housing's target levels of unit subsidy in 1987.

Table 4.7: Target levels of improvement subsidy (1987)

	Hfl
Pre-war dwellings	40,000
Dwellings built between 1946 and 1968	12,000
Dwellings built after 1968	4,000
Thermal insulation	1,500

Source: Unpublished paper from VROM, 'The Housing Situation and Policies in the Netherlands in 1987' p 23a

Table 4.8: Housing investment broken down between new-build and renovation work (Hfl million)

	Out-turn prices			Constant (1980) prices			%	
	New-build	Repair & renovation	Total	New-build	Repair & renovation	Total	New-build	Repair & renovation
1969	3,843	299	4,142	8,108	631	8739	92.8	7.2
1970	4,170	321	4,491	8,424	648	9072	92.9	7.1
1971	4,949	386	5,335	9,303	726	10,029	92.8	7.2
1972	6,328	483	6,811	11,024	841	11,865	92.9	7.1
1973	6,959	613	7,572	11,242	990	12,232	91.9	8.1
1974	6,595	798	7,393	9,713	1,175	10,888	89.2	10.8
1975	6,518	1,071	7,589	8,714	1,432	10,146	85.9	14.1
1976	7,034	1,528	8,562	8,641	1,877	10,518	82.2	17.8
1977	8,693	1,920	10,613	10,038	2,217	12,255	81.9	18.1
1978	9,329	2,323	11,652	10,354	2,578	12,932	80.1	19.9
1979	9,208	2,640	11,848	9,806	2,812	12,618	77.7	22.3
1980	10,609	2,686	13,295	10,609	2,686	13,295	79.8	20.2
1981	10,178	2,558	12,736	9,539	2,397	11,936	79.9	20.1
1982	10,435	2,504	12,939	9,235	2,216	11,451	80.6	19.4
1983	9,961	1,969	11,930	8,572	1,694	10,266	83.5	16.5
1984	10,392	2,022	12,414	8,660	1,685	10,345	83.7	16.3
1985	9,028	2,141	11,169	7,352	1,743	9,095	80.8	19.2
1986	9,273	2,494	11,767	7,539	2,028	9,567	78.8	21.2

Source: Unpublished information supplied by VROM

As in the other countries covered by this study, the proportion of renovation expenditure within the total of capital expenditure has been growing. However, with a new-build programme which has remained more buoyant than elsewhere, the shift from new-build to renovation has been less spectacular in the Netherlands than in the other western countries. Table 4.8 gives expenditure in out-turn and constant (1980) prices in the two categories between 1969 and 1986.

Housing benefits

As in France, Germany and the United Kingdom, the emphasis in subsidy policy has shifted in recent years away from bricks and mortar subsidies to housing benefit support to individuals. Overall, between 1976 and 1984, housing benefit payments increased by a factor of more than four (from Hfl 500 million to Hfl 2,100 million) while bricks and mortar subsidies for rented housing increased by a factor of less than three (from Hfl 1,300 million to Hfl 3,300 million).[12]

Housing benefit is available to all tenants, although there are special schemes for young people, single persons, and occupants of various forms of specialised accommodation such as hostels or caravans. Under the main scheme (which covers private sector and social sector tenants in the same way), the number of housing benefit recipients, and the amounts of benefit both globally and individually have risen sharply since the scheme was introduced in 1970.

Table 4.9 gives information from 1970 to 1985. Since then, government figures show that the number of recipients has continued to climb, topping 800,000 in 1987, with a consequent increase in the total amount of benefits paid to over Hfl 1.4 million. However, as the table shows, the rate of real increase has tended to slow down. Partly, this is due to changes to the rules, which have reduced the benefit rates and the eligibility for benefit. The reduction in the rate of rent increases is also a major influence. In the early 1980s, rents were increasing by between 8% and nearly 10% a year, but in 1984, the increase dropped to 4.9%, and by 1986 it had fallen to 2%.

Table 4.9:   Housing benefits (1986/87)

Year	Number of recipients (thousands)	Total amount of benefit (Hfl million)		Average annual benefit (Hfl)	
		Current prices	Constant (1980) prices	Current prices	Constant (1980) prices
1970/71	30.9	19.2	39.4	622	1,277
1972/73	75.0	80.6	142.0	1,075	1,895
1975/76	248.3	524.8	705.9	1,507	2,027
1978/79	394.7	609.3	690.5	1,544	1,750
1980/81	455.9	628.9	628.9	1,600	1,600
1982/83	628.8	1,069.0	963.1	1,745	1,572
1983/84	635.3	1,131.0	989.1	1,782	1,558
1984/85	661.6	1,166.0	993.4	1,763	1,502

Source: Unpublished paper from VROM, 'The Housing Situation and Policies in the Netherlands 1988' p 20

As elsewhere, the amount of housing benefit depends on household income, the rent level, and the size of family. Table 4.10 shows the way in which the proportion of household income going on rent (after receipt of housing benefit) increases both with income and with the rent level.

Table 4.10: Ratio of rent to income, after receipt of housing benefit (1986/87)

Annual income (Hfl)	Monthly rent (Hfl)					
	250	350	400	500	600	685
21,750	13.06	13.06	13.51	14.34	15.72	17.38
23,250		13.93	14.19	14.97	16.26	17.81
25,250			14.45	16.16	17.35	18.77
28,500				17.68	18.73	20.00
30,500				18.49	19.48	20.66
33,500					20.42	21.49

Source: Unpublished paper from VROM, 'The Housing Situation and Policies in the Netherlands 1988' p 20

Income and expenditure of housing associations

Limited information is available about the income and expenditure of housing associations. Management and maintenance per dwelling in 1982 amounted to Hfl 1,440 (or about £300). Table 4.11 gives a breakdown of the annual account per dwelling between 1975 and 1982. It should be remembered that part of the rent income will have been subsidised through housing benefits (see Table 4.9), but the amount cannot be reliably estimated because Table 4.9 covers all recipients in the private and social sectors, while Table 4.11 covers only part of the social sector which in turn contains some dwellings outside the Housing Act.

Table 4.11: Income and expenditure per dwelling by housing associations in actual and constant (1980) prices (Hfl)

	1975 Actual	Cons-tant	1980 Actual	Cons-tant	1981 Actual	Cons-tant	1982 Actual	Cons-tant
Expenditure								
Management and Maintenance	667	906	1,079	1,079	1,284	1,202	1,440	1,272
Interest and Depreciation	1,693	2,300	2,743	2,743	3,227	3,021	3,758	3,320
Other expenses	486	660	727	727	802	751	805	711
Surplus	282	383	349	349	61	57	-154	-136
Total	3,128	4,249	4,898	4,898	5,374	5,030	5,849	5,167
Income								
Rents	2,021	2,746	3,118	3,118	3,391	3,174	3,713	3,280
Government contributions	580	788	809	809	854	799	1,016	898
Other income	527	716	971	971	1,129	1,057	1,120	989
Total	3,128	4,250	4,898	4,898	5374	5,030	5,849	5,167

Source: *Statistical Yearbook of the Netherlands* 1986, Table D.7, and VROM

V   The buildings

About one in ten dwellings in the social rented sector in 1985/86 dated from the pre-war period. Most of them belong to the larger housing associations and municipal landlord companies. Of the roughly four-fifths of the social rented stock which had then been built since the Second World War, about half dates from before 1969. Table 4.12 gives its age profile compared with the stock as a whole.

Table 4.12: Age profile of the social rented stock compared with the stock as a whole (1985/86)

	Social rented sector Number (thousands)	%	Stock as a whole Number (thousands)	%
Pre-1945	230.8	10.5	1,295.6	24.5
1945-1969	872.3	39.8	1,711.4	32.4
Post-1969	875.9	40.0	1,868.7	35.4
Unknown	211.6	9.7	407.8	7.7
Total	2,190.6	100.0	5,283.5	100.0

Source: *Woningbehoeftenonderzoek 1985/86*, Table 1 (Central Bureau of Statistics, 1987)

Thus, a substantial part of the stock is now over 20 years old. Although the great majority of it is in reasonable or good condition, even a small proportion of poor stock among the great numbers built during this early post-war period can present large financial problems. The Ministry of Housing puts the total bill for up-dating the social rented stock at Hfl 10,300 million (about £2,300 million), of which Hfl 7,000 million is needed for the 1945-1970 stock. Table 4.13 gives detailed information about the condition of the social rented stock. As Section IV explains, its disrepair is being tackled as part of the Multi-year Programme for Urban Renewal.

Table 4.13: Condition of the social rented stock (1984)

Age	Good		Fair		Poor		Very poor		Total	Cost Hfl Md
	No	%	No	%	No	%	No	%	No	%
					(thousands)					
Pre-1945	77	40	69	35	36	18	13	7	195	100	1.6
1945-70	403	40	475	48	100	10	22	2	1,000	100	7.0
Post-1970	541	80	125	18	6	1	4	1	675	100	1.6
Total	1,021	55	669	36	142	7	39	2	1,871	100	10.3

Source: *Tweede Kamer 1986-1987*, **Table 4.2**

In addition to these costs, which represent the backlog of repairs and maintenance, the Ministry of Housing estimates that a further Hfl 2,000 million is needed to bring amenities up to scratch, half that amount for the 1945-1970 stock.

Space and construction standards for the social rented sector have always been those laid down in building regulations for housing generally, although social landlords have normally built to rather higher than these minimum standards in practice. Table 4.14 gives sizes of Housing Act dwellings built between 1964 and 1982 by numbers of rooms (including kitchen), and usable floor area. Over this period, there has been a clear and steady shift towards dwellings with fewer rooms, while the average area increased until 1971 and 1972, since when it has declined again and by 1982 was almost back to 1964 levels.

In comparison with 'premium-assisted' dwellings (see Section II) and non-subsidised dwellings, Housing Act dwellings generally have fewer rooms and are smaller, notably so in comparison with non-subsidised (predominantly owner-occupied) dwellings. The trend over time towards dwellings with fewer rooms has also been much more marked in the social rented sector than elsewhere.

Table 4.14: **Size of Housing Act dwellings by number of rooms and area**

	% of dwellings by number of rooms						Average number of rooms	Average area (m²)
	1+2	3	4	5	6	>6		
1964	0	4	9	50	30	7	5.3	57
1965	1	6	7	57	23	6	5.1	58
1966	1	5	5	62	21	6	5.2	63
1967	0	8	9	59	21	3	5.0	62
1968	1	9	4	58	26	2	5.1	63
1969	0	7	8	59	24	2	5.1	64
1970	1	8	8	48	32	3	5.1	65
1971	1	9	7	48	32	3	5.1	66
1972	1	10	9	54	32	3	5.0	66
1973	1	10	13	52	22	2	4.9	65
1974	3	11	16	51	18	1	4.7	63
1975	5	16	24	43	11	1	4.4	62
1976	7	14	32	34	12	1	4.3	64
1977	9	17	34	31	8	1	4.1	63
1978	8	17	35	32	8	0	4.2	63
1979	6	16	40	30	8	0	4.2	61
1980	6	16	39	31	7	0	4.2	62
1981	6	15	41	32	5	0	4.2	61
1982	6	18	43	30	3	0	4.1	58

Source: 'Some data on house-building in the Netherlands 1986', Table G (VROM, 1987)

Although figures are not available to show the split between housing equipped with baths and housing equipped with showers in France, Germany, and the United Kingdom, baths are undoubtedly much more common than showers in all sectors in these countries. This is not the case in the Netherlands, where baths are the order of the day only in unsubsidised dwellings. Virtually all Housing Act dwellings are equipped with showers rather than baths. On the other hand, all new Housing Act dwellings built since 1971 have central heating, as against new housing generally, where central heating became universal only in 1975. Table 4.15 shows levels of amenity in social rented housing built between 1964 and 1982.

Table 4.15: Amenities in Housing Act dwellings (%)

	Separate		Bath/Shower combined with laundry	Central heating
	Bath	Shower		
1964	0	57	43	31
1965	0	60	40	59
1966	2	71	27	77
1967	0	72	28	84
1968	0	92	8	90
1969	2	93	5	95
1970	1	96	3	98
1971	2	98	0	100
1972	3	96	1	100
1973	2	98	0	100
1974	1	99	0	100
1975	2	98	0	100
1976	1	99	0	100
1977	2	98	0	100
1978	1	99	0	100
1979	5	95	0	100
1980	6	94	0	100
1981	4	96	0	100
1982	5	95	0	100

Source: 'Some data on house-building in the Netherlands 1986', Table H (VROM, 1987)

Although the social rented sector has built a higher proportion of flats than other sectors in the post-war period, houses form a much larger part of the stock than in France and Germany. As Table 4.16 shows, in most years between 1964 and 1982, about two-thirds of the Housing Act dwellings for which approval has been given have been houses, and only during the large building programme of the later 1960s did the proportion fall below 50%. In this respect, social housing in the Netherlands is much more like that in the United Kingdom. Indeed, in only four of the years between 1964 and 1982, were approvals given for more flats than houses.

The flatted housing developments of the late 1960s and early 1970s are, however, just as monolithic as their counterparts in France, Germany and the United Kingdom. Estates made up of serried ranks of long medium-rise and high-rise blocks - 'gallery blocks' - are a characteristic feature of the landscape in the overspill areas around the Randstad economic and industrial heartland in the West of the Netherlands, and around the Growth Cities in other parts of the country (see Section I). Like much medium-rise council housing in the United Kingdom, gallery blocks have the management problems of deck, balcony or corridor access serving large numbers of flats on each level, rather than the separate entrances and staircases - and lifts where necessary - giving access to a few flats on each floor, which is the more prevalent building form in France, Germany and the Soviet Union.

Table 4.16: Built form of Housing Act dwellings

	Total approvals	Proportion Houses %	Flats %	2	3	4	5	6	7	8	>8	Flats in gallery blocks (%)
							Storeys (%)					
1964	56,569	61	39	6	12	38	18	0	4	4	18	48
1965	69,720	49	51	4	8	23	19	2	8	4	32	62
1966	68,057	48	52	2	4	16	13	3	13	3	46	80
1967	66,838	38	62	3	4	12	4	2	17	4	54	86
1968	38,091	46	54	4	2	15	7	4	10	3	55	83
1969	36,875	56	44	4	8	16	7	3	16	5	44	76
1970	40,684	62	38	8	3	14	4	8	14	6	43	98
1971	46,151	63	37	8	2	8	7	5	18	7	45	94
1972	49,161	66	34	10	7	10	13	5	10	5	40	88
1973	48,276	71	29	14	10	7	10	10	5	4	40	85
1974	39,189	75	25	21	16	27	7	2	8	1	18	62
1975	41,792	67	33	22	24	28	9	1	7	4	5	49
1976	35,804	69	31	14	34	38	6	3	2	0	3	48
1977	34,590	65	35	19	33	31	5	5	2	1	4	54
1978	28,750	71	29	24	32	33	6	3	1	0	2	44
1979	38,400	69	31	16	35	28	15	2	1	1	3	44
1980	59,150	67	33	22	29	35	8	1	1	1	3	46
1981	79,400	68	32	14	29	37	13	3	2	1	1	53
1982	69,675	63	37	10	22	37	21	5	2	1	2	43

Source: 'Some data on house-building in the Netherlands 1986', Table F (VROM, 1987)

Table 4.16 gives the total numbers of Housing Act dwellings for which approval was given between 1964 and 1982, showing the split between houses and flats, the number of storeys in blocks of flats, and the proportion of flats which are in gallery blocks. On this basis, it has been estimated that 350,000 dwellings are to be found in complexes of six storeys and more.[13]

This table shows clearly the extent to which high-rise and gallery developments fell from favour in 1974, very much at the same time as the French government issued its circular discouraging large-scale estates. The table also shows the way in which the economies of lift provision militated against blocks of between five and eight storeys.

VI   The tenants

As in Germany, little information is available specifically about the tenants in the social rented sector, but government statistical data cover in some detail the lower income groups from which the tenants are largely drawn.

About three-quarters of a million households drew housing benefit in 1987.[14] This means that about one tenant household in four was living in rented accommodation at rents within the upper and lower price limits, and was on a low enough income to qualify for support. According to the more detailed information available for 1983/84, two out of three multi-person housing benefit recipient households had incomes of no more than the statutory minimum wage, 13% of them received their income under the Public Assistance (General) Act, 37% were 65 or more years old, and 24% were couples of working age. The average benefit was Hfl 1,782 per year. Some 635,000 families received housing benefit, out of a total of perhaps 750,000 who were eligible to receive it. This is a quarter of all tenants.

As in Germany, the proportion of tenants' disposable income which goes on rents has increased significantly in recent years, with higher income tenants paying a significantly larger share. Table 4.17 gives averages for different income groups for 1982/83 and 1986/87. The overall average moved from 11.3% at 1 January 1978 to 16.4% at 1 April 1986. Energy costs have gone up even more sharply, and represented 12.2% of disposable income at 1 April 1986, compared with 5.9% at 1 January 1978. By contrast, the housing costs of owner-occupiers have remained roughly constant as a proportion of disposable income over the same period.[15]

Table 4.17: Trend in ratio of rent to income from 1982/83 to 1986/87

Annual income (Hfl)	1982/83	1986/87
<21,750	11.13	13.06
24,500-25,000	13.40	15.07
29,000-30,000	15.76	17.56
33,000-34,000	16.43	20.01

Source: Unpublished paper from VROM, 'The housing situation
            and policies in the Netherlands 1988' p 20

Unemployment in the 1980s rose steeply, with the number of people drawing benefit rising by a factor of nearly four between 1975 and 1984, but showing a slight fall in 1985. The sharpest increase took place between 1980 and 1983.[16] According to the Netherlands Bureau of Statistics, more than three out of eight of the unemployed in 1983 were young people of under 25 years old, and their numbers had increased rather more than the average since 1980.[17] Table 4.18 gives the total numbers of people drawing unemployment benefit between 1975 and 1985.

Table 4.18: Number of people receiving unemployment benefits

1975	1980	1983	1984	1985	1986
		(thousands)			
181.7	237.8	647.8	690.7	679.2	649.7

Source: *Statistical Yearbook of the Netherlands* 1986, Table V.19,
            and VROM

According to 1981 figures for tenants in both the private and social sectors, their net income was most commonly in the bracket between Hfl 26,000 and Hfl 34,000 a year. This is rather higher than the net 'modal' income (that is, the income of a wage-earner with two children under 16 and a wage just below the premium-income limit of the obligatory sick-fund insurance scheme) which was Hfl 22,027 in 1981. On the other hand, it is considerably above the net statutory minimum wage of Hfl 17,669 in 1981.[18]

However, roughly one in ten tenant households had a net income of under Hfl 14,000. There was a further bulge between Hfl 17,000 and Hfl 20,000 which accounted for about one in twelve tenant households. This bracket includes the statutory minimum wage. Some 38% of tenant households were known to have a net annual income of under Hfl 26,000. The most common bracket for rent was between Hfl 2,400 and Hfl 3,600. By contrast, only 18% of owner-occupier households were known to have incomes below this level.[19] Table 4.19 gives a more detailed breakdown of tenants' incomes in relation to rents, with incomes of owner-occupiers for comparison. The tight relationship between rents and incomes at the various levels may well in part reflect the way in which the housing benefit tables are constructed.

Table 4.19: Incomes and rents (1981)

| Number of households | Net income (Hfl thousands) | | | | | | | | Not known |
	<14	14-17	17-20	20-23	23-26	26-34	34-42	>42	
Owner-Occupiers									
2,064.7	92.2	36.7	89.9	69.0	81.3	265.3	195.3	325.4	909.7
Tenants									
2,875.8	297.2	139.5	231.1	204.0	208.8	462.7	237.0	197.2	898.3
Annual rent*									
<2.4 677.8	117.0	53.7	78.1	59.9	53.2	82.5	31.6	22.5	179.2
2.4-3.6 867.2	91.4	46.7	77.8	71.0	73.7	144.5	63.6	41.8	256.8
3.6-4.8 558.3	37.5	18.5	35.4	37.5	39.8	111.3	56.4	40.7	181.2
>4.8 693.2	38.5	17.7	33.6	33.6	38.8	121.0	83.8	90.6	235.8
Not known 79.2	12.8	2.8	6.3	2.1	3.3	3.4	1.7	1.6	45.3

Note: * Hfl thousands

Source: *Statistical Yearbook of the Netherlands* 1986, Table D.5

In 1983, single parent families totalled 323,900, or 6.4% of all households.   Over one in three single parent families were unemployed, and were in the lowest income bracket, with spendable incomes averaging Hfl 26,100 a year. The number of single parent families headed by women in receipt of assistance rose from 73,600 in 1980 to 116,800 in 1984.[20]

The immigration pattern has been dominated by the influx of people from the former Dutch territory of Surinam, particularly in the late 1940s and early 1950s. However, it remained significant into the 1970s. Out of a total net increase by immigration and emigration of some 72,000 in 1975, just over half (36,700) came from Surinam. Other large immigrant groups came from Turkey (9,500), Morocco (7,100), and Asia (5,500). Five years later, when the net increase was down to some 53,000, nearly a third (16,700) came from Surinam, while almost the same number (14,900) came from Turkey, just over 9,000 from Morocco, and 6,300 from Asia.

Although net immigration dipped to under 10,000 in 1983 and 1984 before rising to just over 24,000 in 1985, the total turnover was much more significant, with nearly 67,000 arrivals in 1983 and 1984, and nearly 80,000 in 1985. The net increase from Surinam slowed down considerably to an average of about 2,200 a year, while there was a net loss of Turks. However, the net increase from Morocco and Asia remained rather higher, at an average of about 2,700 and 4,500 respectively.[21] The proportion of foreign tenants on one estate was 31% in 1984 and rose to 57% in 1985.[22]

VII   Management problems and solutions

Problem estate initiatives

The overall vacancy rate in the social rented sector at 1 October 1986 was quite low at 2.3%,[23] but levels of empty dwellings were as high as 8% to 10% on some problem estates, and on Bijlmermeer (see below), one in four dwellings had been empty at the worst point in 1985.

Rent arrears were roughly constant in the three-year period from 1984 to 1986, at about 2.8% of the rent roll. About a quarter of tenants were in arrear, four out of five of them for the first month only. Table 4.20 gives the rent arrears picture in greater detail.

Table 4.20: Rent arrears

	1984	1985	1986
Gross monthly rent per dwelling (Hfl)	411.0	424.0	431.0
Average rent arrears per dwelling (Hfl)	131.0	139.0	133.0
Rent arrears as % of gross annual rent	2.7	2.8	2.6
% of tenants in arrear	24.4	24.8	24.9
Total rent arrears (Hfl million)	200.0	222.0	220.0

Source: Information supplied by NWR

A study by the Research Institute for Policy Sciences and Technology (OTB) of Delft University of Technology in 1983 showed that overall losses through non-payment of rent in the social rented sector were comparable with the private rented sector. However, on a far from complete set of annual returns by housing associations and municipal landlord companies, the OTB found at least 100 estates where the losses in 1983 amounted to more than 5%. These are post-war estates of more than 50 dwellings, and consisting primarily of high and medium-rise blocks of flats. In 1985, also on the basis of very incomplete annual returns, at least 250 estates had arrears over 5%, though the landlord organisations say that arrears have since fallen sharply.[24]

As was noted in Section III, the Dutch Ministry of Housing has a strictly non-interventionist approach to housing management issues, except where there is a threat of insolvency, and has therefore so far been involved only in the rescue operation for the Bijlmermeer estate (see below). However, as will be seen, the Dutch Ministry of the Interior is funding some projects on social rented housing estates as part of its crime prevention programme. Measures receiving support can involve current expenditure, such as pump-priming help with the first year's salary of an estate superintendent/caretaker as at the Meenthe estate (see below), or capital works to improve security. Central government provides 50% of the funding, with the remainder coming from local sources. It is also possible to draw on other relevant central government programmes for associated measures, such as environmental improvements.

The remainder of this section considers a sample of problem estates where in most cases the landlord organisations on their own initiative have taken a variety of measures to turn them round. As in France and the United Kingdom (though less so in Germany), some landlord organisations have seen major remodelling or even demolition as the only solution to their worst problems. The best known example of major remodelling in the Netherlands is the Schotte flats at Middelburg, where the top 7 storeys of an 11-storey block have been removed. The main intention was to reduce the sense of monotony in this estate of three blocks, all of the same height. The most remarkable feature of this project was that the panels which were removed have been re-used on another site in another part of Middelburg, in order to reduce costs.

Demolition has so far been motivated more by management problems than by major structural defects, and a substantial proportion of the post-war dwellings which have been demolished are houses. The largest estate to be demolished so far is Linnaeusstraat at Leeuwarden (see below), consisting of 430 flats and maisonettes built between 1947 and 1955, which was demolished in 1977. Other estates for which demolition is a real possibility are the 498 Hanze flats in Kampen, the 284 Morgenstond flats in The Hague, and about 1,000 flats at Hoogvliet in Rotterdam. The first two estates suffer from major technical defects, but those in Rotterdam are virtually unlettable because of their situation and reputation.[25]

The initiatives described below show what can be achieved by a variety of more positive approaches to problem estates.

Bijlmermeer, Amsterdam

The Bijlmermeer estate on the south-eastern outskirts of Amsterdam has as great an international reputation as Les Minguettes in France, the Märkisches Viertel in Germany, or Broadwater Farm in the United Kingdom. However, in its national context, Bijlmermeer occupies an even more dominant place than do its counterparts in other countries. Whereas France, Germany and the United Kingdom all have a range of very large post-war problem estates, Bijlmermeer is the only one on this scale in the Netherlands.

Built between 1966 and 1975 on a green field site outside the city limits of Amsterdam but at the instigation of the city council, Bijlmermeer consists of about 13,000 flats, virtually all of them in the social rented sector. The estate was very much the brainchild of Amsterdam municipal planners and architects, inspired by the ideas of Le Corbusier, and consists of 30 10-storey blocks with corridor and deck access, set in extensive landscaped areas with rigid segregation of pedestrians and vehicles.

Until the late 1970s, Bijlmermeer was cut off by poor transport links with the outside world, and with an incomplete range of social and communal facilities. It was managed by 16 housing associations, none of them with offices on the estate, and with poor coordination of service delivery between them and the municipality. Although the estate originally attracted some relatively well-off tenants, there were always difficulties in finding enough applicants for housing there, and the vacancy rate remained at about the 5% level until 1976. The allocation difficulties were compounded by the preponderance of large flats, which in the first instance meant high child densities, but the falling birth-rate, particularly among the Dutch population, later led to a greater concentration of immigrant families and to increasing numbers of empty flats, many of which were then taken over by squatters from the former Dutch colonies.

About half the present tenants are of foreign origin, with one in three coming from the former Dutch colonies in the Antilles or Surinam. Poverty is high, with about 70% of households on the minimum state income level, and consequently on housing benefit. There are high levels of unemployment, while one in five households is a single parent family. In the early 1980s, the vacancy rate began to climb, reaching 24% in 1985. Similarly, turnover rose, reaching 34% in 1984. Rent arrears have been a peristent problem, with about one in three tenants in arrear, and frequent evictions for non-payment of rent.

Bijlmermeer has long since had a reputation for petty crime, and in particular for drug-trafficking, which together with its gaunt design, and often vandalised and litter-strewn environment and garages, contributed to a negative image in the outside world and a sense of stigmatisation among the residents.

In 1983, the central government launched an initiative to turn round Bijlmermeer. A three-pronged approach was adopted; rent reductions, new management, and physical improvements. Central government provided a one-off Hfl 100 million subsidy to reduce rents. The housing stock of 15 of the housing associations was transferred to a single, specially formed housing association, Nieuw Amsterdam, with financial support of Hfl 130 million to pay for physical improvement work, and to cover the losses from excessive vacancies and high turnover, until the new measures were expected to take effect. The Amsterdam city council made grants of Hfl 70 million to improve the landscaping and garages, and to cover the cost of providing them at no charge.

A major transformation has since taken place on Bijlmermeer, but the problems have by no means been solved entirely. The new style management based in an office block on the estate itself clearly provides a quick and relatively unbureaucratic service to potential tenants, who as a special measure, are able to apply direct to Nieuw Amsterdam rather than through the municipality. Many other management functions are now being devolved from this central office to five district offices, in particular, the administration of the all-important block caretakers whose responsibilities include minor repairs and repairs reporting. Management and maintenance activity is considerably more intensive than is normal on Dutch social housing estates, but the national shortage of police resources has meant that hopes of intensive policing have not been realised. As an alternative, the housing association is introducing a trial scheme of 'concierges' to improve supervision, with funding from the Ministry of the Interior's initiative to combat delinquency.

Tenant consultation and involvement have been actively promoted in various ways, and with mixed but perceptible success, despite the high turnover rate. Nearly every block now has its own tenants' association, which acts as a point of communication with the landlord, and in several cases organises social activities. The tenants form the majority on the Nieuw Amsterdam board of management. There is also some specialised tenant-led economic enterprise, for example an export-import business between Surinamese tenants and their relatives in Surinam, afro-hairdressers, video shops, a small cinema, and pubs.

A major change in the economic fortunes of Bijlmermeer came with the opening of a large and comprehensive shopping centre in 1987, and with the move of several commercial enterprises and bank headquarters to new office premises which have been built on the estate (with no special subsidies or tax breaks, apart from a small reduction in the ground rent for those which led the way). Although progress in providing employment opportunities for Bijlmermeer residents is gradual, these developments are already making a useful contribution by bringing people and money from outside into the estate.

There has also been a great physical transformation. The drab facades of the blocks have been given a variety of colour treatments with the twin purpose of improving their appearance and of arresting the deterioration which had started in the concrete. The landscaping has been improved, in particular with a programme of tree planting and the replacement of shrubbed areas with grass to facilitate maintenance. Major insulation work has been completed in order to cut the cost of the district heating scheme which was particularly burdensome to the low income tenants on the estate. Experimental schemes are exploring ways of controlling access and improving visibility on the long balconies. Security is being improved in the garages, and surface parking is being discouraged. Some 700 of the unnecessary and unpopular large three-bedroomed flats are being converted into 1,400 single-bedroom flats at a total cost of Hfl 42 million, or the equivalent of rather less than £10,000 per single-bedroom unit.

Although turnover and rent arrears remain at high levels, the vacancy rate declined at a steady and increasing rate from the 24% peak in 1985 to 17% at the beginning of 1987 and 7% at the end of 1987. Part of the credit for this improvement must go to the wide range of measures which have been developed and implemented to make Bijlmermeer a more attractive place to live. However, it is widely accepted that the vacancy rate on the estate is closely connected with the availability of alternative subsidised housing for rent in the area. The worst period was when completions of new housing were running at a high rate between 1983 and 1985. Subsequently, Bijlmermeer has benefitted from the national and local change in emphasis towards rehabilitation of the older stock, and the sharp cutback in new housing in the social rented sector. Nieuw Amsterdam management are painfully aware of their vulnerability to any future reduction in market demand.

The social and economic future of Bijlmermeer is far from secure in other ways too. With demand effectively limited for the foreseeable future to low-income tenants with no alternative choice, continued social stereotyping is seen as inevitable, with all that that implies for management costs. In addition, the concentrated age profile and type of building mean accelerating and high maintenance costs. Moreover, with turnover, rent arrears, and even empty dwellings - impressive though the reduction has been - remaining at high levels, the need for extensive special subsidies from the community at large is bound to remain, and such subsidies are always particularly susceptible to changes in the political climate. In short, the Bijlmermeer initiative is an ambitious attempt to turn round an estate with problems which are on a unique scale for the Netherlands, but it has no foreseeable prospect of becoming financially viable without massive and continuing public support.

Peperklip estate, Rotterdam

The Peperklip estate consists of about 550 flats in the dock area of Rotterdam south of the river Maas. It is owned and managed by the Rotterdam municipal housing company. As its name suggests, it is in the form of a paper-clip, though one which has been bent outwards, with curved high-rise blocks of six or eight storeys at each of the three extremities, joined by two long four-storey blocks. (An alternative school of thought has it that the name derives from the clippers which used to unload their cargoes of spice in the adjoining dock and whose shape is said to have inspired the architect).

It was built in 1981 on a strip of previously derelict land between the dockside itself and a railway line. Large tracts of the surroundings are still wasteland, and although housing associations are gradually developing the area with other social housing, the area will not be fully developed until the mid-1990s. Despite tensions between the left-wing Rotterdam City Council and the right-wing central government which has come to power since the redevelopment scheme was launched, central government is continuing to fund the environmental work in the area. Shops are gradually beginning to appear, and there is a reasonable bus service into the city.

From the outset, the estate suffered from low demand from the overspill population of the surrounding parts of the city for whom it was intended. Empties remained at about the 100 level throughout the first couple of years, and although the estate has since become fully occupied, there is a turnover rate of about 20%. The economic (and political) pressure to house any applicant, whatever the management considerations, has clearly contributed to this instability. As a result, ethnic imbalances have increased, and there are now families of more than ten different nationalities - but with a minority of them of Dutch origin - living on the estate. Four out of five tenants are over a month in arrears with their rent, and a similar proportion draw housing benefit. The district heating scheme with its contentious individual metering system is a further problem for the poorer tenants in particular.

The unattractive location of the estate is exacerbated by a striking contrast between design of the two types of housing. The low-rise flats are grouped eight to a staircase, with lockable entrance doors and entryphones. The common areas of these flats are well kept, and the flats are relatively popular. On the other hand, there is lift and balcony access to the high-rise flats, with uncontrolled access. The high-rise sections also contain the large family flats, with consequently excessive child densities. Graffitti and vandalism are persistent problems in these parts of the estate, including the rifling of mail-boxes, but otherwise, violence and crime are remarkably low.

The poor standard of maintenance of the open spaces is not helped by the tenants' responsibility to take all their household rubbish by hand to paladins parked in the open around the estate. Demarcation lines between the municipal housing company and other parts of the local authority are clearly inadequate to secure the effective coordination of service.

Within its own responsibilities, the municipal housing company has acted decisively to market tenancies and to provide a good service. There is an estate office, with a steady stream of enquirers. Although its role is management rather than caring, the staff clearly have a good personal rapport with the tenants. They interview and advise housing applicants, and provide accompanied viewing. The office also houses a two-man repairs team to do running repairs, while more serious jobs are contracted out to private firms. The target time for replacing broken windows - which are common - is 48 hours. Graffitti are removed as quickly, while the graffitti-artists are encouraged - with some success - to put their energies into controlled mural activity.

Meenthe estate, Leeuwarden

The Meenthe is a group of three blocks of flats and maisonettes, and about 180 houses totalling roughly 400 dwellings on the Bilgaard complex, which is made up of nine similar groups together with a supermarket, schools and other facilities. It was built in 1968 by the municipality of Leeuwarden, the small provincial capital of Friesland in the north of the Netherlands, on the outskirts of the town. Although Bilgaard is isolated from the town centre - about 20 minutes walk away - by a ring road, and the Meenthe is at the furthest end of the complex, the situation is not unattractive. One side of the estate is bounded by a river, and beyond that is open country.

On completion, the Bilgaard complex was transferred to three housing associations, with the Meenthe group going to the Woningstichting Leeuwarden-Leeuwarderadel (WLL), which owns about 3,000 dwellings in the province. However, most of the other WLL property consists of houses in rural areas, and the urban Meenthe development with its high proportion of flats and maisonettes has always been regarded as an alien element in its portfolio, not least in an area where there has always been a strong tradition of living in houses.

The built form of the nine groups is unpromising. In each, the flats and maisonettes are in three blocks. The least problematic are the terraced houses set around oblong courtyards with car spaces. The high-rise block of twelve storeys are also relatively easy to manage. The long five-storey split-level block of three-floor maisonettes with individual entrances at the lower level, and two-storey maisonettes with balcony access above presents greater difficulties, not least because the only way in which the upper maisonettes can be reached by lift is through the entire length of the third block and then across a windswept walkway. This third block consists entirely of balcony access flats on eight floors, and presents the greatest management problems.

Although the balconies are glazed in both blocks, they are unattractive and threatening, with numerous corners and walls behind which attackers can lurk. In the maisonette block, holes have been cut in the walls as a low-cost experimental measure to increase visibility, and incidentally improve the appearance of the balcony. The two adjoining lifts are a constant source of trouble, and at the time of the visit were completely wrecked by fire. The backlog of maintenance is estimated at Hfl 7,500, or about £1,650, per dwelling. On the other hand, internally, the dwellings are generally felt to be well appointed and in good condition.

The most visible management problems are graffitti, vandalism and fire damage, especially in the staircases and storage areas, scattered refuse, a bleak immediate environment, and a high proportion of vacant flats, especially in the eight-storey block where the housing association is now leaving flats empty as they fall vacant, pending a decision on whether to demolish or improve the building. Overall, about 140 dwellings, or a third of the total, are empty, and half of these have been empty for more than four months.

The turnover rate is high throughout the Meenthe, including the houses, though the 1987 figure of 30% is a distinct improvement on 36% the previous year. Rent levels are comparatively low at a monthly average of Hfl 325 (about £70) with heating and other costs adding a further Hfl 170, and rent arrears are not seen as a serious burden, with less than 2% of rents outstanding for more than four months.

Poverty is high, with 85% of households drawing housing benefit. One out of two heads of household is unemployed, compared with one in five in the town of Leeuwarden as a whole. Immigrants make up 12% of the population, six times the average for the town, and according to the estate superintendent, 22 nationalities are represented on the estate. Some 17% of households are single parent families, and two out of three households consist of one or two persons, whilst 61% of the population is under 25 years of age, with large numbers of children and teenagers. The latter are commonly blamed for the frequent break-ins, muggings and drug abuse. With these levels of economic and social deprivation, it is therefore hardly surprising that the residents find credit hard to come by, and that the estate is regarded by the residents and the community at large as the municipality's dumping-ground for problem families.

The first move to turn the estate round came in 1983 when a group which formed spontaneously among the tenants themselves decided that action was needed. Surprisingly, their first concern was to stem the social decline rather than to improve their material conditions, and that remains their priority. After three years' pressure on the housing association and the municipality - neither of which saw much prospect of tangible financial benefits from supporting them - in 1986 the group managed to secure their sympathetic interest. They have since obtained the half-time services of a worker from a local independent social organisation, funded by the central and local government City Renewal scheme. The housing association has provided an empty flat for meetings, with the running costs met by the municipality. The municipality has also made available some unused school premises for use as an apparently successful community centre with a range of activities designed to teach basic domestic skills.

The housing association has taken steps to improve its management of the estate. An estate superintendent/caretaker has been appointed (with the prospect of some pump-priming support from the Ministry of the Interior's project to combat delinquency).

His personal influence is clearly considerable, as also is that of a part-time policeman. The estate is also patrolled at night by a private security firm. A two-man repairs team is permanently on site in working hours. An increasing amount of consultant advice on management is being bought in from the association's umbrella organisation, the NWR.

As the figures given above show, it is still far too early to predict success, and with a clear excess of social rented accommodation in the Leeuwarden area, it is doubtful whether sufficient demand can ever be stimulated to fill the Meenthe. There are also some major social and administrative gaps which even the most enthusiastic tenants' group is bound to find daunting. Attempts at job creation are dogged by the residents' lack of educational qualifications or skills training. Dealing with such a varied range of funding agencies whose support is perennially at risk is a huge challenge. There is clearly still a frustrating lack of coordination between the housing association and the municipality in the provision of day-to-day services. The Meenthe has long since been such a drain on the financial and management resources of the housing association that it must always be vulnerable to total failure.

Kavel 6 estate, The Hague

The Kavel 6 estate is built on an inner city clearance site. It consists of about 300 flats, maisonettes and houses completed in 1982 between a raised highway and a canal. The layout is varied but dense, with a network of walkways and landscaped areas between the dwellings. The tenants include a substantial number of immigrants, and the child density is high, but there are no signs of widespread social disadvantagement. The estate is owned by a denominational housing association, which by all accounts manages and maintains it effectively. There is no local office, but a monthly visit by a mobile office is planned.

The estate's problems stem from the principle of open access which was central to the original design, and the extensive garage areas and storage rooms along internal corridors which are overlooked by no-one. There is said to be considerable drug abuse, but little reported crime.

The impetus for action came from the tenants' growing fear of crime and personal attack, which led to a successful application for help under the Ministry of the Interior's programme (see above). Following an approach by the active tenants' association to the municipality and the housing association, a committee of all three interests was formed, and including representatives of the relevant municipal services such as the police and the parks department. Arrangements for staircase by staircase consultation were set up. The measures which have been agreed and implemented are mainly physical changes, concentrating on restricting access and improving visibility. Porches with locking front doors and entryphones have been installed on each staircase. Unnecessary walkways have been removed. Landscaping has been modified to deter intruders. The lighting in the storeroom corridors has been improved, with mirrors and glazing to provide better visibility. The garage areas have been divided into smaller units with better lighting and electronic access.

Management measures are few. The housing association is doing some social engineering by giving preference to applicants with local connections. There has also been some increase in tenant involvement, with a tenant taking on the responsibility for locking and unlocking the garden area night and morning, and tenants accompanying repairs staff on their monthly check of the estate.

The total cost is Hfl 570,000, or about £400 per dwelling, nearly a third of it going on the garage improvements. The project is being evaluated by a research team on behalf of the Ministry of the Interior.

Oranjeplein estate, The Hague

The Oranjeplein estate has more evident social problems. It consists of 179 flats, maisonettes and houses in the larger Schilderswijk area which was cleared of 19th century slum tenements in the mid-1970s. Oranjeplein was redeveloped by a housing association, various non-governmental bodies, and the municipality in the late 1970s and early 1980s. The scheme includes a comprehensive range of communal facilities; schools, a shopping centre, a sports complex, a community centre, and some attractive landscaped areas. The estate is managed from the housing association's local office which serves all its property in the Schilderswijk area.

It became apparent, however, as early as 1984 that the new estate was in serious social difficulties, mainly because of insensitive allocations policies. Half the population were immigrants, and there was a high level of poverty. There were widespread reports of crime - especially drug abuse, with 250 known pushers in the immediate area of Schilderwijk - and prostitution. Vandalism and graffitti were taking a large toll. Gangs of young people were terrorising the residents. As at Kavel 6, the measures taken by the municipality and the housing association - with about Hfl 400,000 support from local government programmes - have largely taken the form of physical improvement work, though the housing association is funding intensified caretaking arrangements. Unnecessary walkways and external staircases have been removed. The garages have been divided into smaller units with better lighting and electronic access. Through routes have been restricted to deter outsiders.

There have clearly been difficulties in funding staff to promote the social development which the community needs, and in coordinating the activities of the various agencies which are working on the estate or providing resources. However, some work experience has been provided for young unemployed people.

Molenwijk estate, The Hague

The Molenwijk (Mill Quarter) estate belongs to De Goede Woning, a Protestant housing association with about 8,000 dwellings (and a further 1,000 under construction) throughout the Hague. The association has developed its own local management approach very similar to that of the Priority Estates Project, with local offices which provide all the main management functions including repairs by a local repairs team. A key figure is the 'Huismeester' who does odd jobs and is the main point of contact for the tenants on day-to-day matters.

The Molenwijk estate is in an inner city area of the Hague. Previously the site of about 1,700 social rented dwellings built in 1915, the area has been the subject of extensive clearance and redevelopment since 1976 under the Urban Renewal legislation. By that time, the dwellings themselves were in a poor state of repair, and the area was in serious social decline. Those who could afford to move out did so, and were replaced by increasing numbers of the economically and socially disadvantaged from clearance schemes which were already taking place, and by immigrants from Surinam and the poorer countries of the Middle East and around the Mediterranean, who eventually formed half of the population, many of them unemployed.

About nine out of ten of the present residents of the Molenwijk lived there before it was redeveloped. Intensive local management was therefore seen by De Goede Woning as essential if the redevelopment scheme was to prove a lasting success. Their part of the scheme consists of about a 1,000 new-build flats, maisonettes and houses. (There is also one of the original blocks which the municipality of the Hague has renovated and still manages.) With the exception of two sheltered blocks for older people, the new dwellings are mainly in long four-storey blocks. The buildings are attractive, as is their setting between two canals, and also the surface treatment and landscaping between them.

The detailed design and layout have visibly improved as the scheme has progressed, and the lessons of experience and consultation have been learned. Anti-graffitti treatment, locking front doors and entryphones are now standard. There are separate central heating installations for each dwelling, and the tenants receive detailed instruction in how to operate their heating systems economically and avoiding condensation.

The local management team of 10 or 11 people has part-time social worker support to provide general advice and individual counselling. There are good links with the local schools, where special attention is paid to the needs of the minority ethnic groups. At the working level in particular, the relationship between the local office and the municipality is said to be close, with effectively coordinated arrangements for street cleansing and rubbish removal. In its capacity as the overall lead agency for urban regeneration schemes, the municipality also has its own social role on the estate, and has provided a surprisingly successful animal compound for the benefit of the local children, which is maintained by their parents.

At the more mundane level of routine housing management, the intensive local approach is often necessary just to hold the line. Some tenants individually and collectively need frequent encouragement to fulfil their responsibilities to keep their landings and staircases clean. This is a major point of principle with the housing association, as also is a speedy repairs service and the removal of graffitti. Effective links need to be maintained with the police to contain the spread of nuisance and petty crime, including some drug abuse.

The Molenwijk is an estate where intensive local management was introduced to forestall the risk of serious problems on a newly built estate rather than to cure them. As such, it is a rare and largely unheralded initiative both nationally and internationally.

Conclusion

Although the Dutch Ministry of Housing is rarely directly involved in housing management issues, it is concerned about the condition of the stock and indeed is pressing for a change of emphasis towards rehabilitation in the new housing policy which was adopted from the beginning of 1988. Resources from the Multi-year Programme for Urban Renewal described in Section II have therefore been directed towards improving the physical condition of problem estates, which is generally acknowledged to be one of the major sources of management difficulty.

This programme is, however, only marginally directed towards the long-standing lack of maintenance which is regarded by many as one of the root causes of the growing management problems. Indeed, the withdrawal of the open-ended subsidy system (see Section IV) could even reduce still further the amount spent by landlords on maintenance, while at the same time exacerbating the sense of poor value for money felt by tenants.

Apart from the exceptional measures taken to deal with the Bijlmermeer estate, the only major intervention by central government is through the Ministry of the Interior's crime prevention programme which, as has been shown above, is supporting a range of capital and revenue housing management measures on rundown estates.

The development of new approaches on the ground to the management problems of rundown estates has so far been on the initiative of the individual landlord organisations. However, the two umbrella organisations are becoming increasingly involved, and are providing support to their members, mainly in the form of advice and consultancy activity.

NOTES

1. *Prominent Facts on Housing and the Building Industry in the Netherlands 1980-1985* published by the Department of Information and International Relations, Ministry of Housing, Physical Planning and Environment

2. *Statistical Yearbook of the Netherlands 1986*, table 13

3. *Statistical Yearbook of the Netherlands 1986*, table 14

4. Background paper by Nederlands Christelijk Instituut voor Volkshuisvesting (NCIV), p 1

5. 'The Housing Situation and Policies in the Netherlands 1988,, unpublished background paper by Loek Kampschöer, Deputy Inspector General of Housing, Ministry of Housing, Physical Planning and the Environment, p 4

6. *Comparative Study of Urban Renewal Policy*, Ministry of Housing and Physical Planning, July 1982, p 15

7. *Growth Centres and Growth Cities*, Ministry of Housing and Physical Planning, 1981, p 5

8. *Social and Cultural Report* 1984, table 6.2

9. 'The Housing Situation and Policies in the Netherlands 1988', unpublished background paper by Loek Kampschöer, Deputy Inspector General of Housing, Ministry of Housing, Physical Planning and the Environment, pp 17-19

10. *Social and Cultural Report* 1984, Appendix 3 to Chapter 6 'Housing'

11. 'The Housing Situation and Policies in the Netherlands 1988', unpublished background paper by Loek Kampschöer, Deputy Inspector General of Housing, Ministry of Housing, Physical Planning and the Environment, p 7

12. 'The Financing of Housing and Housing Subsidies in the Netherlands', Ministry of Housing, Physical Planning and Environment, October 1984 - December 1985, p 20

13. Paper given by N van Velzen to International Symposium, 30 May 1986

14. 'Financial Aspects of The Netherlands Housing Policy', paper by Peter Albers

15. 'Social Problems and Management', paper by Dr Jan van der Moolen to IFHP conference in Nottingham, 14 May 1988, table 2

16. *Statistical Yearbook of the Netherlands 1986*, p 134, diagram H1

17. 'A Statistical View of The Netherlands 1983', leaflet published by Central Bureau of Statistics

18. *Statistical Yearbook of the Netherlands 1986*, p 89, table 5; and *Some Data on House-Building in The Netherlands 1986*, Ministry of Housing, Physical Planning and Environment, table 1

19. *Statistical Yearbook of the Netherlands 1986*, p 89, table 5

20. *Statistical Yearbook of the Netherlands 1986*, pp 359 and 360, derived from tables 27 and 28

21. *Statistical Yearbook of the Netherlands 1986*, p 52, table 49

22. Information supplied by Dr Jan van der Moolen (NWR)

23. 'Housing in the Netherlands: at the crossroads', paper by Prof Hugo Priemus, OTB Delft, December 1987, table 3, derived from Central Bureau of Statistics data

24. Information provided by Prof Hugo Priemus, OTB Delft

25. 'Post-War Public housing in the Netherlands', paper by Prof Hugo Priemus, OTB Delft, p 39

five

THE SOVIET UNION

I   The general background

Population and housing stock

According to the 1987 edition of the Soviet statistical year-book, the population of the Soviet Union in mid-1987 was 283.1 million.[1] This is over 100 million more than the 181.6 million figure for early 1951 provided by the Soviet Government to the United Nations Economic Commission for Europe (UN ECE) in 1987,[2] and is not far short of twice the population of 159.2 million in pre-revolutionary Russia in 1913.[3]

The population is growing, with the natural increase per thousand having fluctuated widely over the past half-century. From 13.2 per thousand in 1940, it rose to 17.8 in 1960 before falling to 9.2 in 1970, since when it has risen again slightly, reaching 10.2 in 1986.[4] However, the regional variations are wide, with natural increase rates in some of the central Asian republics seven or eight times those in European parts of the USSR such as the Baltic republics or the Ukraine.[5]

It is therefore not surprising that household sizes also vary considerably, from 2.9 in the Baltic republics of Estonia and Latvia to about 4.5 in the central Asian republics. The average size of household in urban dwellings - which are almost all flats - is 3.3, with a density of 1.4 persons per room (excluding kitchen and bathroom).

The report to the UN ECE puts the total stock of individual dwellings at over 80 million, with hostel accommodation available in addition to this (see Section II) for about seven million people. However, the most commonly used measure of the housing stock is its total area in square metres. The 1987 statistical year-book puts the total at the end of 1986 at 4,190 million square metres, 63% of which is situated in urban areas.

As will be seen, there are great differences in housing conditions between urban and rural areas, and between the 15 individual republics. In urban areas, more than four out of five households now live in self-contained dwellings - compared with less than 30% in the mid-1950s[6] - while in rural areas, virtually all households have their own self-contained accommodation, but often with low levels of amenity.

With the persistent shortage of accommodation in urban areas which the foregoing figures imply, and the resulting high levels of sharing of dwellings and facilities by three generations, and often by two or more families, the concepts of housing units and household size in the USSR are of less significance than in the other countries covered by this study. Thus, as suggested above, the accent in Soviet statistics is more on the total area of the housing stock, and the share of that area occupied by individuals. On this basis, according to the 1987 statistical year-book, the average floor space per head in 1986 was 14.3 square metres in urban areas, and 16.1 square metres in rural areas, with an overall national average of 14.9 square metres per person.

Urbanisation and industrialisation

At the outbreak of the war between the Soviet Union and Nazi Germany in 1941, less than a third of the population of the USSR lived in urban areas. Taking into account the great increase in population which had taken place since the Revolution, even in 1941, there had already been a massive migration from the countryside to the towns. However, the post-war period has seen an even more dramatic shift of population to the towns and cities, and the urban population now accounts for two-thirds of the national total. The speed and recent nature of the urbanisation process is thrown into sharp focus by Table 5.1, which traces population trends from before the Revolution until mid-1987.

Table 5.1:   Trends in urban and rural population 1913-1987

	Total (million)	Urban (million)	(%)	Rural (million)	(%)
1913	159.2	28.5	17.9	130.7	82.1
1917	163.0	29.1	17.9	133.9	82.1
1940	194.1	63.1	32.5	131.0	67.5
1959	208.8	100.0	47.9	108.8	52.1
1970	241.7	136.0	56.3	105.7	43.7
1971	243.9	138.8	56.9	105.1	43.1
1979	262.4	163.6	62.3	98.8	37.7
1981	266.6	168.9	63.4	97.7	36.6
1986	278.8	182.9	65.6	95.9	34.4
1987 1 Jan	281.7	186.0	66.0	95.7	34.0
1 Jul	283.1	187.5	66.2	95.6	33.8

Source: *Narodnoye Khozyaistvo SSSR za 70 let 1917-1987*, p 373

Despite a policy to steer industry, and so people, to small and medium-sized towns, large towns and cities continue to dominate. Out of a total of some 6,000 cities and towns in 1986, the 278 cities with a population of over 100,000 account for 60% of the urban population. Indeed, the larger the city, the greater the tendency to grow. The number of cities with a population of more than one million inhabitants has risen from 9 in 1970 to 23 in 1987.[9] Although the pace has now slackened, there has also been a spate of new towns across the Soviet Union. In the early 1960s, they were being started at the rate of over 30 a year, and nearly 20 a year were being started in the early 1970s.

The process of industrialisation which led to this mushrooming in the urban population was begun in earnest with the series of Five Year Plans, dating from 1929. From this time, housing investment as a proportion of total capital investment was 12.8% at its lowest during the Second Five Year Plan of 1933-37, and reached a peak of 23.5% during the Sixth Five Year Plan of 1956-60. As will be seen in later sections, this was the time at which the mass housing programme also began to make real headway in volume terms, and the post-war period has seen the construction of no less than 80% of the total urban living space.[8]

Much of the building in the immediate post-war years was to make good the enormous losses during the period when the Soviet Union was involved in the Second World War (1941-45), much of it under the rigours of German invasion. During these years - known in the USSR as the 'Great Patriotic War' - 70,000 villages and hamlets are said to have been destroyed, along with 1,710 towns and urban settlements. Buildings totally destroyed in urban areas are put at 70 million square metres, or about one-sixth of the urban housing stock at that time, with at least the same amount damaged. Those killed in the war are estimated at 20 million, while 25 million were rendered homeless. The physical losses were quickly made good, with the housing stock in the ravaged towns virtually back to its pre-war level by 1952. However, the demographic effects continue to be felt, with women still outnumbering men by over 16 million in 1987.[9]

Tenure

Under Article 44 of the 1977 Constitution, Soviet citizens have a right to housing, and a duty to take good care of it. Apart from minor categories such as some housing on state and collective farms, there are three main tenure sectors in which they can exercise this right and this duty; renting from the state, building cooperatives, and private ownership. In urban areas, just over 70% of housing is rented from the state, while in rural areas, about the same proportion is privately owned. By far the largest part of the owner-occupied housing in rural areas consists of small wooden single-storey detached houses in their own plots, many dating from before the Revolution, and many - despite their often picturesque external appearance - in poor condition with low levels of amenity. Table 5.2 gives a detailed breakdown between the sectors.

The proportions vary considerably according to republic and town. For example, over 80% of the urban stock in Estonia, Latvia and the Russian Federative Republic (by far the largest of the republics, and including Moscow and Leningrad) is rented from the state, while in the Ukraine, and Azerbaijan and Tajikistan - two of the southern republics - only about two-thirds of the urban stock is rented from the state.[10] The larger cities usually have little if any owner-occupied housing. In rural areas, the share of housing rented from the state is rising, from 23% in 1980 to 29% in 1986,[11] but again with substantial geographical variations.[12]

Table 5.2:   Tenure (1985)

	Urban %	Rural %
Rented from state	71.4	21.8
Building cooperatives	6.0	0.2
Collective farms		4.3
Privately owned	22.6	73.6

Source: Constructed from page 27 of *Prospects and Main Trends
of the Development of Human Settlements in the USSR in
the period ending in 2000*, Report to the 10th Session of
the UN Commission for Human Settlements
(HABITAT), Moscow 1987.

Partly for economic reasons which will be discussed in greater
detail in Section IV, the Soviet government is encouraging the
development of the owner-occupied and cooperative sectors.
However, the authorities are also motivated by the belief that
people who have some sort of personal stake in their homes will
take better care of them.   In December 1988, the Soviet Politburo
decided to allow public sector landlords (see Section III) to sell
flats to sitting tenants.   Typical prices will be between 10,000
roubles and 16,000 roubles - that is, a multiple of four to seven
times the average annual income - with a down-payment of half
that amount, and the remainder to be paid off over ten years.[13]
    Taken to its logical conclusion, the policy to encourage
cooperatives and private ownership could lead towards at least
some degree of social residualisation as is happening in the western
European countries considered in earlier chapters, with the 'haves'
buying their way into better housing.
    The immediate attractions at least of the policy to sell to sitting
tenants are not, however, obvious.   Moreover, despite government
pressure to promote the house-building cooperative sector, in
practice this share of the market has until very recently at least been
declining.   Between 1981 and 1986, the private and cooperative
sectors accounted for 21% of total housing construction, compared
with 25% in the 1970s and 38% in the 1960s.[14]
    The shortage of housing land within the boundaries of the larger
cities, in particular Leningrad and Moscow, means that building for
owner-occupation is a possibility only on their fringes.   Elsewhere,
in smaller towns and in rural areas, suitable plots are more easily

available. Building plots are typically 600 square metres (15 metres by 40 metres). They are allocated free of capital cost by the local soviet (municipality), at a nominal annual rent of 1% of the cost of building the house. In one example outside Moscow, attractive alpine style houses with three rooms cost about 17,000 roubles (about seven times the average annual income) to build, while five-room versions cost about 28,000 roubles (about 12 times the average annual income). Anecdotal evidence indicates that the market value of such a property may be about twice these costs.

New privately owned houses are normally built in traditional materials - often wood - employing local artisans on a private basis. Soft loans are available from the state bank at a typical interest rate of 3%, and with lower rates for privileged categories, such as war veterans and meritorious workers. Private houses can be inherited, or sold on terms agreed between the vendor and purchaser. Most existing and new houses in the owner-occupied sector are main homes, whose occupants often depend to a great extent on the produce of their plots for part of their food or income.

There is, however, also a long and extensive tradition of a second, usually quite modest, home (a 'dacha') in the countryside for city dwellers at all social levels. Kudryavtsev in his booklet *I Hereby Apply For an Apartment* (in English) puts the cost of a prefabricated 'dacha' at 2,500 roubles, plus 800 roubles for foundation and assembly costs. Unofficial estimates put the proportion of Leningrad families with a second home at one in four or even one in three. Gregory Andrusz's comprehensive study *Housing and Urban Development in the USSR* (Macmillan, 1984) talks of three million second homes in the - admittedly large - administrative region surrounding Moscow. Many second homes have become available as a result of the population drift from the coutryside to the towns.

The Soviet constitution prevents the individual from owning (rather than renting) more than one home, and from exploiting such an asset for an 'unearned' financial gain. **Private renting** in the sense of landlords who own and let housing as a business therefore does not exist in the Soviet Union. However, tenants have a constitutional right - for example under Article 76 of the Housing Code of the Russian Federative Republic - to sub-let part of a rented (or owner-occupied) dwelling to other parties, and provision is officially made for people who need to leave their flat temporarily - for example, to take up a job for a spell in another part of the country - to retain their tenancy and to sub-let the flat in the meantime. There are no figures to show the amount of sub-letting which goes on, but it is generally held to be considerable. An article in the international Soviet weekly news-sheet *Moscow News* in May 1988 refers openly to a family which has rented a one-room flat for 50 roubles a month, which is vastly higher than the official rent (see Section IV).

Although house-building **cooperatives** are largely financed by the state, they are universally seen in practice as a separate form of tenure. Their chequered political history - and that of the 'leasing cooperatives' which were abolished in the inter-war years - is traced in detail in Gregory Andrusz's book which is cited above.

As Table 5.2 shows, they are largely an urban phenomenon, and with one in five families in urban areas still living in shared accommodation, they are usually seen as a way of jumping the queue for those who can lay hands on the money for the deposit. However, in an economy where personal savings are at high levels (see Section VI), parents are often ready to help, not least when this means that they will then be able to live in less cramped conditions themselves. Alternatively, as will be seen, employers can offer financial help. Membership is therefore open to a wider range of society than may at first appear. House-building cooperatives will be considered in greater detail in Section III.

Table 5.2 also shows that the **state rented sector** is the dominant form of tenure in the cities and towns, but that it caters only for a small minority in rural areas. As the equivalent of the social rented sector in the western European countries covered by the rest of this report, it will be considered in detail in subsequent sections of this chapter. However, it is worth underlining at this point that, as in other countries, there are two categories of social landlord organisations. In the Soviet Union, these are the municipalities, or 'soviets' on the one hand, and employers, such as state enterprises and government ministries on the other. As will be seen, there are considerable differences and tensions between these two categories.

II   The history of the social rented sector

Urban housing before the Revolution

Unlike the western European countries covered by this report, the Soviet Union can look back on no 19th century attempts to improve the living conditions of working people in the newly industrialised cities. To a great extent, this is because of the much slower development of social reform generally in Tsarist Russia. The feudal system of serfdom was abolished only in 1861, releasing more than 20 million people from bondage to the land. As Sir Donald Mackenzie Wallace reports in the 1912 edition of his *Russia*, it was this mass of newly emancipated workers who provided "an unlimited supply of cheap labour" to feed the industrial revolution which overtook Russia in the latter part of the 19th century.[16]

With rare exceptions such as a typically unrealised scheme in 1906 to put up cheap and hygienic dwellings,[19] there were few signs of an active social conscience about the living conditions of this newly emerging industrial workforce in the final decades of Tsarist Russia. This is not least because the land-owning classes were themselves accustomed to living in cramped and often primitive conditions during their winter stays in St Petersburg and Moscow (although they lived in much greater comfort on their estates during the rest of the year).

Moreover, as the accounts of more than one 19th century traveller to Russia have shown, housing conditions and urban planning came relatively low in the national priorities. Describing Moscow, Mackenzie Wallace says that "dilapidated buildings which in West European cities would hide themselves in some narrow lane or back slum here stand composedly in the face of day by the side of a palatial residence",[18] while in provincial towns, the "houses are built of wood or brick, generally one-storied.... Many of them do not condescend to turn their facades to the street".[19] Gregory Andrusz quotes a French traveller at about the same period in very similar vein.[20]

However tendentious subsequent accounts of pre-revolutionary urban housing conditions may be, there is enough evidence from earlier writers such as Mackenzie Wallace and the novelist Lev Tolstoy (see below), for us to be sure that the living conditions of those who had migrated from the land to work in the new industries in the towns and cities were at least as bad as those in any of the western European countries covered by this study. Nonetheless, it should be borne in mind that these people had rarely lived in conditions of bucolic ease on the land, and even before the prospect of industrial employment began to be opened up, it had been traditional practice for large numbers of men to travel long distances in search of work, and when they found it, to spend long periods away from their families.

It was therefore no new hardship for the new industrial migrant workers to be housed in over-crowded and insanitary barrack style accommodation. Describing the 'enormous blocks' in pre-revolutionary St Petersburg, Mackenzie Wallace says,

> Those built for the working classes sometimes contain, I am assured, more than a thousand inhabitants. How many cubic feet of air is allowed to each person I do not know; not so many, I fear, as is recommended by the most advanced sanitary authorities.[21]

Similarly, describing a visit to a hostel in one of the poorest areas of Moscow in the 1880s, Tolstoy talks in shocked tones of a huge building with separate dormitories for men and women, full of bunks "like those in the third class on the railway", with the inhabitants suffering from cold and hunger. However, relating his experience to a friend on his return home, he is assured that such conditions are an inevitable consequence of civilisation, and that London has worse to offer.[22]

According to the Soviet housing economist, E M Blekh, people living in the working-class areas of towns and cities had on average between two and two and a half square metres of living space, and according to figures which he cites from the 1912 census, 18% of the population of Moscow was living in a total of 23,300 flats - that is, an average number of 12 people to each flat.[22] He also says that only 10% of pre-revolutionary urban housing blocks were connected to a mains water supply, only 2%-3% had mains drainage, and 5% had electric lighting.

Much of this housing was provided by employers, near to their factories or mines, or the new industrial complexes such as the oilfields of Baku on the Caspian Sea. As has already been shown in Section I, this tradition of housing provided by employers has lived on under Soviet rule, as also has communal living in flats with shared facilities (which is still the way of life for 15% of urban families). Similarly, migrant labour still exists in a major way, and probably accounts for a large part of the seven million places in hostels to which Section I refers.

From the Revolution to the end of the Second World War

Before the October Revolution, the stage was already set (if only just) for the new Bolshevik government to provide low-rent housing through the local soviets (or municipalities as they will be termed from now on). During the First World War, the Tsarist government had gone the same way as governments in western Europe by imposing rent control, and after the overthrow of the Tsarist government in March 1917, Kerensky's Provisional Government issued a decree which among other things gave local authorities a responsibility to make low-rent housing available.

In the first instance, the municipalities approached their task by taking over existing accommodation, most of it housing owned by private landlords. However, some of it was housing considered to be under-occupied by owner-occupiers who were forced to share their homes or in some cases to leave them altogether. Nonetheless, it would be wrong to think that owner-occupiers were generally expropriated, even in the towns and cities. While a decree in August 1918 announced that 30% of urban housing was to be taken over by the state and a further 50% by the municipalities to hand over to tenant management committees, 20% was to be left in the hands of owner-occupiers.[24]

Indeed, owner-occupation received a new lease of life with Lenin's return to a partial free-enterprise economy in the New Economic Policy (NEP) of 1921 to 1928, and despite the growing political risks to private ownership after Stalin succeeded Lenin in 1924, owner-occupation continued to make a vastly larger contribution than the state sector through the 1920s and into the 1930s. According to the 1926 census, less than half (47%) of the area of the urban housing stock at that date belonged to the state, while 53% belonged to individuals.[25] Moreover, during the inter-war period (which for the Soviet Union lasted until 1941), private house-building exceeded that by the state by a factor of more than two. Some 281 million square metres of housing were built for owner-occupation between 1918 and the middle of 1941, compared with a total of 127.9 million square metres built by the state.[26]

After a brief flirtation with totally rent-free housing between early 1921 until the spring of 1922, the Soviet government reverted to a low-rent policy which survives to this day, and which will be considered in greater detail in Section IV. However, as a corollary of low rents, tenants were made responsible for the cost of day-to-day repairs and maintenance - for example, decoration - both in order to inculcate a greater respect for public property and to help balance the books financially.

The New Economic Policy also saw the birth of housing cooperatives of two types. The first was the 'leasing cooperative' (Zhilishchno-arendnoye kooperativnoye tovarishchestvo, or ZhAKT), which leased not only their housing accommodation from the state, but also other facilities such as crèches. However, the form of tenure represented by the ZhAKT was not only ideologically suspect from the outset, but also increasingly came to be thought deficient in practice, and was abolished by a 1937 decree.

The other type of cooperative, the 'house-building cooperative' (Zhilishchno-stroitel'noye kooperativnoye tovarishchestvo, now generally known by the acronym ZhSK) has proved more durable, even though it too has not always enjoyed full political confidence, and underwent a period of eclipse between 1937 and the early 1960s. House-building cooperatives will be considered in greater detail in Section III. However, as a measure of the contribution of both types of cooperative during their brief inter-war heyday, it is estimated that in 1931, about 4% of the work-force of the Soviet Union were members of housing cooperatives.[27]

The inter-war years also saw a variety of initiatives - many of which progressed no further than the drawing-board - to establish new forms of housing provision and tenure in keeping with the 'new man' whom the advent of communism was to create. International interest in the architectural potential of this pioneering society was considerable. Le Corbusier visited Moscow in 1929, and as a letter to the Vesnin brothers shows, was enthusiastic about the opportunities.[28] The German Bauhaus school also exerted an influence (see Chapter 3, Section II).

The formation of the first house-building cooperative - the Sokol cooperative - in 1921, which involved such prestigious figures as academician V. A. Vesnin (see previous paragraph), is claimed to have served as a far-reaching prototype for the garden city concept in the Soviet Union.[29] On the other hand, utopian plans for collectivised living soon fell by the wayside. Kudryavtsev quotes the example of one of the schemes for the new town of Magnitogorsk which involved the complete collectivisation of life.[30] There was to have been communal catering, and children would have been brought up separately from their parents so that the adults could labour more effectively to build the new society. This scheme did not come into existence, and the reality of life in a communal flat no doubt was and still is like the description by Ilf and Petrov in their satirical novel, *The Golden Calf*, with its tensions between tenants, sub-let rooms and parts of rooms, and a kangaroo court to mete out summary justice to the tenant who habitually fails to turn off the light in the communal lavatory.[31]

It is therefore not surprising that despite its long traditions going back to an enforced way of life before the Revolution, communal living in the inter-war period and subsequently has been generally regarded by the Soviet government as a temporary expedient, although communal flats remained the standard form of housing until the late 1950s. Nonetheless, official housing policy has since 1961 been to provide a separate flat for each family. Economic exigencies have meant that the target date has constantly receded. As will be seen, the present aim is to achieve this goal - which since 1981 has also included the aim of a separate room for each member of the family - by the millenium.[32]

The post-war period

As has been shown in Section I, in the 1950s, more than seven out of ten urban families were still living in shared accommodation. There were three main reasons. First, as has been seen, housing construction was limited in the inter-war years, during which time there were also some substantial losses, especially through damage during the Civil War which saw the loss of about 360,000 buildings,[33] and later through clearance of slum property and the start of some grandiose new town plans.

Second, mainly as a result of the programme of heavy industrialisation which took priority in the 1930s, there was an enormous shift of population from the countryside to the towns and cities. The urban population more than doubled between 1917 and 1940.[34]

Third, as has been shown in Section I, the Second World War saw the loss of about 70 million square metres of housing, or no less than a sixth of the urban housing stock which existed at the outbreak of war in 1941. Table 5.3 shows the development of the urban housing stock and population between 1913 and 1986.

Table 5.3:   Development of the urban housing stock and population 1913-1986

	Total area (m²)	State (m²)	%	Of which Private (m²)	%	Population (million)	Average space per person (m²)
1913	180	-	-	180	100	28.5	6.3
1926	216	103	47.7	113	52.3	26.3	8.2
1940	421	267	63.4	154	36.6	63.1+	6.7
1950	513	340	66.3	173	33.7	73.0	7.0
1955	640	432	67.5	208	32.5	88.2	7.3
1960	958	583	60.9	375	39.1	108.3	8.8
1965	1,238	806	65.1	432	34.9	123.8	10.0
1970	1,542*	1,046	67.8	496	32.2	136.0+	11.3
1975	1,875*	1,352	72.1	523	27.9	155.1	12.0
1980	2,202*	1,655	75.2	547	24.8	168.9	13.0
1986+	2,640	2,050	77.7	590	22.3	182.9	14.4

Notes: + Figures from 1987 published statistics
          * Figures revised in 1982 published statistics probably to take account of
          increase in urban population with widening of some urban boundaries

Sources: G D Andrusz *Housing and Urban Development in the
          USSR* pp 22-23; *Narodnoye Khozyaistvo SSSR za 70 let
          1917-1987*, pp 373 and 517

As this table shows, the post-war housing programme took off in earnest in the mid-1950s. This was the period of the Sixth Five-Year Plan, beginning in 1956. According to these official statistics, more housing was produced in the five years between 1956 and 1960 than in the whole of the inter-war period, and in 1960, house-building in the state (rented) sector exceeded that by individuals for owner-occupation. As Table 5.4 shows, house-building for rent has risen throughout the post-war period, while building by individuals for owner-occupation has declined steadily, apart from 1985 and 1986 when the trend sems to have been reversed. (Although it is outside the scope of this report, it will also be noted that there has been a steady increase in house-building on collective farms.)

As noted above, house-building cooperatives were relaunched in the early 1960s, since when, their share of new housing construction has fluctuated slightly above 5%, though it too increased in 1985 and 1986 when it reached about 7%.

Table 5.4:   Total housing construction (urban and rural) 1918-1986
             (million m²)

	Total (m m²)	State for rent		Building cooperatives		Private		Collective farms and 'rural intelligentsia'*	
		(m m²)	(%)	(m m²)	(%)	(m m²)	(%)	(m m²)	(%)
1918-1940 (inc 1st half of 1941)	408.9	127.9	31.3	-	-	281.0	68.7	-	-
1 July 1941 to 1 Jan 1946	102.5	41.3	40.3	-	-	13.6	13.3	47.6	46.4
4th FYP+ (1946-50)	200.9	72.4	36.0	-	-	44.7	22.2	83.8	41.7
5th FYP (1951-55)	240.5	113.0	47.0	-	-	65.1	27.1	62.4	25.9
6th FYP (1956-60)	474.1	224.0	47.2	-	-	250.1	57.8	-	-
7th FYP (1961-65)	490.6	287.0	58.5	13.4	2.7	184.9	37.7	5.3	1.1
8th FYP (1966-70)	518.5	318.9	61.5	33.6	6.5	153.8	29.7	12.2	2.4
9th FYP (1971-75)	544.8	374.7	68.8	32.6	6.0	120.8	22.2	16.7	3.1
10th FYP (1976-80)	527.3	386.4	73.3	27.4	5.2	91.4	17.3	22.1	4.2
11th FYP (1981-85)	552.2	403.7	73.1	32.8	5.9	80.3	14.5	35.4	6.4
1986	119.8	86.2	72.0	8.2	6.8	17.4	14.5	8.0	6.7

Notes: + FYP - Five Year Plan
             * The category 'rural intelligentsia' is applicable only to the figures
             between 1 July 1941 and 31 December 1955

Source: *Narodnoye Khozyaistvo SSSR za 60 let 1917-1977*, p 492;
             Narodnoye Khozyaistvo SSSR za 70 let 1917-1987, p 508

Table 5.5 gives subsets within the foregoing figures for urban house-building between 1955 and 1986. Although disaggregated figures for house-building cooperatives are not available, it can be assumed that nearly all the cooperative activity detailed in Table 5.4 took place in towns and cities. The table also underlines the small and declining amount of private house-building in urban areas. The inclusion of some house-building activity on collective farms from the 1970s tends to support the footnote to Table 5.3 about widened urban boundaries.

Table 5.5: Urban house-building 1955-1986 (million m²)

	Total (m m²)	State for rent and cooperatives (m m²)	(%)	Private (m m²)	(%)	Collective farms (m m²)	(%)
5th FYP (1951-55)	129.8	91.0	70.1	38.8	29.9	-	-
6th FYP (1956-60)	241.7	181.0	74.9	60.7	25.1	-	-
7th FYP (1961-65)	291.6	240.8	82.6	50.8	17.4	-	-
8th FYP (1966-70)	335.5	299.1	89.2	36.4	10.8	-	-
9th FYP (1971-75)	377.4	345.0	91.4	32.4	8.6	-	-
10th FYP (1976-80)	378.7	345.9	91.3	31.2	8.2	1.6	0.4
11th FYP (1981-85)	384.8	350.7	91.1	29.3	7.6	4.8	1.2
1986	82.9	75.5	91.1	6.8	8.2	0.6	0.7

Source: *Narodnoye Khozyaistvo SSSR za 60 let 1917-1977*, p 493; *Narodnoye Khozyaistvo SSSR za 70 let 1917-1987*, p 509

As will be seen in Section V, major changes have taken place since the 1950s in higher space standards and in the built form where there has been a huge shift towards high-rise construction. Coupled with rent levels which have remained unchanged since 1928, these changes have had a major effect on housing finance. This is discussed in Section IV.

It is worth noting at this point, however, that Soviet commentators unanimously see the development of industrial building systems and a large-scale capacity for producing lifts in the 1960s as the breakthrough to the huge high-rise 'mikrorayon' peripheral housing estates which dominate the skyline around the major cities and towns of the USSR, and which in many places have taken over large tracts of inner cities.

The 'mikrorayon' concept evolved in the 1950s as a self-sufficient housing complex, with its own infrastructure of shops, schools, clinics, communal and sporting facilities, with transport links to enable residents to reach their place of work within half an hour. In addition to these social and economic benefits, such high-density living complexes are also supposed to provide economies in the use of land, and to avoid the cost of building the extended transport and mains services infrastructure which would be inevitable with low-rise housing development. However, as will be seen in later sections, the provision of the necessary non-housing facilities has often lagged behind in the Soviet Union as it has in the other countries covered by this study, while high-rise housing has been found to involve relatively high management and maintenance costs, which too will ring a familiar note elsewhere.

III   The landlord organisations

As was explained in Section 1, apart from various forms of financial help by the state to individual owner-occupiers, the state housing sector as such consists of two main forms of tenure; rented accommodation, and house-building cooperatives. Section I also pointed to the fundamental division in the state rented sector proper between municipal landlord organisations on the one hand, and state enterprises, government ministries and the like on the other. For the sake of brevity, this second category of landlord organisations will be termed employers from now on. This section considers these two forms of landlord organisation and house-building cooperatives in greater detail. Table 5.6 gives a breakdown of ownership of the urban stock in percentage terms.

Table 5.6:   Ownership of the urban housing stock

	%	
Renting	71.2	
of which,		
employers		37.6
municipalities		32.8
communal organisations		0.8
Building cooperatives	5.1	
Owner-occupied	23.8	
Total	100.0	

Source: Derived from E M Blekh, *Povysheniye effektivnosti ekspluatatsii zhilikh zdani'*, Table 4, p 19

Municipalities

The municipalities or 'soviets' have several separate functions in the field of rented and cooperative housing. First, they are responsible for commissioning the construction of new housing (or major capital repair work) of which they are directly the landlords. This is regulated by allocations of capital finance authorised by the central - USSR - government and the government of the appropriate individual republic. The work is done by a variety of construction enterprises, but increasingly by some 500 specialist organisations known as 'domostroitel'niye kombinaty' or DSKs, which concentrate on the manufacture and assembly of large panel systems which account for more than half the present-day housing output in the Soviet Union.[35]

Second, the municipalities are responsible for the management and maintenance of their own housing. Their management structure is considered in greater detail below, but in essence is not dissimilar from the management structure in much of British local authority housing management, with the ultimate responsibility for the various management functions divided between separate and largely autonomous municipal departments. However, as will be seen, there have been various moves in the Soviet Union in recent years to decentralise housing management.

In particular, the departments which handle planned maintenance and repairs seem remarkably similar to British local authority direct labour organisations. They in turn call on specialist enterprises for such major categories of maintenance work as, for example, lifts. With a 100,000 lifts in Moscow alone, such specialised enterprises are clearly needed, and by common consent, lift maintenance in Moscow is efficiently handled. The maintenance organisation claims that people trapped in lifts are freed within half an hour at any time of day, and repairs usually completed within 24 hours (although housing specialists readily admit that other towns and cities do not always reach the same standards).

As is explained in Section II, tenants are responsible for minor repairs and internal decoration. However, at an average expenditure of 11 roubles a year (less than half of 1% of average income) they clearly spend little out of their own pockets on the upkeep of their homes.[36] Offices to take minor repairs orders are a frequent sight in Soviet towns and cities, and statistics showing why tenants get repairs done privately show that difficulty in getting to the repairs office is the cause of only 1.5% of housing repairs in urban areas which are done independently. However, delays in getting the work done are the reason for half the repairs for which tenants resort to self-help.[37] As will be seen in Section VII, less than a quarter of tenants' average expenditure on repairs is with the official maintenance organisations.

As in other countries, this is where there is the greatest friction between tenants and their landlord organisations. Blekh endorses the way in which their respective responsibilities have often been set out in formal agreements, but notes that limited capacity has sometimes led to tenants' being pushed into doing more than they can legally be required to do.

Third, the municipalities are responsible for allocations and lettings not only of their own housing, but also of housing belonging to employers and to cooperatives. As will be seen, their relationship with employers is sensitive and sometimes imprecise, not least in respect of allocations and lettings. Employers often do what they can to minimise the municipalities' involvement in the allocation of what they regard as their housing, existing for economic rather than social reasons. Indeed, this difference of approach is often seen as representing the crucial divide between municipal housing and that owned and managed by employers - with municipal housing having something approaching a 'residual' role to cater for retired people, single mothers, and others not in regular work.

On the other hand, it should be noted that the seven million places in hostel accommodation are almost wholly the responsibility of employers, and it is this form of housing which is generally regarded as taking those who are the most disadvantaged socially - migrants from the countryside and the more far-flung republics - although they also cater for substantial numbers of students and full-time employees without families.

In the case of house-building cooperatives, the municipalities are responsible for registering and vetting applications from people who are seeking to join cooperatives as individuals rather than as members sponsored by their place of work (see below). Although no clear evidence is available, individuals sometimes claim that municipal housing officers tend to see cooperatives as a reflexion on their own service, and as a resort for the economically privileged. This alleged defensive attitude on the part of the municipal authorities is often cited as a reason for the slow progress of house-building cooperatives.

Applications for new lettings in the municipal stock are made to the housing district where the prospective tenant wants to live within the municipality. However, it is apparently possible to apply to more than one district. Applicants provide basic information about their household, and priorities are determined almost exclusively by the existing conditions in which the family is living, in particular the amount of floor space available for each person. For example, the million people in Moscow with less than 5 square metres (in comparison with a city average of 17.4 square metres in 1987) have the highest priority.[38] Similarly, people with less than 6 square metres have priority in Leningrad. Most people at this level of housing need will be sharing flats, often with other members of their families, and often in communal accommodation.

Length of residence is also a criterion. For example, in the major cities such as Leningrad, a minimum of ten years' officially authorised residence may be required before a family can be considered for a separate flat. Here too, there can be complications, as is shown by the case of the family described in *Moscow News* (see Section I). Usually, they are caused by people dying or moving out of a shared flat and so altering the space standards of those remaining, or by difficulties between the municipality and the employer about the applicant's status and who is responsible for allocating accommodation to him or her.

Some privileged groups get special priority from most municipalities, for example, war veterans or those with badly needed skills. The ageing population of Moscow and Leningrad has led to special measures to attract young skilled workers. Although the folklore has it - and possibly not without some justification - that families with more than three children get favoured treatment, no allowance is made for socially disadvantaged categories such as single-parent families, though those responsible for allocations say that they pay particular attention to their needs when providing them with flats, typically by grouping families so that they can support one another.

Abuse of the system is not unknown. Kudryavtsev openly cites cases where local officials have been disciplined for favouritism in allocating housing unfairly to their families and friends.[39]

Over the Soviet Union as a whole, 1,762,000 households improved their living conditions in 1986, 1,575,000 of them moving off the housing waiting-lists. This represented 12.6% of the total number of households who were on waiting-lists. However, the scale of the challenge still facing Soviet housing authorities is evident from the continuing demand for housing. On 1 January 1987, 12,660,000 households, or 22.3% of all Soviet households, were on housing waiting-lists.[40]

By extension, the allocations and lettings functions of the municipalities include some responsibility for tenant mobility. Tenants have a statutory right to exchange under the laws of the individual republics, for example under Article 67 of the Housing Code of the Russian Federative Republic. However, there are virtually no arrangements to facilitate domestic moves and exchanges between one city and another, not least because of varying allocations criteria. Thus, unless they are moving for job reasons and the employing enterprise (see below) has accommodation available, tenants wanting to move to another part of the country have to make their own arrangements for an exchange, usually by advertising in the local newspaper.

For moves within the area of a municipality, there are usually structured arrangements, with an office responsible for taking exchange applications in each housing district. In some cases, bulletins are published periodically by the municipal lettings office, and some of the bigger municipalities claim to have computerised exchange facilities. Kudryavtsev[41] reports that the Moscow exchange system organised 100,000 such moves in 1983 within the city's total of about 2,750,000 flats,[42] while Leningrad housing officials put their annual number of exchanges at about 60,000.

Despite the official arrangements for exchanges, it appears that many of them are the result of self-help. Although they are technically illegal, hand-written advertisements attached to fences near metro stations and in other prominent places are a common sight in large Soviet housing estates.

Fourth, although there are still some areas where this remains the responsibility of ministries and enterprises, the municipalities are responsible for providing and maintaining the great bulk of the social and communal infrastructure on which their own housing depends. This includes shops, schools, crèches, clinics, and sport and recreational facilities, as well as services such as refuse collection and the maintenance of the open space. They are not responsible for providing public transport services, but clearly need a closely coordinated relationship with the local transport undertaking in order to ensure that this crucial service to the residents of every housing development is in place and functioning effectively.

Municipal housing practitioners readily admit that the coordination of service delivery could often be better, but point to the superiority of their management performance over that of the employers (see below) in their often fragmented housing stock. The management and maintenance arrangements of the municipalities have been the subject of continual debate over many years, and since 1959 there has been a trend for municipal housing in the larger towns and cities to be devolved to local offices - known variously under such names as Direktsia po ekspluatatsii zdani' (DEZ), Zhilishchno-ekspluatatsionnaya kontora (ZhEK) or Domo'upravleniye - serving typically between 2,000 and 3,000 flats.[43] They are responsible for commissioning repairs, cleansing, environmental maintenance, snow-clearing and the like.[44]

More recently, some large municipalities have been experimenting with more intensive and integrated local management teams, such a the PZhRO in Moscow, with a target-oriented approach and some degree of payment by results. The aim of these experiments is to achieve a balance of economies of scale and responsiveness to the tenants' requirements. Blekh cites examples in Leningrad where greater financial transparency of maintenance work linked with better incentives to the workers and a conscious effort to provide an effective service to the tenants resulted in a reduction of 7%-10% in repairs orders and 30% less complaints.[45]

Such improvements are being supported by strengthening the communications centre (dispecherskaya) arrangements, a traditional feature of Soviet municipal housing management for funnelling tenants' requests. The most significant innovation in this respect is the network arrangement known as ODS (Ob'edinennaya dispecherskaya sistema) which cities such as Moscow and Leningrad are installing in every 'mikrorayon' estate. This includes direct telephone links to the office from the entrance-halls of all blocks of flats. Blekh points to the significant economic advantages which these arrangements can offer, for example in reducing wastage of water because of leaks (where he puts the saving at no less than 75%), avoiding duplication of maintenance work, and the reduced risk of major fires.[46]

Tenant involvement in management issues is largely advisory. Block committees are a common feature, and apparently can be quite influential in their representations to the municipality about issues of concern to the residents. (In housing owned and managed by employers, they operate through the trade unions.) In addition to their advisory function, they may have some executive responsibilities, for example to deal with some repairs.[47]

As the current 'perestroika' process is revealing elsewhere in the Soviet economy, a shortage of people with management training and skills has long been a barrier to greater efficiency in the management and maintenance of housing. Housing staff are thinner on the ground, and of lower calibre than most other workers.[48] Although they more than doubled in numbers between 1965 and 1985, from 1,321,000 to 2,834,000, the urban living area for which they are responsible more than trebled. Blekh calculates a current staff shortfall of 22%. He also notes an over-representation of women and older workers among housing staff. Housing workers are markedly less well qualified that the average, and their pay which stood at 91% of the service sector average in 1965 had fallen to 80% of the service sector average by 1985 (which in itself is well below the national average). It is therefore not surprising that there is a particularly high turnover among housing staff, and that this and their generally low morale is considered to be a major reason for inefficient housing management.

Employers

As was shown in Table 5.6, overall, employers own the majority of the urban rented accommodation nationally. However, the proportions vary greatly from place to place, and in Moscow and Leningrad in particular, the municipal sector is by far the largest. According to figures supplied by the respective city councils, 65.4% of the Moscow housing stock belongs to the municipality, with 24.5% belonging to employers, while in Leningrad, 70.8% of the stock belongs to the municipality, and only 10.4% to employers (with a further 4.4% in the process of being transferred to the municipality). It is therefore not surprising that employers in Leningrad have an arrangement to buy nomination rights from the city council. Conversely, cities and towns where the local economy is dominated by a very few employers, as for example Togliatti with its car-assembly plant, tend to have the bulk of their housing owned by employers.

Mainly because their primary purpose is to run a business or service organisation, and their allegiance is to the republic or national government rather than to the local community, employers are demonstrably less interested than municipalities in the standard of their housing provision and in its maintenance. It is a frequent complaint that enterprises are unwilling to shoulder their responsibility to provide for the social and transport infrastructure. To quote Kudryavtsev:

> The managements of enterprises are sometimes very reluctant to finance the development of communal amenities and services, building of utility networks and thoroughfares (which, incidentally, is why the kindergarten in our neighbourhood was 'overlooked').

He goes on to cite other examples.[49]

The space standards in housing owned by employers are lower than in the municipal sector. On average, the total floor area per person in housing provided by employers is 14.6 square metres, compared with 15.7 square metres in municipal housing.[50] It is also in poorer physical condition, with 3.1% unfit, compared with 2.3% of municipal housing.[51] Employers' housing also scores significantly worse than municipal housing in terms of all the main amenities.[52]

There is also clear evidence that employers are considerably less efficient than municipalities in the management and maintenance of their stock. Blekh shows that their ability to generate income from their landlord activities - rent collection, leasing of shops and other facilities, and the like - in 1985 was significantly below that of the municipalities, while their expenditure on management, maintenance and repairs was higher in all respects, and had got worse over the years.[53]

To a great extent, this is because of the fragmented and dispersed nature of much of their stock. Gregory Andrusz calculates that in the Russian Federative Republic in 1980, employers had 21,000 offices in comparison with 3,000 municipal offices, but with only twice as much stock to manage and maintain. It is generally accepted in the Soviet Union that a multitude of offices means worse rather than better service.

In 1957 and 1967, legislation was passed to promote the housing role of the municipalities against that of employers. In part, this move may have been intended to resolve the persistently tense relationships between employers and municipalities about the blurred demarcation line between them on nomination rights to each other's housing. However, the main motive behind this shift in policy was undoubtedly to achieve more effective and economical management and maintenance of the employers' housing stock.

In the event, little progress has been made in transferring housing owned by employers to the municipalities. Over recent years in Moscow, no more than 2% of the employers' stock has changed hands, while nationally in 1985, only 1.4% of the total area of the employers' stock was transferred.[54] It is sometimes suggested that this is partly because the municipalities are unwilling to take over housing which manifestly has a substantial backlog of maintenance and repair,[55] and anyone who has been involved in the 1980 transfer of GLC housing to the London boroughs will recognise the relevance of such concerns. However, it is just as likely that inertia and reluctance on the part of the employers to lose this attractive bargaining counter in the competition for scarce labour is at least as influential.

Although the municipalities are ultimately responsible for issuing the allocation orders which entitle applicants to housing, it is clear that employers have more discretion to pick and choose their tenants than have the municipalities. They keep their own waiting-lists which are vetted by the trade unions who have a responsibility to see fair play. Significantly, the waiting-list can be used as a management tool. Kudryavtsev refers to waiting-list demotion as a form of sanction against poor performance at work.[56]

House-building cooperatives

As was shown in Section I, house-building cooperatives were put into political hibernation for a quarter of a century after 1937 until they were given new legitimacy under the Cooperative Law of 1 June 1962.

Proposals for cooperatives usually originate at the members' place of work, but it is the responsibility of the municipality to form the cooperatives themselves and to approve their constitutions. The municipalities also retain a right to intervene in the running of cooperatives if they have reason for concern about the efficiency of their management.

They are self-financing, both in terms of capital expenditure and in their management and maintenance accounts. Members often do a substantial proportion of the running repairs and maintenance work, although the municipal repair and maintenance organisations do major capital work and other maintenance if necessary.

House-building cooperatives are usually quite large, assuming responsibility for commissioning and supervising the building of a block of perhaps 200 flats, almost invariably as part of a much bigger estate of rented and other cooperative housing. The main design work is done by the municipal architect's department, and the building work is done by a state construction firm.

In the case of larger cooperatives, their constitution will provide for periodic full-scale meetings of the membership, with day-to-day decisons taken by an elected committee. This level of democratic control is said to be effective in securing completion of the construction work more quickly than in the state rented sector, and in providing for efficient management. It enables cooperatives to decide on higher levels of service than in the state rented sector; for example to appoint and pay for a 'concierge', or to use the skills of members to provide an efficient repairs service. The committee also has a decisive say in the selection of new members put forward by the municipality, and in exerting pressure on members who are socially or financially irresponsible.

Employers - factories, enterprises, ministries and the like - have power to offer their employees support with the capital and running costs of joining a housing cooperative. Where such help is given, it is often in the form of a soft loan to help with the down-payment to the cooperative. This is negotiable, but usually at least 25% of the capital cost. The repayment period is also negotiable, and typically ranges between 10 and 20 years. Interest rates vary between 0.5%

and 3% according to the social status of the borrower, with war veterans for example paying a lower rate.

When the loan is paid off, the member's outgoings are reduced to the rent level which would be paid on a similar flat in the state rented sector (see Section IV). If the member dies, his family can inherit the flat if they are already living there. In the case of other disposals - normally when the member moves to another town - it is a matter for the cooperative to find a new member, and the previous member receives a refund of his capital outlay. However, under the economic reforms now under discussion, the government is looking at the possibility of permitting a market in housing cooperative flats.

Taking the actual example of a two-room Moscow flat of 32 square metres, plus kitchen, bathroom and entrance hall, the total cost was 200 roubles per square metre, or 6,400 roubles in all. In this case, with a down-payment of 45% or some 3,000 roubles, the monthly repayments of capital and interest at 2% on the balance over 15 years, together with a contribution of 5 roubles to a sinking fund for eventual capital repairs, come to between 25 and 30 roubles.

This is probably six times the rent of an equivalent flat in the state rented sector, and is no doubt a major reason for the slow growth of the cooperative sector despite its obvious benefits. Cost was cited as the reason why the 'typical family' described in *Moscow News* (see above) could not consider moving into a cooperative. However, it is important to recognise that perceptions of 'opportunity costs' are far from similar in east and west Europe. People who in west Europe would be on quite low take-home pay are often surprisingly well-off in the USSR. Most wives work, and some employees manage to hold down two jobs. Moreover, as noted elsewhere, in an economy which despite its low - by western European standards - average wage of about 200 roubles a month, still offers limited scope for satisfying consumer demands, savings ratios are high, and parents are often willing to contribute their savings towards the down-payment if it means getting their own flat to themselves.

In practice, the opportunity to jump the long housing queue seems to be the main motivation for joining a cooperative. As will be seen, cooperative members can also enjoy better space standards than tenants in the state rented sector who are allocated housing according to tightly drawn rules about their entitlement to living space. However, the standard of the accommodation itself between the two sectors in terms of amenity and finish is identical.

It should also be borne in mind that with interest rates as low as they are in the Soviet Union, in the long run the housing cooperative member is little worse off financially. Eventually, he or his family are refunded their capital outlay.

Although membership of a housing cooperative depends on the ability to afford the down-payment and considerably higher monthly outgoings than in the state rented sector, it is widely held that they are not socially divisive. This view is borne out by the difficulty for an outsider at least in identifying on a visit to an estate which blocks - and their occupants - belong to cooperatives, and which are in the state rented sector. As will be seen, blocks belonging to housing cooperatives seem to fit broadly into the same social pecking order as the estates on which they are situated, which we will be considering later in this chapter.

Well established and officially encouraged though they are in the housing structure of the Soviet Union, housing cooperatives have so far made only a limited impact. Table 5.2 puts their share of the urban housing stock at 6%, while Table 5.4 shows that since they were resuscitated in the 1960s, their contribution to the new-build programme has hovered about this level, though it has been significantly higher in such cities as Moscow and Leningrad where they account for 8% and 10% of the stock respectively. Nationally, there are about 25,000 house-building cooperatives.[57]

As has already been indicated, this is no doubt partly because of the substantial down-payment which cooperative members have to put down, and the higher monthly payments than for normal renting, both of which may conflict with the individual's aspirations towards car-ownership in particular. However, despite central government policies to promote cooperatives, it is clear from conversations with members of cooperatives, and with local government officials, that the latter are still not altogether enthusiastic in their support for new cooperative ventures.

The role of central government

As indicated at the beginning of this section, the central - USSR - government is responsible for the overall planning of the housing construction programme, and in consequence for making the financial resources available. The overall body responsible for state planning, including the development of the Five-Year Plans, is

'Gosplan', while the construction part of the plans is the responsibility of the main central State construction organisation, 'Gosstroi'. Resource allocation within the plans is being increasingly devolved to the individual republics, who deal with the municipalities and employers.

Since the 1970s, there has been a clear trend to give the municipalities greater influence in the direction of housing resources, not least because of the way in which resources going to employers have traditionally been re-directed to other purposes. Housing finance allocated to employers is now earmarked to be used for the designated housing purposes.

As part of a long-standing succession of attempts to improve the quality of mass housing and to achieve greater economy in its construction and subsequent maintenance, in 1963 the Soviet government set up a national organisation 'Gosgrazhdanstroi' (the State Committee on Civil Construction and Architecture) under Gosstroi. Gosgrazhdanstroi, recently renamed 'Goskomarkhitektury' or State Committee for Architecture, is primarily concerned with the development of cost-effective construction methods for the wide variety of climate, building conditions, and housing needs which are to be found across the Soviet Union.

Gosgrazhdanstroi research and development work - which includes economic and urban planning as well as architectural design and building methods - is done at seven institutes situated in various parts of the country. These institutes provide planning advice and design services to municipalities and construction enterprises, and in several cases, such as the car manufacturing town of Togliatti, have taken on the entire green-fields development of new towns and cities.

IV Finance

Capital provision

As explained in the previous section, finance for new housebuilding and major capital repairs and renovation work by the municipalities and employers alike comes in the form of budget allocations from the central government through the appropriate republic government. Although some of this capital is raised in the form of loans from the state construction bank (Stroibank), and (in the case of employers' housing) some is provided by the employers, for practical purposes, the servicing of the debt is handled by the government and affects neither the landlord organisation nor the tenant directly.

Nor does the availability of capital finance appear to be a major concern in Soviet housing circles. Although officials inevitably list it in conversation as a constraint on their activity, they usually regard it as less important than the availability of the necessary physical resources, the capacity of the local construction enterprise, the DSK, to provide the labour and materials, and the capacity of the local transport system to cope with the development of the project and to serve its residents subsequently.

The main problem posed by the capital financing of the housing programme has been and remains the soaring cost of new-build construction. To a great extent, this is due to the steady improvement in space standards which has taken place throughout the post-revolutionary period. Table 5.7 shows the amount of state capital investment in rented and house-building cooperative housing between 1918 and 1986, together with the available information about the number of flats built and their average size. Although the calculations of average costs per flat and per square metre are bound to be unreliable within each time span, they show a clear trend - after an aberration at the start of the series - not only towards dearer unit costs through increasing size standards, but also to escalating costs of construction.

The reduction in costs per square metre in the late 1950s and early 1960s is coincided with a decline in space standards at that time. It is indeed probable that the move towards standardised low-rise communal housing of basic standard in the early post-war years did lead to some economies at the time (although, as is now beginning to emerge, leading to high remedial costs for later generations).

The remorseless increase since then is due to a variety of causes. As the Table demonstrates, higher space standards are not the whole story, although it should be noted that ceiling heights have risen significantly as well as floor areas. The quality of provision has also improved, with particular attention being given to sound insulation.   However, there are frequent allegations that the escalating costs are due in part to expensive materials which architects are using unnecessarily for aesthetic reasons.

Table 5.7: Total capital investment (at comparative prices) in rented and house-building cooperative housing, with numbers and sizes of flats, from the 6th to the 11th Five-Year Plan (FYP)

	Capital investment (Rm²) (R)	Number of flats (k)	Average cost per flat (R)	Average area (m²)	Average cost per square metre
6th FYP					
(1956-60)	33,183	5,126	6,473	43.7	148.1
Of which, 1960	8,066	1,331	6,060	41.9	144.6
7th FYP					
(1961-65)	42,635	7,319	5,825	41.1	141.7
Of which, 1965	9,326	1,511	6,172	41.8	147.7
8th FYP					
(1966-70)	59,906	8,141	7,359	43.3	169.9
Of which, 1970	13,629	1,723	7,910	44.5	177.8
9th FYP					
(1971-75)	76,715	8,859	8,660	46.0	188.3
Of which, 1975	16,402	1,778	9,225	46.8	197.1
10th FYP					
(1976-80)	87,487	8,388	10,430	49.4	211.1
Of which, 1980	18,195	1,667	10,915	50.4	216.6
11th FYP					
(1981-85)	106,258	8,274	12,842	52.8	243.2
Of which, 1985	22,919	1,638	13,992	54.1	258.6
1986	25,355	1,743	14,547	54.2	268.4

Source: Constructed from pp 510 and 514 of *Narodnoye Khozyaistvo SSSR za 70 let 1917-1987*

Nonetheless, the standard of finishing by the construction enterprises is notoriously inadequate, leading to significant capital repair payments by the landlord organisations - ultimately at state expense - at 4% of the cost of the building.[58] This is despite a guarantee period which was extended from one year to two years in the 1970s precisely to provide an incentive to better quality control. Moreover, the tenants themselves typically need to pay between 700 and 900 roubles (about four times the average monthly income) to put right defects when they move into new flats.[59]

264 The Soviet Union

Despite the claimed savings in notional land and foundation costs with high-rise building, it is clear that the construction costs of the high-rise panel systems which now account for the majority of state new-build housing are considerably higher than was housing built with the older traditional construction methods. In part, this is no doubt because industrial building systems are proving to be intrinsically more costly, not least with the need to install lifts and other facilities such as refuse chutes which were not needed in low-rise housing. However, as Gregory Andrusz argues, the chronic labour shortage in the construction industry and the high turnover as people take jobs on building sites almost literally as a passport to living in the big cities, has been a major contributory factor to housing costs, and one which is readily accepted informally by Soviet housing experts.[60]

In addition to this cost escalation in new construction work, in recent years, the Soviet government has also increasingly had to come to terms with the cost of renovation work needed on old housing - particularly the pre-revolutionary stock in the city centres, much of which has so far been used as communal flats. Close behind comes the older housing built since the Revolution, especially the cramped and unpopular low-rise walk-up flat blocks of the 1950s and 1960s. Coping with the cost of modernising housing which is less often physically defective than out of tune with present-day expectations (suffering from 'moral obsolescence' in Soviet terminology) is now recognised as one of the major financial challenges facing the country.

Kudryavtsev refers to state expenditure of 2,500 million roubles in 1982 on capital repairs to a total of 70 million square metres of housing, and claims that the modernisation of the five-storey stock will add greatly to this expenditure.[61] In discussion, Gosgrazhdanstroi officials put the annual current expenditure on capital repairs at 4,000 million roubles, for 60 million square metres of housing.

Some of the cost of the social and communal infrastructure to which Section III refers may be met out of the national 'social budget' (Obshchestvenniye fondy potrebleniya) which provides for such services as education, health and social security. In the case of employers' housing, such facilities can also be topped up from the profits of the enterprises, although as we have seen, such housing tends in practice to be worse off in this respect than that belonging to the municipalities. In 1986, the social fund amounted to the equivalent of 554 roubles per person, or (at an average of 989 roubles per worker) the equivalent of nearly half the average annual wage.

Income and expenditure

The social budget is also responsible for meeting the increasing deficit in the national housing revenue account. As shown at the beginning of this section, the cost of servicing capital expenditure on new construction or major repairs is excluded from the equation (apart from a small contribution to a sinking fund towards the cost of future major repairs, which in 1985 amounted to 1.5% of total management and maintenance costs).[62] The sharply rising trend of state expenditure to cover this deficit between income from rent and other sources on the one hand, and management and maintenance expenditure on the other is shown in Table 5.8. In total, it has risen from 100 million roubles in 1940 to 9,800 million roubles in 1986, or by 10 times per square metre, while its share of the total social budget has risen by nearly three times.

Table 5.8: State subsidies to the running cost of rented housing

	1940	1960	1970	1980	1985	1986
Total subsidy (Rm)	100	1300	3400	6900	9300	9800
Area of rented stock (million m²)	267*	583*	1072*+	1969	2414	2507
Subsidy per square metre (R)	0.4*	2.2*	3.2*	3.5	3.9	3.9
Share of social budget (%)	2.2	4.8	5.3	5.9	6.3	6.3

Notes: * Figures of total area for 1940, 1960 and 1970 exclude rural rented stock. The subsidy per square metre for these years was therefore marginally lower than the figures given in the Table.
+ Figure taken from 1977 Yearbook, which is revised downwards from 1132 in 1972 Yearbook.

Source: Constructed from p 641 of *Narodnoye Khozyaistvo SSSR 1958*; p 544 of *Narodnoye Khozyaistvo SSSR 1972*; p 496 of *Narodnoye Khozyaistvo SSSR za 60 let 1917-1977*; and pp 435 and 517 of *Narodnoye Khozyaistvo SSSR za 70 let 1917-1987*

The main cause of this escalating deficit has been the virtual freezing of rent levels since 1928, though this has been exacerbated by the outdated method for calculating rents. At the same time, management and maintenance costs have risen considerably despite the downwards pressure on the numbers of housing workers and their wages, which is described in Section III.

Rent levels vary slightly from one republic to another, and between towns and cities of different sizes. The overall range is between 3.0 and 4.4 kopeks (1 rouble = 100 kopeks) per month per square metre of 'living area'. 'Living area' excludes kitchens, bathrooms, entrance halls and built-in cupboard space. At current levels of income, rent payments (including the costs of services, see below) typically come to less than 3% of family incomes, compared with an intended 10% when they were originally fixed 60 years ago.[63]

As Blekh puts it with conscious understatement, "The existing arrangements for determining rent levels are not without their contradictions". The criterion of 'living area' was introduced at a time when the great majority of families were sharing such facilities as bathrooms, kitchens and other common areas of communal flats. Thus, with the great shift which has now taken place towards a separate flat for each family, most people now enjoy these expensive facilities at no cost. Nor is there any difference between rents in old unimproved property and those in modernised or new flats.

Moreover, when space standards are increased - as happened for example in the Russian Federative Republic in 1984, when they went up from 9 to 12 square metres per person - the total rent goes down as tenants cease to be liable to pay the marginal rent level of about three times the standard level on any space which they occupy above their entitlement. Finally, as suggested above, rent levels themselves have remained virtually unchanged for sixty years, while average incomes have multiplied by a factor of more than six.

It is therefore not surprising that despite the obvious political sensitivities about the long cherished policy of low rents, there is now considerable discussion in the press and in everyday conversation about the increasing anomaly of the existing level and structure of rents.

Landlord organisations have been able to increase their charges for utilities - mainly, heating, water (including hot water), and electricity - but these are still provided at greatly less than their cost. For example, tenants get their electricity and water at about 10% of their cost, and as suggested in Section III, are profligate in their use.[64] The cost of providing utilities nearly doubled - from 1.88 roubles to 3.4 roubles per square metre - between 1965 and 1985.[65] In the same period, charges for these services rose from 0.09 roubles to 0.73 roubles, leaving a substantial gap to be filled.[66]

Landlord organisations have a third source of income in the form of leasehold payments by organisations which lease accommodation in housing blocks. For the most part, these are state shops serving the local community, but they also include offices. Municipal landlord organisations derive more of their income from leaseholders than do employers, but it is a declining share, as is shown in Table 5.9 which summarises their sources of income between 1965 and 1985.

Table 5.9: Sources of annual income of municipal landlord organisations, 1965-1985 (Roubles per square metre, and percentages)

	1965 R/m²	%	1970 R/m²	%	1975 R/m²	%	1980 R/m²	%	1985 R/m²	%
Rent	1.52	60.4	1.58	54.5	1.64	54.2	1.68	53.3	1.59	50.0
Utilities	0.09	3.6	0.40	13.9	0.48	15.9	0.60	19.1	0.73	23.0
Lease holders	0.90	35.9	0.92	31.7	0.91	30.0	0.87	27.6	0.86	27.0
Total	2.51	100.0	2.90	100.0	3.03	100.0	3.15	100.0	3.18	100.0

Source: E M Blekh, *Povysheniye effektivnosti ekspluatatsii zhilikh zdani'*, Table 17, p 102

Kudryavtsev offers the other side of the coin from his own personal circumstances.[67] As a tenant of an untypically large Moscow flat with a 'living area' which works out at 80 square metres (and a kitchen of 10.5 square metres), his family of four pays a basic rent of 7.40 roubles per month. Before the 1984 increase in space standards in the Russian Federative Republic, his rent was 8.50 roubles. Central heating costs 3.20 roubles, hot and cold water cost 2.40 roubles, the telephone costs 2.50 roubles, and electricity - mainly because the family's cooking is by electricity rather than gas - costs on average about 6.00 roubles per month.

Expenditure on management and maintenance increased between 1965 and 1985 by a factor of 3.7 in all, although a large part of the increase was due to the growth in the size of the stock. Table 5.10 gives a breakdown of expenditure per square metre over this period, which shows the costs of management personnel remaining roughly static, while the costs of maintenance activity such as sweeping, grass-cutting, snow-clearing and refuse removal rose by about three-quarters, and running repair costs more than doubled. Apparently, a large part of the additional expenditure is due to the special problems of managing and maintaining high-rise blocks and their surrounding area, with lift repairs and grounds maintenance as prominent items.

Table 5.10: Annual management and maintenance expenditure, 1965-1985 (Roubles per square metre and percentages)

	1965		1970		1975		1980		1985	
	R/m²	%	R/m²	%	R/m²	%	R/m²	%	R/m²	%
Administr-ative staff and workers	0.76	29.3	0.94	32.9	0.90	30.4	1.05	32.7	1.03	30.4
Local services	0.36	13.9	0.37	12.9	0.42	12.2	0.48	14.9	0.59	17.4
Running repairs	0.72	27.8	1.13	39.5	1.29	43.6	1.45	45.2	1.54	45.4
Other	0.75	28.9	0.42	14.7	0.35	11.8	0.23	7.2	0.23	6.8
Total	2.59	100.0	2.86	100.0	2.96	100.0	3.21	100.0	3.39	100.0

Source: E M Blekh, *Povysheniye effektivnosti ekspluatatsii zhilikh zdani'*, Table 22, p 114

Comparison of the line showing rent income in Table 5.9 with the total of management and maintenance expenditure in Table 5.10 demonstrates vividly the growing gap between the two. By 1985, management and maintenance costs were more than twice rent income. Moreover, as Table 5.9 also shows, the income from leaseholders is declining, while it has already been shown that the landlord organisations make further losses from the provision of utilities. It is therefore hardly surprising that the subsidy to cover the gap on the revenue account in 1985 amounted to a massive 9,800 million roubles, or the equivalent of 3.85 roubles per square metre of the rented and house-building cooperative stock (the latter do not receive subsidy but are not disaggregated in the statistics).[68] As a note in the 1987 *Statistical Yearbook* points out, altogether tenants pay less than a quarter of the actual cost of managing and maintaining their homes. This is apparently taking major maintenance work into account as well as day-to-day work as shown in Table 5.10.

There have been several attempts over the years to contain costs, and as has been shown in Section III, some far-reaching attempts have been made to introduce more cost-effective management structures. In Section VII, we will consider the scope which has been identified for reducing losses through rent arrears and empty dwellings. However, despite the savings which are undoubtedly possible on the supply side, there is a clear mood in housing circles and among the general populace that after six decades of frozen rents, rent increases and new rent structures cannot now be long delayed.

V   The buildings

Age profile and condition

As Tables 5.3, 5.4, and 5.5 in Section II show, the state rented sector is in volume terms very much a phenomenon of the post-war years. It can be reliably estimated that in 1986, some 90% of the rented (and house-building cooperative) stock - both overall and in urban areas - had been built in the last three decades.

This estimate assumes that of the roughly 10 million square metres of housing which since the mid-1960s have annually been the subject of demolition programmes, a considerable proportion consists of stock which was municipalised or hastily constructed in the early post-revolutionary period.[69]

As in the United Kingdom, although less so elsewhere, there has been a substantial clearance programme of older housing either because it was dilapidated beyond recall or to fit in with contemporary ideas of town planning, and often for both these reasons. Moreover, as was shown in Section I, some 70 million square metres of housing was lost during the Second World War.

Nonetheless, even if the present pre-revolutionary and early post-revolutionary stock is a relatively minute proportion - certainly less than a twentieth part - of the area of the present rented stock as a whole, the changing trend towards refurbishment rather than replacement over recent years has caused technical and economic headaches in the Soviet Union which are far from unfamiliar in western Europe.

This housing consists predominantly of blocks of brick-built construction between two and five storeys in height, and which is physically in poor condition to the extent that some of it is having to be demolished.[70] Much of it has been used as communal flats, which are increasingly unpopular. The city of Moscow has set up an institute with the task of drawing up plans for modernising this stock where it is economic to do so. As suggested in Section IV, work is already underway on some of the pre-revolutionary stock, though at high cost.

The second generation of rented housing which is causing concern consists of walk-up blocks, mostly five storeys in height, the majority of which is stock built in the early 1950s although some was built in the 1930s, again mostly of brick and much of it of fundamentally solid, if unattractive, construction. This is another small part of the stock, again certainly less than a twentieth of the rented stock as a whole. It too is often in poor physical condition, and lacking in amenities. Because it is of non-standardised design, it is often difficult to modernise or convert into individual flats. Its future too is therefore questionable.

The third generation consists broadly of the stock built during the Sixth and Seventh Five-Year Plans, that is in the late 1950s and early 1960s. At over a fifth of the present rented stock, it is a matter of much greater concern. Like the previous category, it consists predominantly of walk-up blocks of five storeys, but built according to standard designs, usually of brick. Levels of amenity are mostly high, but the quality of construction was generally poor. The rehabilitation and modernisation of this stock is seen as a high priority,[71] but it is accepted that a sizeable proportion is beyond recall and will need to be demolished.

The mid-1960s saw a fundamental change in housing design with the advent of industrialised building systems. Over 70% of the 1986 urban rented stock was built after 1965, and probably more in Moscow (where 87% of the stock was built between 1960 and 1985).[72] In 1970, large panel systems already accounted for 38% of urban house-building, and the national building institute TsNIIEP Zhilishcha which comes under Gosgrazhdanstroi (see Section III) predicts that by the end of the century, the proportion will rise to three-quarters. In the mid-1980s, about 55% of the urban rented stock was basically of brick-built construction, with the remainder constructed in various forms of industrialised systems, with about 30% of the whole in large panel systems.[73]

The last two decades have therefore changed the face of the urban landscape, not only on the peripheries of all the major towns and cities, but also within many urban areas, where high-density medium and high-rise housing estates have replaced much of the traditional low-rise housing.

The apparently uninterrupted rings of high-rise estates around such cities as Moscow and Leningrad are the most conspicuous feature of this systems-building boom of the last two decades. Typically, such housing is in long blocks of varying heights in the range between 10 and 16 storeys. Like their counterparts in France and the German Federal Republic, but unlike some Dutch and a large part of the British flatted stock, modern Soviet blocks of flats have lifts serving a few flats on each landing. Balcony, corridor and deck access is rare. Entryphone systems also seem to be unknown, although some blocks have lockable main doors.

Despite the enthusiasm with which Soviet architects and planners have embraced high-rise building, low and medium-rise building - often also using industrialised systems - has continued, particularly in the towns and smaller cities. They are also used sometimes to add variety to what is readily acknowledged to be the monotonous sky-lines of unbroken high-rise developments in the larger cities. In 1985, the average height of the urban stock had reached 6.2 storeys, having risen annually by 1.2% since 1970, while the average height of the Moscow stock in 1984 was 8.9 storeys, a rise of 35% since 1971.[74] This is an even more remarkable change for anyone who can still remember the Moscow of 1910 when 91% of Moscow's housing was single-storey.[75] Table 5.11 gives the current height profile of the Moscow stock.

Table 5.11: Height by number of storeys of Moscow housing stock

Number of storeys	Percentage of stock
1-2	0.3
3-5	25.8
6-9	33.4
>9	40.5

Source: Figures provided by Moscow city council

The clear relationship between height and age is shown by Table 5.12 which gives the age profile of the Moscow stock.

Table 5.12: Age of the Moscow housing stock

Age	Percentage of stock
Pre-1918	4.0
1918-1940	3.7
1941-1965	30.1
Post-1965	62.2

Source: Figures provided by Moscow city council

The Soviet view of the economic and social advantages of high-rise housing have already been cited in Section IV - lower land and foundation costs, lower infrastructure costs, and greater proximity to work, shops and communal facilities. Town planners and architects also often cite aesthetic benefits, though - as suggested above - they and others are not unaware of the risk of monotony.

However, increasing experience of the management and maintenance costs of high-rise housing has raised question marks about it as a panacea. It has been calculated that each 1% addition to the number of storeys increases management and maintenance costs by 0.1%, while each 1% increase in the 'equipment index' (in practice, lifts, rubbish chutes, and electric - as against gas - cookers) adds a further 0.7% to management and maintenance costs.[76]

Thus, while the current repair costs of this latest generation of housing are - at 0.11 roubles per square metre per year - lower overall than for the older generations of housing described above, the differences are not all that great when the relative ages are taken into account. For example, housing built in the late 1950s and early 1960s costs 0.13 roubles per square metre per year in current repairs, while the oldest housing costs 0.32 roubles. Moreover, some elements in the modern housing, such as doors and windows, electrical equipment, and walls are proportionately more costly to maintain than in the older property. The joints between panels give particular problems, not least in extreme winter conditions.[77]

It is therefore not surprising that even without the open public (if not always tenant) disillusionment with high-rise housing in much of western Europe, Soviet housing authorities have ceased to regard ever higher buildings as a panacea for their housing problems. By the late 1970s, the enthusiasm was already on the wane, and since 1981, new house-building of over 9 storeys in height has been restricted to Moscow (where the average height of new housing blocks in 1988 was still 16.5 storeys), Leningrad and Kiev.[79] Even in Moscow, the high-rise policy is being questioned. An article in Moskovskaya Pravda in May 1988 contains criticism by a local housing official of the prevalence of blocks 16 to 22 storeys high, which he claims are being built to suit the interests of the providers rather than those of the community.[80]

Size

As was noted in Section IV, the average size of flats has tended to grow since the beginning of the 1960s, although those built in the early years of this period were rather smaller than their predecessors. This increase in size coincides with the transition to industrialised building methods which began at this time.

In the **rented sector**, the proportion of one-room (that is, living room and bedroom) flats increased slightly between 1971 and 1986, and the proportion of flats with three and more rooms increased considerably (see Table 5.13). On the other hand, the proportion of two-room flats went down even more significantly. These changes can be associated with demographic trends which will be examined in greater detail in Section VI. In essence they show an overall increase in the number of births from 1970, with an increase in families with three or more children from 1980 (though with considerable variations between the different republics). Divorce has also been on the increase, with the rate doubling between 1960 and 1970, and continuing to increase until 1980 since when it has fallen slightly.[81]

The trend in the sizes of house-building **cooperative** flats has been significantly different. Overall, cooperative flats tend to be rather larger than rented flats, which as was shown in Section II, is one of the attractions of this sector. In contrast with the rented sector, the proportion of one-room flats has fallen rather than increased, and while the proportion of two-room flats has fallen as well, it has done so less sharply than in the rented sector. The increasing trend in flats with three and more rooms is greater in the cooperative than in the rented sector. At first sight, these differences in trend suggest that cooperatives tend to cater for families with children rather than couples or single people. This may well be the case. However, they may also suggest simply that smaller households are using the cooperative form of tenure as a way of improving their living standards. Possible differences between tenants in the rented and cooperative sectors will be considered further in Section VI. Table 5.13 gives a breakdown of the sizes (by number of rooms) of rented and cooperative flats built between 1971 and 1986.

Table 5.13: Sizes of flats by number of rooms - built in the rented and house-building cooperative sectors 1971-1986

	Number of flats built (thousands)	1-room (%)	2-room (%)	3-room (%)	>3-room (%)
Rented sector					
8th FYP 1971-75	6,936	19	45	31	5
Of which, 1975	1,388	19	43	33	5
9th FYP 1976-80	6,698	19	42	34	5
Of which, 1980	1,348	20	40	34	6
10th FYP 1981-85	6,654	20	38	36	6
Of which, 1985	1,316	20	38	36	6
1986	1,402	20	37	37	6
Cooperatives					
8th FYP 1971-75	667	21	46	29	4
Of which, 1975	114	21	44	31	4
9th FYP 1976-80	512	19	42	34	5
Of which, 1980	94	19	41	34	6
10th FYP 1981-85	580	18	41	35	6
Of which, 1985	137	18	41	35	6
1986	142	18	40	36	6

Source: *Narodnoye Khozyaistvo SSSR za 70 let 1917-1987,* p 511

Table 5.14 gives the floor areas of flats built in the rented and cooperative sectors respectively between 1976 and 1986, showing that the space standards of flats of all types increased over this period, and that cooperative flats generally are larger than rented flats. The almost general progressive decline in 'living area' as a proportion of the total area is a further indication of improved space standards, as it demonstrates an increase in kitchen, bathroom and hall space.

Table 5.14: Floor area of flats in the rented and house-building cooperative sectors 1976-1986

Rented sector	Overall	1-room	2-room	3-room	>3-room
9th FYP 1976-80					
Average area (m²)	51.6	32.4	48.2	62.5	77.9
Proportion of which is 'living space' (%)	63	55	62	66	68
Of which, 1980					
Average area (m²)	52.5	32.9	49.2	63.5	77.5
Proportion of which is 'living space' (%)	62	55	60	65	67
10th FYP 1981-85					
Average area (m²)	54.3	34.1	50.0	65.7	82.2
Proportion of which is 'living space' (%)	61	53	59	64	66
Of which, 1985					
Average area (m²)	55.3	35.0	50.6	66.8	83.1
Proportion of which is 'living space' (%)	60	52	59	63	66
1986					
Average area (m²)	54.4	34.4	50.7	66.7	84.0
Proportion of which is 'living space' (%)	60	52	59	63	65
Cooperatives					
9th FYP 1976-80					
Average area (m²)	53.0	33.1	49.0	64.7	83.4
Proportion of which is 'living space' (%)	62	55	61	64	66
Of which, 1980					
Average area (m²)	54.1	33.5	49.5	65.4	85.6
Proportion of which is 'living space' (%)	61	54	60	63	66
10th FYP 1981-85					
Average area (m²)	55.5	34.6	50.5	66.5	88.4
Proportion of which is 'living space' (%)	60	53	59	63	67
Of which, 1985					
Average area (m²)	55.8	35.1	50.9	66.6	87.5
Proportion of which is 'living space' (%)	60	53	58	63	67
1986					
Average area (m²)	56.2	35.6	51.2	66.5	87.0
Proportion of which is 'living space' (%)	59	52	58	61	65

Source: *Narodnoye Khozyaistvo SSSR za 70 let 1917-1987*, pp 512-513

Amenities

The period between 1970 and 1986 has seen considerable progress in connecting those urban areas which were previously not provided with the basic services to mains water supplies, mains drainage, and gas, while there has been dramatic progress in rural areas. Table 5.15 shows the numbers of communities of different types which were connected to these services at the end of 1970, 1980, 1985 and 1986.

Table 5.15: Number of communities provided with mains water, mains drainage and gas 1970-1986

	1970	1980	1985	1986
Mains water				
Cities and towns	1,787	2,041	2,143	2,157
Urban settlements	2,579	3,294	3,428	3,433
Rural settlements	3,424	7,583	10,722	21,792
Mains drainage				
Cities and towns	1,283	1,647	1,804	1,851
Urban settlements	1,120	1,829	2,090	2,132
Rural settlements	N/A	2,650	3,270	6,345
Gas				
Cities and towns	1,720	2,011	2,095	2,099
Urban settlements	1,866	2,885	3,133	3,184
Rural settlements	38,100	144,500	165,800	169,600

Source: *Narodnoye Khozyaistvo SSSR za 70 let 1917-1987*, pp 521-522

Within the urban rented sector, there has also been a major improvement in the provision of the main amenities, in particular of running hot water (from district heating systems), baths, and gas. Table 5.16 shows progress in providing the rented and house-building cooperative stock in urban areas with the basic amenities between 1970 and 1986.

Table 5.16: **Proportion of urban rented and house-building cooperative stock with basic facilities 1970-1986 (% by total area)**

	1970	1980	1985	1986
Mains water	78.9	89.8	91.8	92.2
Mains drainage	75.8	87.8	89.7	90.2
Central heating	73.6	86.5	88.9	89.3
Gas	64.6	79.4	78.3	78.1
Running hot water	33.8	57.1	71.2	72.4
Baths	60.7	79.9	83.2	84.1

Source: *Narodnoye Khozyaistvo SSSR za 70 let 1917-1987*, p 521

The sharp increase in the proportion of housing with running hot water, baths and gas is clearly because these are standard features of housing built with industrialised building methods, but which were less common in the earlier stock. The slight decline in the proportion of housing equipped with gas since 1980 can probably be attributed to safety considerations, a supposition which is reinforced by a footnote to the table in the Soviet statistical yearbook, pointing out that the number of flats equipped with electric cookers doubled to 5.7 million between 1980 and 1986. Other possible factors are the diversion of gas to export markets in western Europe, and the increased availability of electricity generated in nuclear power stations.

VI   The tenants

Although Soviet statistics provide some valuable information about the population as a whole, there are no disaggregated data by tenure. Nor is there much hard information about relative advantage and disadvantage. There is however some useful information about demographic trends, from which some reasonable inferences can be drawn.

Demographic trends

In Section V, we looked briefly at the relationship between the sizes of flats and recent demographic trends. The period from 1960 to 1986 saw a drop of nearly a quarter in the marriage rate, while the divorce rate nearly trebled. The latter trend may well be associated with the domestic pressures in a society where three generations of the family are often sharing cramped flats. In the same period, the birth-rate, and the number of births, including births of a third or subsequent child, fell and then rose again. However, significantly, the rise in the birth-rate in urban areas was much less pronounced than in rural areas. Mortality rose between 1960 and 1985, but fell back slightly in 1986.

Table 5.17 summarises these trends, which point to a growth in the numbers of one-person households, of larger families, and of older people, all of which are significant for Soviet housing policy.

Table 5.17: Major demographic trends 1960-1986

	1960	1970	1980	1985	1986
Marriages (per 1,000 population)	12.1	9.7	10.3	9.8	9.8
Divorces (per 1,000 population)	1.3	2.6	3.5	3.4	3.4
Births (per 1,000 population)	24.9	17.4	18.3	19.4	20.0
Of which, in urban areas	21.9	16.4	17.0	17.4	17.9
Deaths (per 1,000 population)	7.1	8.2	10.3	10.6	9.8
Natural increase (per 1,000 population)	17.8	9.2	8.0	8.8	10.2
Births (thousands)	5,341	4,226	4,851	5,374	5,611
Of which, third or subsequent child	1,857	1,334	1,070	1,344	1,453
Third or subsequent births as % of all	35	32	22	25	26

Source: *Narodnoye Khozyaistvo SSSR za 70 let 1917-1987*, **pp 404 and 405**

As was noted in Section I, population growth rates vary considerably geographically, from between 4.0 and 6.6 per thousand of the population in two of the Baltic republics to between

28.5 and 35.2 in the Central Asian republics. The national average in 1986 was 10.2.[82]

Further demographic information is provided by the numbers of mothers receiving special allowances because they have large families. After declining from the high levels of over three million such families which existed between the 1950s and 1970s, they seem to have stabilised at about two million in the 1980s. However, as Table 5.18 shows, the number of four-child families is now on the increase.

Table 5.18: Number of mothers receiving allowances for large families 1950-1986

	1950	1970	1980	1985	1986
Total	3,079	3,211	2,150	1,941	1,953
Of which,					
four-child families	1,449	1,172	717	794	818
five-child families	839	782	472	431	444
six-child families	440	546	325	266	262
>six-child families	351	711	636	450	429

Source: *Narodnoye Khozyaistvo SSSR za 70 let 1917-1987*, p 437

The housing authorities are becoming increasingly aware of the cumulative effect of these various demographic trends on their housing policies. An article in *Moskovskaya Pravda* discussing Moscow's housing plans up to the year 2000 talks of the growing numbers of single-person and 'complex' families - for example, those consisting of a mother and son, or a sister and brother - which now account for 43% of all Moscow families. As a result, the existing two-room stock is being used inefficiently.[83]

Social disadvantagement

Information about single parent families has not been published separately since 1965, at which time, the numbers had been falling steadily since the late 1950s, mostly no doubt because families bereaved in the war were now growing up. In 1965, there were 1,595,000 single mothers,[84] compared with 3,286,000 in 1958.[85] The only present indicator is the level of payments to large and single parent families which appear as a combined figure in the 1987 *Statistical Yearbook*. These payments fell from 500 million roubles in 1960 to 300 million roubles in 1980 before rising again to 600 million roubles in 1985 and 1986. Although these figures provide no conclusive evidence about the trend in the number of single parent families, they suggest an increase rather than a decrease. It may also be significant that the 1980 figures for social security payments include for the first time an allowance for children in 'deprived families' (na detei maloobespechennym sem'yam). This totalled 1,100 million roubles in 1980, and 1,000 million roubles in 1985 and 1986.

As noted above, little information is available to assess other forms of social disadvantagement. Officially, unemployment was eradicated in the early 1930s, having fallen from 1,576,000 in 1928 to 1,081,000 in early 1930 and 240,000 in late 1930.[87] Indeed, whatever the inefficiencies in the deployment of labour, the Soviet Union still suffers from a shortage of workers.

Similarly, although homelessness officially does not exist, privately it is readily acknowledged that quite apart from the vagrants who are recognised as a social problem, large numbers of people lack any accommodation which they could reasonably describe as home. Indeed, although they are unquantified, the concept of people 'with no fixed abode' is so well ingrained in Soviet society that they are known by the acronym of the Russian term, 'BOMZh' (Bez opredelennogo mesta zhitel'stva). It is also worth noting that the number of gypsies - who form a recognised national group - rose from 132,000 in 1959 to 175,000 in 1970, and to 209,000 in 1977; it may well be that these figures include some who would be classified as homeless in this country.

As Gregory Andrusz emphasises, from pre-war days, the interests of women have played an important part in Soviet housing policy, and it is probably no exaggeration to include them among the socially disadvantaged. Although according to the statistical table,[88] men and women spend exactly the same time at their paid work, women on average spend over three hours each working day on shopping and housework, compared with less than an hour spent by men on these activities. Inadequacies in the social and communal infrastructure, and in the design and amenity levels of flats, therefore bear particularly hard on women, and it has traditionally been an explicit part of Soviet housing policy to look after their interests.

In discussing social advantage and disadvantage, it is important to bear in mind the importance of geographical location in the Soviet Union. Although there are also advantages in living on the land, the rural population is in many ways significantly worse provided for than are city dwellers. Furthermore, those who live in small and medium-sized towns fare worse than those living in the large cities. Those who live in the 'closed' cities or who volunteer to work on the new projects in Siberia enjoy compensating benefits, such as better infrastructure, cultural and recreational facilities, housing, and career prospects.

Social stratification and tenure

As far as tenure is concerned, Soviet housing specialists and laymen insist that there are no social distinctions between sectors, and therefore that house-building cooperatives for example, are in no way the preserve of, say, the intelligentsia. Nonetheless, some broad generalisations can be made with reasonable confidence, based on the available statistical data and on personal observation and discussion.

In doing so, it should be borne in mind that Soviet perceptions of relative social status are by no means the same as those in western Europe (where too, there are great differences in attitude towards different jobs from one country to another).

Notwithstanding the absence of social data broken down by tenure, and the no doubt justifiable claims of Soviet authorities that there is no social discrimination in the allocation of housing, it is reasonable to suppose that pecking orders do exist, though in a less marked and discernible way than is usually the case in western Europe. Indeed, as has already been noted, municipal rented housing caters for marginalised social groups as well as those in full-time employment, while employers - almost by definition - cater for their own workers and so are able to avoid taking the poorer tenants.

As will be seen in Section VII, Soviet housing estates acquire just as clear a good or bad image among the population as do their western counterparts, and it is hard to think that those with social leverage will readily accept accommodation on an unpopular estate. Conversely, those with least leverage such as migrant workers will tend to find themselves in hostels. For example, quoting unofficial reports of an incident in the Pechatniki district of south Moscow on 20 February 1988, *The Independent* speaks of a clash between a gang of Russians and migrant workers from Soviet Central Asia living in hostel accommodation. The increasing need to bring in workers from the non-Russian republics and from further afield - for example, Vietnamese refugees - for the large construction projects in cities such as Moscow and Leningrad and elsewhere in the European republics can only fuel such potential racial conflicts.

House-building cooperatives

It is clear that there are no social bars to membership of house-building cooperatives. However, as individuals who are members will testify, a considerable degree of persistence and resilience can be needed on the part of members, not only to persuade the authorities to register the cooperative, but also to get the housing built. Members of house-building cooperatives also need to display more commitment to the efficient management and upkeep of their housing than may be the case with residents in state rented accommodation.

On the other hand, it is easy to exaggerate the importance of the relatively high cost of belonging to house-building cooperatives as a factor in determining their social composition. As was explained in Section III, parents and relatives are often happy to help with the down-payment, if only to get their offspring out of the flat which two or three generations may already be sharing. Employers too can offer financial help, and as suggested above, personal savings are high. The number of urban savings bank accounts more than doubled between 1970 and 1986, and the average level of individual deposits in 1986 was 1,327 roubles, which is over half the typical down-payment on a flat in a house-building cooperative. The capital cost of entry therefore does not seem to be a major obstacle.

As far as the higher day-to-day costs of belonging to a house-building cooperative are concerned, it is important to remember that pay relativities in the Soviet Union vary greatly from those in western Europe, so that for example, transport workers earned on average 17% more than the national average income in 1986, while construction workers earned 25% more. On the other hand, white-collar workers often earn considerably less.[89] Moreover, in an economy with negligible income tax, cheap or free housing, health care and education, and limited supplies of many of the dearer consumer goods and durables, people often have more cash than they can easily spend - as seen by the high savings rates. Affording the cost of living in a cooperative is therefore less of a problem for many Soviet citizens than an outsider might expect.

Rural housing

As has been shown, about one in five of the population still lives and works on the land, where the traditionally predominant form of tenure is owner-occupation, usually in individual wooden houses, many of them old and dilapidated. Although the level of amenities is inevitably lower than in the urban stock, space standards are rather higher, and those who live on the land almost invariably have their own plots on which they can grow produce. These are a subject of envy among town dwellers, some of whom share the ambition of their western counterparts to move to a home with a garden, despite the longer time spent in getting to work. As was shown in Section I, large numbers of town dwellers have weekend cottages in the countryside.

Over 70% of the rural stock was privately owned in 1986 (1,093 million out of 1,550 million square metres). Against this volume of private housing, the 8 million square metres of rented housing provided by collective farms in recent years is hardly likely to make a significant impact.

Moreover, with increasing incomes and improving conditions on the land (as part of a deliberate policy to stabilise the working age of the rural population), there is likely to be a greater trend towards home ownership. In 1986, average rural incomes at 192 roubles per month were 98% of the average national income, compared with 70% in 1940, 83% in 1970, and only 88% as recently as 1980. It should also be noted that in contrast with urban incomes, few rural incomes are significantly below the average.[90] It is therefore not surprising that the number of rural accounts in the savings banks nearly doubled between 1970 and 1986 despite the reduction in the population, and that average individual deposits in savings bank accounts have been above the urban average since 1970. In 1986, they stood on average at 1,473 roubles.[91]

Tenants' attitudes

While by all accounts, the ambition of most occupiers of social rented flats in western Europe is to live in a house with a garden, the Soviet equivalent is the family in rooms in a communal flat dreaming of the day when they will have a flat of their own. For those who already have self-contained family accommodation, indifferent caretaking and environmental maintenance is of relatively little account, and tenants in the Soviet Union apparently have a low level of dissatisfaction with standards of housing size and quality, providing that they have reached the goal of a flat of their own.

Nonetheless, housing is often a burning topic in everyday conversation in the Soviet Union, and individuals' complaints are aired quite prominently in the press and television programmes, usually to illustrate how far there is still to go. Current plans for dealing with the persistent housing shortage, and the management problems which are emerging in the existing rented stock, will be considered in Section VII.

VII Management problems and solutions

Previous sections have emphasised that in contrast with the western European countries covered by this report, the Soviet Union still has a serious overall housing shortage, particularly in urban areas. Large numbers of flats are occupied by different households within the same family, often with three generations sharing accommodation so cramped that the living-rooms serve also as bedrooms, and the various groups within the household compete for use of the kitchen and bathroom facilities. The article in the international Soviet weekly news sheet *Moscow News* which has been cited in previous sections gives a remarkably frank account of the stresses on a typical four-person family living in a two-room flat of 31 square metres, which officially they also share with the wife's 85-year old grandmother, her sister and her sister's daughter.[92] The pressures are even greater in the substantial remaining rump of communal flats, where several unrelated families have to share these facilities.

As has been seen, a formidable construction programme has already done much to answer these needs, and the authorities are constantly reminding the public about the way in which living conditions are improving. Section VI has highlighted the extent to which this is happening, while also pointing to the size of the remaining problems. In these conditions, it is to be expected that people's ambitions are centred more on getting under a roof of one's own than on the quality of that roof and of the accommodation beneath it. This is a far cry from the over-capacity of the social rented sectors in many areas of western Europe, where the quality of life on housing estates is often perceived as stagnant or deteriorating, and where even in areas of shortage, there is now little new building.

It must also be borne in mind that in the cities and towns of the countries in western Europe which are covered by this report, there are substantial owner-occupied and - in some cases - private rented sectors which provide alternative housing, however unattainable it may be for many tenants in the social rented sector. For the Soviet town dweller, particularly in the large cities, the alternative is in practice usually confined to the house-building cooperative sector. It is perhaps a measure of the Soviet public's expectations of the state as the main provider of low-cost housing, if not necessarily of general satisfaction with that provision, that the cooperative sector remains so small despite its apparent attractions.

In part, this may be because cooperative housing - outwardly at least - is virtually indistinguishable from rented housing. Indeed, an urban built form which consists almost entirely of flats adds to the lack of perceptible alternatives, and so further limits the scope for dissatisfaction. Moreover, whether or not one takes at their full face value the claims of Soviet commentators that there is no social stratification in the rented or cooperative sectors, it is clear that because of its numerical dominance alone, the state rented sector must cover the whole urban social spectrum, whatever social concentrations may exist within it.

Preferences, pressures and causes of unpopularity

As in other countries, those with the least social leverage inevitably find themselves in the least popular housing. Young people and migrant workers are to a great extent accommodated in hostels, while other less favoured families stay in, or are eventually allocated, rooms in communal flats which almost by definition are in old and poorly equipped property. In the last resort it is also normal practice to transfer persistent rent arrears cases, and some others who in western Europe would be dubbed 'problem families' to hostel accommodation.

As was explained in Section III, while employers still provide large amounts of housing for their own workers, the municipalities have traditionally housed non-workers such as pensioners and single parent families, as well. There is therefore some social distinction between these two main branches of the state rented sector, although as has been seen, municipal tenants have significant advantages in the higher standard of accommodation and management services provided by the municipalities.

It is clear that there are significant variations in the attractiveness of urban housing which affect the social make-up of the residents. As has been seen in Section V, many (but by no means all) of the pre-war and early post-war five-storey walk-up blocks are a highly unpopular form of accommodation, whether they are communal flats or individual flats.

In discussion, however, Soviet housing experts readily acknowledge that even the more modern estates (mikroraiony) consisting of individual flats vary greatly in their attractiveness to tenants, characteristically and tellingly describing the popular ones as more 'prestigious' (prestizhniye). Most of the reasons given for these variations will be familiar. The unpopular estates often have poorly developed social and communal services such as schools, clinics, and sports and recreational facilities. Public transport links may still be lacking, and there are examples of previously unpopular estates which were transformed as soon as the metro line to them was completed. Limited or indifferent shopping facilities were often mentioned.

An unpublished survey of tenants' attitudes in Leningrad showed that top of their list of priorities was proximity to the metro, followed by access to green space in the case of families, with social and communal infrastructure, especially good quality shops, as a further high priority. The least popular housing estates are those affected by industrial pollution in the east of the city.

In a glowing report in June 1988 about the new Novokosino estate in Moscow, the Moscow evening newspaper significantly plays up its many social amenities, though revealing that for the time being, some of them are to be housed in temporary accommodation.[93] More prosaically, the Leningrad housing policy statement for 1986-2000 which is used to illustrate much of this section recognises that there are still considerable deficiencies in the provision of such amenities, going back to estates built in the 1960s. The policy statement is frankly realistic about the prospects of bringing some amenities up to standard in the short term. For example, while pre-school facilities should fully meet needs by 1991, the provision of schools and clinics will only be up to 85% of requirements by that time, hospitals 75%, and cinemas 50%. (Although the cinema may well be losing out to television as a form of entertainment, it still offers a refuge to young people wanting to escape the lack of privacy in their over-crowded flats.)

As in the western European social housing estates, tenants are said to be well satisfied with their flats as such, but sometimes less so with the standard of caretaking and environmental maintenance. The condition of entrance halls, staircases, and paved and grassed areas often looks similar to that on unpopular housing estates in western Europe. It is clear from the literature that caretaking and environmental maintenance are causes for concern.[94] It was therefore interesting to note during an unaccompanied visit to one unpopular Leningrad estate (which, like so many unpopular western European housing estates has an ironically optimistic name, in this case, the 'Cheerful Settlement'), that landscaping and newly planted shrubs were a striking feature of the current programme to up-grade the area.

It was equally striking that part of this area has been turned into a cooperative, including an infill development of brick-built houses. In casual conversation, the members were positive if not wildly optimistic.

As elsewhere, location is an important factor in determining the relative popularity of an estate. In some cases, there are special factors such as the industrial pollution affecting the estate described above. On the plus side, peripheral estates are often liked because they offer easy access to the open countryside, or because of special situations such as the Leningrad estates built on the shores of the gulf of Finland.

As a general rule, however, people are said to prefer to live in the centres of towns and cities (as long as it is not in a communal flat), rather than in the peripheral estates. The most frequently quoted reason is the ease of getting to theatres, cinemas and other places of entertainment, but it was sometimes suggested in discussion that there is a tendency towards 'gentrification' in the inner city areas. This is where - because of the lower provision of schools and facilities for children - smaller and older families are often allocated housing, while there is a growing concentration of families with young and teenage children on the peripheral estates, which are better served to cater for their needs.

Thus, although Soviet housing experts vigorously, and no doubt justifiably, deny that there is any form of social discrimination in the allocation of state housing, it is not unlikely that some degree of segregation takes place through self-selection and because of the pecking-order which inevitably exists in the allocation of any commodity which is in short supply. Although the clash on a south Moscow estate reported in *The Independent* (see Section VI) may have been an isolated incident, it is perhaps significant that it appears at least partly to have been racially inspired, with a gang of Russians from a named estate fighting with migrants from Soviet Central Asia living in hostel accommodation.

Indicators of management problems

With the enormous unfulfilled demand for housing in the Soviet Union which is described above and in other sections, it is to be expected that empty dwellings would not be a problem. However, as in some areas of high demand in the United Kingdom, and for apparently similar reasons, major vacancy rates are not unknown. In Leningrad, which as we shall see later has some of the most intense housing problems in the Soviet Union, it is common if unofficial knowledge that about 200,000 square metres of housing is unoccupied. This is the equivalent of roughly 4,000 flats. It is mainly communal housing in the central area, mostly low quality and in need of conversion and modernisation, but one of the reasons for its remaining empty is said to be the prospective tenants' awareness that if they accept such accommodation, that is where they will stay for the foreseeable future.

Offical figures put 109,600 square metres of the 'living area' of the Moscow municipal stock as empty in mid-1980.[95] Although this is a vacancy rate of only a fraction of 1%, it represents a direct annual loss of about 217,000 roubles even on low Soviet rents. Moreover, it is the equivalent of more than 2,000 empty flats in another of the most hard-pressed cities of the Soviet Union. In this case, the reason given for the vacancies is unnecessarily slow lettings procedures.

In a two page article outlining the city of Moscow's housing plans up to the year 2000, *Moskovskaya Pravda* emphasises the importance of speeding up the letting of new flats and those which have fallen vacant, which it claims could make an additional 40,000 to 50,000 square metres of accommodation available.[96] The same article also points out that about 22,000 out of the city's 250,000 hostel spaces are unoccupied; the equivalent of 8,000 rooms for family use.

Despite the low incomes of certain groups, especially some pensioners, it is also to be expected that low rent levels would be accompanied by low levels of rent arrears. However, the level is significant and tending to rise. The 1985 figure for outstanding rent amounted to 14.5% of the rent due.[97] On 1 January 1988, the level in Moscow was 12.7%.[98] With the penalty for arrears at only a tenth of 1% of the outstanding amount, and with virtually absolute security of tenure, such a level of rent arrears is not as surprising as it may at first have seemed. Although it is possible to obtain a court order to deduct arrears direct from pay or pension payments, it appears that to a great extent they are simply added to the deficit of the landlord organisations.

Statistics on the incidence of crime such as burglary are not available. However, one of the most common alterations which tenants make to their homes at their own expense is to change the locks, while one of the items singled out as a cause of the mounting running repair expenditure in the state rented sector is the cost of lock repairs. It was also significant that in discussion, one landlord organisation raised the suggestion that higher rents would enable landlords to spend money on security measures against vandalism. Thus, although the break-ins and vandalism cannot be quantified, there are at least firm indications that they are recognised as problems. However, they are usually regarded as social problems linked to the attitudes and behaviour of young people generally, rather than as housing problems as such.

Towards a solution of the housing problem

Previous sections have shown that the Soviet Union is suffering from broadly similar housing problems in the social rented sector - that is, the state rented sector in this case - as do the four western European countries considered in this report, although as has been seen, each country is doing so in varying degrees. They fall into three main areas which are closely related; housing finance, the condition of the existing stock, and the continuing need for a massive new-build programme.

Housing finance

First, as elsewhere, the social rented sector is in serious economic trouble. The inexorably rising capital cost of providing the housing has been examined in Section IV. This is clearly a matter of growing concern within government, even though rising capital provision for housing is still invariably publicised as an unquestioned virtue.

For example, the total cost of no less than 25 billion roubles for Leningrad's housing programme up to the year 2000 which is analysed in Table 5.19 is covered in a final 11 line paragraph of a newspaper article nearly two pages long.[99] Similarly, the article reporting the equivalent plans for Moscow gives 18 lines to a total investment of 44 to 48 billion roubles by the year 2000.[100] In both Leningrad and Moscow, the construction costs of the housing itself are about a quarter of the total.[101]

Table 5.19: Housing capital expenditure programme in Leningrad 1986-2000

	R million
New housing construction	7,500
Capital repairs	3,700
Social and communal infrastructure	3,800
Ground preparation and services	10,000
Total	25,000

Source: Vechernii Leningrad, 17 May 1988

The breakdown of this total expenditure shows the same awareness of social and communal infrastructure needs as the example of the estate in Moscow quoted above. As Table 5.19 demonstrates, social and communal infrastructure expenditure at 3,800 million roubles is planned. That is more than half the 7,500 million roubles which are destined for the actual construction costs of the new housing. Moreover, a further 2,800 million roubles of the 10,000 million planned for physical infrastructure will go on transport construction. The capital expenditure on the housing itself is therefore less than half the total cost of the programme.

The escalating running costs of rented housing, and the increasing shortfall between them and rent (and other) income are publicly seen as matters requiring solution. Previous sections have pointed to the growing emphasis on management on the supply side, for example to develop organisational structures which are more cost-conscious and efficient in the basic management tasks of ensuring that the stock and its environment is effectively let, maintained and cleaned, that rents are properly collected, and that above all, running repairs are carried out more economically. In all this, there is a growing awareness that a 'tenant-friendly' approach by the landlord organisations can pay real financial dividends. For example, in line with the recent changes in management practices described in Section III, the Leningrad policy statement described above attaches high priority to developing management arrangements which will improve tenant satisfaction and the active involvement in the way in which their housing is run. The proposed measures include the promotion of a greater sense of commitment on the part of housing workers (with higher pay to attract better quality staff financed out of reduced complements), and a major increase in the capacity to deal with tenants' repair orders.

As will be recalled, minor repairs are the tenants' responsibility, and a subject of some frustration. Payments by Leningrad tenants to the official repair organisations in 1985 came to a total of 4,893,000 roubles, or about 2.70 roubles per household; the capacity is to be nearly doubled by 1990, and to multiply by a factor of more than five by the year 2000.

As has been shown in Section IV there is also a growing awareness and acceptance, not least among the public generally, that the current rent levels and rent structure are hopelessly out of date, and that not only will rents have to be increased from the levels at which they have been frozen since 1928, but also that they need to be related much more closely to the wide variations in the quality of housing.

The condition of the existing stock

As has been seen in Sections IV and V, the second major task in Soviet housing policy is to come to grips with the deteriorating condition of the existing stock. This problem is particularly acute in Leningrad where, as Table 5.19 shows, a total expenditure of 3,700 roubles is planned between 1986 and 2000. This amounts to the equivalent of nearly half the amount scheduled for new-build.

This is partly because Leningrad has a larger proportion of older housing than the average, particularly in the city centre - the old St Petersburg - where much of it needs to be preserved, often at a high cost because of its great architectural value. Some 25% of the Leningrad rented and cooperative stock dates from before 1950, compared with a national urban average of about 10%. In central Leningrad, three-quarters of the total housing stock, or some 7,000 buildings with a total floor area of 15.2 million square metres, dates from before 1950. As stated above, perhaps 200,000 square metres of it is standing empty. Apart from its low level of amenity and physical deterioration, this housing consists largely of communal flats. Four out of five of the inner city population of about 820,000 now live in such accommodation.

Much work has already been done in the post-war period to rescue the older stock - which suffered particularly badly during the siege and bombardment of Leningrad - and 11.4 million square metres of housing, or about 137,000 flats, have already been fully or partly modernised throughout the city at a total cost of 2,000 million roubles or about 15,000 roubles per unit. This is considerably higher than the new-build costs outlined in Table 5.7. The present target is to provide a further 154,000 modernised flats with a total floor area of 15.15 million square metres, many of them by conversion of communal accommodation, by the year 2000. With a total planned expenditure of 3,700 million roubles (see Table 5.19), this makes an average unit cost of about 24,000 roubles, about double the projected cost per unit for the new-build programme (see below).

Although the programme will involve the loss of 4.26 million of older housing through demolition or change of use, it is accepted that the magnitude of the task means that the unpopular five-storey walk-up flats built in the 1960s with industrialised systems will have to be retained for the foreseeable future.

The priorities in Moscow are rather different, probably because the age profile of the stock is more modern. Here, according to the plans outlined in *Moskovskaya Pravda*, there are 10,860 five-storey blocks with a total living area of 36.1 million square metres, 20.5 million of which is in housing built with the early industrialised systems. Although the plans for dealing with this property are still at a formative stage, it and the 1,340,000 people still living in communal flats are seen as the top priorities.

The new-build programme

The third major task is to achieve the goal of a separate flat for every family by the year 2000. This involves a continuing and massive new-build programme. In Leningrad, the 1986 stock stood at 80.6 million square metres, with an annual rate of increase at that time of 1.5 million square metres. To provide the 630,000 flats which are needed in Leningrad itself to meet the estimated shortfall between dwellings and households in the year 2000, a total new-build programme of 32.4 million square metres is needed. According to this programme, this annual rate of increase will have to rise to 1.8 million square metres during the current Twelfth Five-Year Plan. As shown in Table 5.19, the budgeted amount over the whole period to 2000 is 7,500 million roubles, which works out at rather less than the recent average national cost per square metre calculated in Table 5.7.

Similar increases are planned in other towns and cities. The Moscow plan, based on detailed demographic analysis, involves the completion of between 720,000 and 750,000 flats by the year 2000, and the loss of 130-150,000. Considerable conversion work will also be necessary to cope with the mismatch between an increase in larger families and a shortage of larger accommodation.

Huge demands are being placed on the construction industry. For example, the construction rate in Moscow will need to increase from 3.3 million square metres a year to 3.8 million square metres. Not surprisingly, there are some commentators who are privately sceptical about the capacity of the construction industry to deliver a programme at such costs and on such a scale. Considerable efforts are therefore being made to provide the necessary manpower and material resources, including those to do the design work on the rehabilitation programme outlined above. Table 5.20 shows the present tenure breakdown for Leningrad, and the contribution by tenure sector to the programme.

This table contains two interesting features. First, although there is to be a major increase in activity by house-building cooperatives, no private provision is envisaged, despite the central government's policy of promoting private building which was re-affirmed as recently as 11 February 1988 in a resolution by the Council of Ministers. In Leningrad, the absence of private activity is no doubt because of the acute shortage of building land in the city.

294 The Soviet Union

Table 5.20: Tenure in Leningrad in 1986, and planned addition to
each tenure sector by the year 2000 (including outskirts)

	Existing stock (1986) m m²	%	Planned additions by 2000 Units (thousands)	%
Rented from state	69.0	85.6	535.0	81.1
Of which,				
employers	8.6	10.7	144.7	21.9
municipality	60.4	74.9	390.3	59.2
House-building				
cooperatives	10.4	12.9	125.0	18.9
Owner-occupied	1.2	1.5	-	-
Total	80.6	100.0	660.0	100.0

Source: Constructed from information in Vechernii Leningrad,
            17 May 1988

Second, despite the central government policy of transferring the
responsibility for providing rented housing from employers to the
municipalities, one in four new flats in the state rented sector will
be provided by employers. Here too, Leningrad, like Moscow (see
Section III) is something of a special case, with an abnormally low
proportion of housing owned by employers in the city's existing
stock. However, the Moscow plan stresses the need for adequate
coordination between the sectors, and for management
responsibility to be the province of the municipal authorities. It
claims that this will produce an average reduction in manpower
from 1.3 to 1.1 management and maintenance workers per 1,000
square metres.

The planned provision by employers contains an element which
amounts in effect to a new form of tenure which has been
developed since the mid-1970s. This is the 'youth housing
complex' (Molodezhny zhiloi kompleks, or MZhK) which is
planned to contribute 21,000 units. The MZhK is a form of
cooperative self-build organisation of young people with materials
and finance provided by their employers. Membership is restricted
to people between the ages of 18 and 30, and is highly competitive.
This combination of youth and self-help with support from
employers is intended to further government policy by encouraging
labour stability and young families, while at the same time offering
selected young people an opportunity to jump the housing queue.

Nationwide, over 150 MZhK projects are already in existence or under construction.

Of the three main problem areas described above, it is not surprising that the one in the forefront of the public mind is the need to increase the total provision sufficiently to meet the current goal of providing every family with its own flat by the year 2000. This means building a total of 2,500 million square metres or 36 million flats,[102] 26 million of them in urban areas and 10 million in rural areas, between 1986 and 2000.[103] This is the equivalent of a 60% addition to the existing stock in 1986. At the same time, the aim is to increase space standards to one room and about 20 square metres per person, as against the 1986 average of about 15 square metres. There is also increasing awareness of the special housing needs of older people and the handicapped.

However, as has been shown, housing officials are just as preoccupied with rising capital costs, with the growing gap between income and expenditure on the housing revenue account, and with the increasing obsolescence of the existing stock. It is therefore not surprising that housing design - for example, the mix of medium and high-rise blocks - and innovations in housing management and maintenance are developed largely in terms of economic efficiency, while social needs are usually regarded as a matter of adequate and timely provision of the necessary educational, health, recreational, transport and shopping facilities.

With the intensification in management problems which many western European countries have seen as they achieved a rough balance between dwellings and household numbers, it is an open question whether the Soviet Union will begin to experience similar difficulties as the millenium comes nearer. However, for the time being, few Soviet commentators seem to see any reason to question the present overall strategy.

NOTES

1. *Narodnoye khozyaistvo SSSR za 70 let: Yubileinii statisticheskii yezhegodnik* (Moskva 'Finansy i statistika' 1987) p 373

2. 'Human Settlements in the USSR: Position, trends and policies': National monograph for the Committee on Housing, Building and Planning of the UN ECE (Moscow, 1987)

3. *Narodnoye khozyaistvo SSSR za 70 let: Yubileinii statisticheskii yezhegodnik* (Moskva 'Finansy i statistika' 1987) p 373

4. *Narodnoye khozyaistvo SSSR za 70 let: Yubileinii statisticheskii yezhegodnik* (Moskva 'Finansy i statistika' 1987) p 407

5. *Narodnoye khozyaistvo SSSR za 70 let: Yubileinii statisticheskii yezhegodnik* (Moskva 'Finansy i statistika' 1987) pp 406-7

6. E M Blekh, *Povysheniye effektivnosti ekspluatatsii zhilykh zdanii* (Moskva Stroiizdat 1987) p 133

7. *Narodnoye khozyaistvo SSSR za 70 let: Yubileinii statisticheskii yezhegodnik* (Moskva 'Finansy i statistika' 1987) p 376

8. G D Andrusz, *Housing and Urban Development in the USSR* (Macmillan 1984) pp 20-23

9. *Narodnoye khozyaistvo SSSR za 70 let: Yubileinii statisticheskii yezhegodnik* (Moskva 'Finansy i statistika' 1987) p 379

10. 'Prospects and main trends of development of human settlements in the USSR in the period ending in 2000. National actions and international cooperation in the field of human settlements': Report to the 10th Session of the UN Commission for Human Settlements (HABITAT) (Moscow 1987) p 27

11. *Narodnoye khozyaistvo SSSR za 70 let: Yubileinii statisticheskii yezhegodnik* (Moskva 'Finansy i statistika' 1987) p 517

12. *Narodnoye khozyaistvo SSSR za 70 let: Yubileinii statisticheskii yezhegodnik* (Moskva 'Finansy i statistika' 1987) p 520

13. *Financial Times*, 7 December 1988

14. *Narodnoye khozyaistvo SSSR za 70 let: Yubileinii statisticheskii yezhegodnik* (Moskva 'Finansy i statistika' 1987) p 508

15. *Moscow News*, No 20 1988, p 9

16. Sir Donald Mackenzie Wallace, *Russia on the Eve of War and Revolution* (Vintage Russian Library 1961) p 500

17. G D Andrusz, *Housing and Urban Development in the USSR* (Macmillan 1984) p 9

18. Sir Donald Mackenzie Wallace, *Russia on the Eve of War and Revolution* (Vintage Russian Library 1961) p 204

19. Sir Donald Mackenzie Wallace, *Russia on the Eve of War and Revolution* (Vintage Russian Library 1961) p 175

20. G D Andrusz, *Housing and Urban Development in the USSR* (Macmillan 1984) p 8

21. Sir Donald Mackenzie Wallace, *Russia on the Eve of War and Revolution* (Vintage Russian Library 1961) p 219

22. L N Tolstoi, *Tak shto nam dyelat'?* (Collected works, Vol 16 Moskva 1964) pp 164-170

23. E M Blekh, *Povysheniye effektivnosti ekspluatatsii zhilykh zdanii* (Moskva Stroiizdat 1987) p 8

24. Christophe Sanson, *La politique du logement en Union Soviétique* (from L'Etat et le Logement, published by L'Arbre Verdoyant) p 206

25. G D Andrusz, *Housing and Urban Development in the USSR* (Macmillan 1984) p 31

26. *Narodnoye khozyaistvo SSSR za 70 let: Yubileinii statisticheskii yezhegodnik* (Moskva 'Finansy i statistika' 1987) p 508

27. G D Andrusz, *Housing and Urban Development in the USSR* (Macmillan 1984) p 42

28. E Kudryavtsev, *I Hereby Apply for an Apartment* (Progress Publishers, Moscow 1986) p 92

29. E M Blekh, *Povysheniye effektivnosti ekspluatatsii zhilykh zdanii* (Moskva Stroiizdat 1987) p 11

30. E Kudryavtsev, *I Hereby Apply for an Apartment* (Progress Publishers, Moscow 1986) p 45

31. I Il'f i Ye Petrov, *Zolotoi Tyelyonok* (Tula 1965) pp 125ff

32. Christophe Sanson, *La politique du logement en Union Soviétique* (from L'Etat et le Logement, published by L'Arbre Verdoyant) p 208

33. E Kudryavtsev, *I Hereby Apply for an Apartment* (Progress Publishers, Moscow 1986) p 88

34. *Narodnoye khozyaistvo SSSR za 70 let: Yubileinii statisticheskii yezhegodnik* (Moskva 'Finansy i statistika' 1987) p 373

35. E Kudryavtsev, *I Hereby Apply for an Apartment* (Progress Publishers, Moscow 1986) p 111

36. *Narodnoye khozyaistvo SSSR za 70 let: Yubileinii statisticheskii yezhegodnik* (Moskva 'Finansy i statistika' 1987) p 499

37. *Narodnoye khozyaistvo SSSR za 70 let: Yubileinii statisticheskii yezhegodnik* (Moskva 'Finansy i statistika' 1987) p 506

38. Information supplied by Moscow City Council

39. E Kudryavtsev, *I Hereby Apply for an Apartment* (Progress Publishers, Moscow 1986) pp 25-26

40. *Narodnoye khozyaistvo SSSR za 70 let: Yubileinii statisticheskii yezhegodnik* (Moskva 'Finansy i statistika' 1987) p 519

41. E Kudryavtsev, *I Hereby Apply for an Apartment* (Progress Publishers, Moscow 1986) pp 54ff

42. *Moscow in Figures 1987* (Leaflet published by Moscow City Council)

43. G D Andrusz, *Housing and Urban Development in the USSR* (Macmillan 1984) p 57

44. E M Blekh, M G Gel'baum, V P Naumov, *Spravochnoye Posobiye* (Moskva Stroiizdat 1984)

45. E M Blekh, *Povysheniye effektivnosti ekspluatatsii zhilykh zdanii* (Moskva Stroiizdat 1987) p 170

46. E M Blekh, *Povysheniye effektivnosti ekspluatatsii zhilykh zdanii* (Moskva Stroiizdat 1987) pp 60ff

47. E M Blekh, *Povysheniye effektivnosti ekspluatatsii zhilykh zdanii* (Moskva Stroiizdat 1987) p 33

48. E M Blekh, *Povysheniye effektivnosti ekspluatatsii zhilykh zdanii* (Moskva Stroiizdat 1987) pp 46-49

49. E Kudryavtsev, *I Hereby Apply for an Apartment* (Progress Publishers, Moscow 1986) pp 37ff

50. E M Blekh, *Povysheniye effektivnosti ekspluatatsii zhilykh zdanii* (Moskva Stroiizdat 1987) p 13

51. E M Blekh, *Povysheniye effektivnosti ekspluatatsii zhilykh zdanii* (Moskva Stroiizdat 1987) p 23

52. G D Andrusz, *Housing and Urban Development in the USSR* (Macmillan 1984) p 59

53. E M Blekh, *Povysheniye effektivnosti ekspluatatsii zhilykh zdanii* (Moskva Stroiizdat 1987) p 20

54. E M Blekh, *Povysheniye effektivnosti ekspluatatsii zhilykh zdanii* (Moskva Stroiizdat 1987) p 21

55. G D Andrusz, *Housing and Urban Development in the USSR* (Macmillan 1984) p 59

56. E Kudryavtsev, *I Hereby Apply for an Apartment* (Progress Publishers, Moscow 1986) p 29

57. E M Blekh, *Povysheniye effektivnosti ekspluatatsii zhilykh zdanii* (Moskva Stroiizdat 1987) p 21

58. E M Blekh, *Povysheniye effektivnosti ekspluatatsii zhilykh zdanii* (Moskva Stroiizdat 1987) p 28

59. E M Blekh, *Povysheniye effektivnosti ekspluatatsii zhilykh zdanii* (Moskva Stroiizdat 1987) p 28

60. G D Andrusz, *Housing and Urban Development in the USSR* (Macmillan 1984) pp 172-3

61. E Kudryavtsev, *I Hereby Apply for an Apartment* (Progress Publishers, Moscow 1986) pp 116-7

62. E M Blekh, *Povysheniye effektivnosti ekspluatatsii zhilykh zdanii* (Moskva Stroiizdat 1987) p 123

63. E M Blekh, *Povysheniye effektivnosti ekspluatatsii zhilykh zdanii* (Moskva Stroiizdat 1987) p 103

64. E M Blekh, *Povysheniye effektivnosti ekspluatatsii zhilykh zdanii* (Moskva Stroiizdat 1987) p 99

65. E M Blekh, *Povysheniye effektivnosti ekspluatatsii zhilykh zdanii* (Moskva Stroiizdat 1987) p 100

66. E M Blekh, *Povysheniye effektivnosti ekspluatatsii zhilykh zdanii* (Moskva Stroiizdat 1987) p 102

67. E Kudryavtsev, *I Hereby Apply for an Apartment* (Progress Publishers, Moscow 1986) p 50

68. *Narodnoye khozyaistvo SSSR za 70 let: Yubileinii statisticheskii yezhegodnik* (Moskva 'Finansy i statistika' 1987) pp 517 and 435

69. G D Andrusz, *Housing and Urban Development in the USSR* (Macmillan 1984) p 205; and E Kudryavtsev, *I Hereby Apply for an Apartment* (Progress Publishers, Moscow 1986) p 62

70. E M Blekh, *Povysheniye effektivnosti ekspluatatsii zhilykh zdanii* (Moskva Stroiizdat 1987) p 152

71. *Izvestia*, 15 October 1986

72. E M Blekh, *Povysheniye effektivnosti ekspluatatsii zhilykh zdanii* (Moskva Stroiizdat 1987) p 22

73. E M Blekh, *Povysheniye effektivnosti ekspluatatsii zhilykh zdanii* (Moskva Stroiizdat 1987) p 24

74. E M Blekh, *Povysheniye effektivnosti ekspluatatsii zhilykh zdanii* (Moskva Stroiizdat 1987) pp 24-25

75. G D Andrusz, *Housing and Urban Development in the USSR* (Macmillan 1984) p 8

76. E M Blekh, *Povysheniye effektivnosti ekspluatatsii zhilykh zdanii* (Moskva Stroiizdat 1987) p 28

77. E M Blekh, *Povysheniye effektivnosti ekspluatatsii zhilykh zdanii* (Moskva Stroiizdat 1987) p 155

78. E M Blekh, *Povysheniye effektivnosti ekspluatatsii zhilykh zdanii* (Moskva Stroiizdat 1987) pp 67ff

79. G D Andrusz, *Housing and Urban Development in the USSR* (Macmillan 1984) pp 182ff

80. *Moskovskaya Pravda*, 18 May 1988

81. *Narodnoye khozyaistvo SSSR za 70 let: Yubileinii statisticheskii yezhegodnik* (Moskva 'Finansy i statistika' 1987) p 404

82. *Narodnoye khozyaistvo SSSR za 70 let: Yubileinii statisticheskii yezhegodnik* (Moskva 'Finansy i statistika' 1987) pp 406-407

83. *Moskovskaya Pravda*, 18 May 1988

84. *Narodnoye khozyaistvo SSSR 1965* (Moskva 'Finansy i statistika' 1966) p 606

85. *Narodnoye khozyaistvo SSSR 1961* (Moskva 'Finansy i statistika' 1962) p 610

86. *Narodnoye khozyaistvo SSSR za 70 let: Yubileinii statisticheskii yezhegodnik* (Moskva 'Finansy i statistika' 1907) p 629

87. *Narodnoye khozyaistvo SSSR za 70 let: Yubileinii statisticheskii yezhegodnik* (Moskva 'Finansy i statistika' 1987) p 11

88. *Narodnoye khozyaistvo SSSR za 70 let: Yubileinii statisticheskii yezhegodnik* (Moskva 'Finansy i statistika' 1987) p 427

89. *Narodnoye khozyaistvo SSSR za 70 let: Yubileinii statistiche-skii yezhegodnik* (Moskva 'Finansy i statistika' 1987) p 431

90. *Narodnoye khozyaistvo SSSR za 70 let: Yubileinii statistiche-skii yezhegodnik* (Moskva 'Finansy i statistika' 1987) p 431

91. *Narodnoye khozyaistvo SSSR za 70 let: Yubileinii statistiche-skii yezhegodnik* (Moskva 'Finansy i statistika' 1987) p 448

92. *Moscow News* No 20, 1988

93. *Vechernyaya Moskva*, 14 June 1988

94. E M Blekh, *Povysheniye effektivnosti ekspluatatsii zhilykh zdanii* (Moskva Stroiizdat 1987) p 76

95. E M Blekh, *Povysheniye effektivnosti ekspluatatsii zhilykh zdanii* (Moskva Stroiizdat 1987) p 104

96. *Moskovskaya Pravda*, 25 March 1988

97. E M Blekh, *Povysheniye effektivnosti ekspluatatsii zhilykh zdanii* (Moskva Stroiizdat 1987) p 105

98. Information supplied by Moscow City Council

99. *Vechernii Leningrad*, 17 May 1988

100. *Moskovskaya Pravda*, 25 March 1988

101. *Moskovskaya Pravda*, 18 May 1988
102. Yurii Batalin, quoted in *Pravda*, 26 May 1988
103. Information supplied by Gosgrazhdanstroi

conclusion

SOCIAL HOUSING AT THE CROSSROADS

Historical divergences

As we have seen, after similar beginnings in the latter half of the
19th century, the social rented sector took different paths in the five
countries covered by this study. However, the path taken by the
United Kingdom was markedly different from the others in several
ways.

First, mass housing in this country made a much earlier start
than in France and the Netherlands. More than one dwelling in five
in the social rented sector in England was built before the Second
World War, compared with under one in twelve in France, and
about one in ten in the Netherlands. (In the Soviet Union, over 16
times as much rented housing has been built in the post-war than
between the wars, but the conditions are so different that
comparisons have little force.) Although the pre-war social rented
sector in Germany was on about the same scale as in the United
Kingdom, the stock belonged to a vastly greater number of small
landlord organisations.

Second, the social rented sector in the United Kingdom became
a matter of party political debate after the First World War, when
central government decided to make local authorities directly
responsible for the development, ownership, and management of
the great bulk of the stock. Although in their different ways, their
counterparts in the other western countries have a key role in social
rented housing in their localities, they have nothing like the same
scope for active party political involvement.

Third, the later rent surpluses generated by this early stock, and the increasingly monolithic character of municipal landlordism made it possible for the high costs of the post-war housing programme to be cushioned through rent pooling, which whatever its accounting attractions, broke any perceived link in the minds of tenants and landlords between cost and the quality of the product.

Fourth, the built form of the inter-war period consisted largely of garden city developments of houses, except for London where the London County Council pioneered the low- and medium-rise balcony-access blocks of flats which in later variations on the same theme throughout the country were to prove much more difficult to manage than their continental counterparts with more restricted and controllable access arrangements.

Fifth, the British quickly identified a social engineering role for council housing, which from the early days was used to re-house people from slum clearance areas as well as the 'deserving poor' whom the continental landlord organisations have traditionally sought as the main body of their tenants.

Differences in management approach

The extent to which the local authorities in the United Kingdom have always been landlords of last resort may well be the most potent factor contributing to the evidently greater relative scale of their management problems among the four western countries. (As has been shown, Soviet municipalities also tend to take the more dependent members of the community, but generally have more effective management arrangements than do the employers' landlord organisations.) However, even if the signs of outright dereliction and depression are less intense and frequent on social rented housing estates in France, West Germany and the Netherlands than they are in the United Kingdom, there is a growing sense among many continental landlord organisations - especially those linked with local authorities - that they too are increasingly having to cope with problems of 'residualisation'. Almost inevitably, any discussion with housing managers in these countries quickly turns to the question of how to deal with 'problem families'.

The debate usually centres on the extent to which the landlord organisations need to develop a welfare role. Generally, they are less inclined to do so in the neighbouring countries than in the

United Kingdom where since the days of Octavia Hill, professional housing managers have tended to adopt a paternalistic stance towards their tenants. Although the French approach towards problem estates relies heavily on the promotion of greater social well-being, and although some German landlord organisations are providing social worker support for their more vulnerable tenants, such initiatives seem far more innovative in these countries than they would in the United Kingdom.

Although as has been seen, there are limited moves towards structured professional training for housing managers in France, West Germany and the Netherlands, the courses are still in their infancy, and it remains to be seen whether they will have the social slant of the Institute of Housing professional qualification in the United Kingdom. Meanwhile, the tendency among continental landlord organisations is more to promote the concept of the tenant as a customer for their products, whose aspirations should be fulfilled within the bounds of a mutually understood business relationship, and in particular, one where there is a perceived link between the cost to the tenant and the quality of the accommodation and the service.

It is common on the Continent for large estates to be owned and managed by more than one landlord organisation. Again, as has been seen, there are few complaints about demarcation problems even on rundown estates. The main exception is Bijlmermeer, near Amsterdam, where a new housing association was formed to replace the 16 previous landlord organisations, but rationalisation of management and ownership does not figure in the wide variety of projects backed by the National Commission in France. On the other hand, few people in these countries appear to see positive merit in the multiple ownership and management of estates, and as has been seen, tenants and housing managers rarely have any sense of competition between the various landlord organisations to provide a better service.

Very few of the landlord organisations in France, West Germany and the Netherlands have their own repairs organisations, while the Soviet Union has arrangements similar to British direct labour organisations, often with problems of efficiency and accountability which are a subject of current debate. In France, West Germany and the Netherlands, several landlord organisations, including some of the biggest landlords, have dispensed with their own repairs organisations, and now put out their repairs to specialist contractors. Invariably, the reason given is that it is cheaper and more efficient to put out to private contractors any repairs which the caretaker cannot do.

Indeed, one of the strengths of the housing management arrangements in France, West Germany and the Netherlands appears to be the resident block caretaker/superintendent who is responsible typically for about 100 dwellings. As well as ensuring that the block and its surroundings are kept clean and tidy, the caretaker is the accepted point of contact between the tenants and the landlord organisation for day-to-day management matters. In particular, he is responsible for reporting repairs, and often does small running repairs himself. It is probably because this arrangement is so effective that local management offices are normally found only on the most difficult estates.

Financial differences

It may also be relevant to housing management that the housing benefit arrangements described in the individual national chapters are less far-reaching in the other western countries than they are in the United Kingdom, even after the reforms of 1988. In France, West Germany and, to a lesser extent, the Netherlands, the general (non-housing benefit) income support systems are still based on the social insurance principle of contributions by employer and employee (with some government support) providing benefits related to previous earnings.

These benefits are expected to cover at least a part of housing costs. Thus, the levels of general income support rarely cover direct housing costs to anything like the same extent as they do in the United Kingdom. For example, housing benefit levels in West Germany - for the small minority of tenants who receive it - are designed to reduce the proportion of income going on rent to just under 20%. In consequence, as has been shown in the individual national chapters, tenants in other countries are considerably more concerned about the cost of their housing, and in particular of changes to it, than are tenants in the United Kingdom.

It is also arguable that social landlord organisations which have to operate as independent and self-balancing cost centres, as do those on France, West Germany and the Netherlands, are likely to have a more cost-conscious ethos than many British local authority housing departments. Until recently they were able to meet deficits on their housing revenue accounts with contributions from the local rate-payers generally. Certainly, the figures given earlier in this study indicate that continental landlord organisations spend less than British local authorities and housing associations on the management and maintenance of their stock, and apparently with results which are at least as good.

It was suggested in Chapter 1 that the higher costs in the United Kingdom may in part be due to transfers from the housing revenue account to other departments of the local authority for services which they provide for the tenants. It may also reflect on the performance of the local authority direct labour organisations which are responsible for carrying out much of the repair work on the housing. In the continental countries, it may be that some of these costs are paid by the tenants in other ways. However, despite evident individual cases of local demarcation problems, the generally accepted and understood separation of functions between the municipal authorities and the landlord organisations appears to make for clear and accountable - and hence probably more economical - relationships between the providers of the various services and their clients.

Despite the scope for a two-tier (or more) quality of housing provision in the statutory financial regimes of all five countries, there is little real sign that tenants are seriously interested in paying more for a different standard of accommodation or service within the social rented sector, except in the Soviet Union, where it is possible to jump the housing queue by joining a cooperative. The Soviet and German cooperatives, and some of the British housing associations perhaps come nearest to two-tier social rented housing.

Priorities on problem estates

Previous chapters have shown that one country's problem estate would be unexceptional elsewhere. Local perceptions and relativities are far more important. Thus, the prospect of a still apparently trouble-free estate going wrong - as with some of the examples in West Berlin, most notably the Märkisches Viertel - is clearly just as relevant in local terms as are serious actual disturbances at Les Minguettes near Lyons or Broadwater Farm in London. Moreover, as the work of the Urban Housing Renewal Unit/Estate Action in England has shown, in considering whether an estate is in need of priority measures or not, inter-regional comparisons within the same country are of as little relevance as are comparisons on the international scale.

Apart from a general concern about empty dwellings, there are remarkably few common denominators internationally between the many estates considered in this study. Beyond that, as the Urban Housing Renewal Unit/Estate Action has found, it is axiomatic that each estate's social and physical make-up, and hence its problems and solutions, are different. Social disadvantage may consist of very varying combinations and levels of unemployment, age patterns among tenants, single parent families, and concentrations of minority ethnic communities on the estate. The built form of problem estates may be high-rise blocks, slab blocks, or even individual houses with gardens. They may be found in city centres as well as on the periphery.

Even more surprising, the one point which came through time and time again - except in the Soviet Union - was the tenants' satisfaction with the layout and internal standard of their dwellings, and their dissatisfaction with the outside appearance of the blocks and with the surrounding environment. It is therefore understandable that priority is being given in virtually every project to improving the facades of the buildings and to making their surroundings attractive and easy to maintain.

Differing approaches to problem estates

It may however be useful to devote a few paragraphs to exploring the differences in approach to problem estates in the United Kingdom on the one hand, and in the continental countries on the other, and to suggest some reasons for these differences.

Where the original starting-point of the Urban Housing Renewal Unit was the need perceived by government to promote improvements in the housing management and diversification of tenure on problem estates, these needs are felt much less keenly on most of the continental estates. Some of the large landlord organisations - typically, but not exclusively, those with 50,000 or more dwellings - have come to recognise that their management structures are over-centralised and bureaucratic, and are actively pursuing decentralisation policies. However, while responsive local management arrangements are just as much a key feature of National Commission schemes in France as they are of Estate Action schemes in England, it should be remembered that most continental estates start with a different landlord and management structure which may be (but not always is) adapted in other ways to achieve the desired result.

In the predominantly flatted built form of the continental estates, piecemeal sales to sitting tenants are just as unlikely as they have been on flatted estates under the Right to Buy in the United Kingdom. As has been shown in the individual chapters, some governments are encouranging their landlord organisations to sell individual dwellings on a voluntary basis, and some are ready to do so, usually for financial reasons. However, there appears to be little real interest on either side. It is rather more surprising to find how little interest there is among continental landlord organisations to sell chronically empty blocks of housing to private developers for improvement and resale to owner-occupiers, even in conditions resembling those where such schemes have been particularly successful in England. This may be because the continental countries generally have a less buoyant - and speculative - market in the owner-occupied sector, but even in cities like Paris where the market is strong, developers seem to see little opportunity to emulate British experience.

Although there are some major exceptions, a further important difference between the United Kingdom and our continental neighbours towards the regeneration of rundown estates lies in the extent to which British tenants are actively consulted and indeed encouraged to participate in the renewal process. In continental schemes, the starting-point for consultation is usually the likely effect of the proposals on rent levels, and some of the most imaginative project leaders regard active tenant involvement as at best a desirable but dispensable luxury, and at worst so alien to the local culture as not to merit serious consideration. It was not only the more paternalistic landlord organisations who frequently suggested either that there was little point in consulting people who were unlikely to be there to see the results of the scheme, or that their tenants had no communal sense, and saw themselves only as consumers of a service.

As has been seen in the examples described in previous chapters, the most effective tenant consultation and participation schemes are usually to be found on estates where an independent consultant has been installed to promote active tenant interest and involvement. Such consultants inevitably have to tread a thin line between raising undue expectations among the tenants and seeming to be no more than an extension of the landlord organisation. Although some

landlord organisations (and municipal authorities) are evidently
nervous about this risk of divided loyalties, there are few if any
substantiated reports of such fears being realised in practice.

Governments at the crossroads

The **United Kingdom** government's policies towards rundown
estates have been incremental and pluralistic, building on the
experience gained in a variety of initiatives to develop new ones.
As in France, central governments have traditionally taken an
interventionist stance, with the Housing Services Advisory Group
and the Housing Services Advisory Unit in the Department of the
Environment acting as brokers of good management practice since
the mid-1970s. The establishment of the Priority Estates Project in
1979 added a development and demonstration role to the central
government contribution, which in turn was augmented by the
creation of the Urban Housing Renewal Unit (later renamed as
Estate Action) in 1985. Although an important part of the Estate
Action remit is to promote greater variety of tenure on problem
estates, in essence these various initiatives have been designed to
develop solutions within the existing framework of local authority
ownership and management.

At the same time, throughout the 1980s, the government has
simultaneously been seeking to develop alternative forms of
ownership and management for the ownership and management of
the rented stock belonging to local authorities and new town
corporations - if not to housing associations. These initiatives have
not been confined to problem estates, although tenant
dissatisfaction has been a powerful impetus behind them. One
strand has consisted of the 'housing trust' formula to convert public
sector housing into a new form of private renting with a high level
of tenant involvement, as at Stockbridge Village and Thamesmead.
Housing Action Trusts are a development of this principle.
Another is to promote cooperatives, in particular tenant
management cooperatives, for example as at Cloverhall and in
Glasgow.

However, the main thrust of the government's policies will have
the effect of bringing the overall management structure of the social
rented sector very much into line with what has traditionally
prevailed in the three continental countries. Tenants Choice, and
the wholesale transfer of some councils' and new towns' stock to

housing associations, are intended at one and the same time to break the political mould of public sector landlordism and to introduce diversity of management - and thus competition - to housing estates.

Previous chapters have underlined the shift from indiscriminate bricks and mortar subsidies towards targetted subsidies to the individual which the governments of the various countries have made or started to make over the last decade. For France (and the Netherlands), it is the escalating cost of these personal subsidies which has brought the social rented sector to the cross-roads in the late 1980s.

For **France**, the reassessment of the subsidy mechanisms is taking the form of fine-tuning the more radical initiatives which were taken in the previous decade, in particular the wide-ranging restructuring of benefits and rents linked with modernisation - the 'conventionnement' system - which was initiated in 1977. The government's decisions on the Laxan report's recommendations for the social rented sector are clearly intended to contain the rise in housing benefit costs without major effects on tenants or the progress of modernisation.

At the same time, the National Commission programme for regenerating rundown estates continues along the established path which apparently has all-party support. With its emphasis on social and economic regeneration, it is the most ambitious and far-reaching of all the government sponsored initiatives described in this study. Although sales to sitting tenants are mooted from time to time, mainly for financial reasons, there is no indication that the government intends to press such proposals, at least to the extent of giving tenants the right to buy their homes. The social rented sector in France therefore seems to be continuing along well trodden and accepted paths.

In the Federal Republic of **Germany**, the gradual decline of the social rented sector is pre-ordained in the subsidy system which releases landlords from the obligation to let dwellings to nominees from the local municipal housing office when the subsidised loans on them have been paid off. At the same time, this shrinking social rented sector is coming under increasing pressure from applicants among the seriously disadvantaged people now living in housing at the bottom end of the private rented sector as it too declines with the tendency of landlords to improve it and go up-market. Increasing numbers of immigrants from eastern Europe are also placing heavy demands on the social rented sector.

Despite its constitutional position, the central government has supported some experimental initiatives on estates, but most intiatives are taken at the local level. For the most part, the measures taken in Germany have concentrated on physical improvements to the buildings and their surroundings. However, in a country where tenants are particularly sensitive to rent levels, there have also been several cases in which the rents on unpopular estates have been reduced to attract tenants. There are mixed views on the extent to which such reductions are necessary or ultimately helpful. As in the Netherlands, the federal government mood is non-interventionist, and its policy of allowing local government influence on allocations to wither away or even to accelerate this process indicates that it too is inclined to turn to the right.

The **Netherlands** has already passed over one major crossroads with the switch in responsibility for providing social rented housing from the municipalities to the housing associations in the mid-1960s. With a social rented housing new-build programme which lasted for longer than in all the other countries, the Netherlands continues to face heavy bricks and mortar subsidies as well as a huge bill for housing benefits. Cost-cutting is therefore the order of the day. The housing benefit rules have already been tightened. New-build activity virtually ceased from the start of 1988, and plans for modernising the existing stock have been cut back.

On problem estates, the government has been heavily involved in the major initiative to rescue the country's one huge estate - Bijlmermeer, near Amsterdam - and is alone among the three continental countries in sharing the British government's concern with crime on estates.   Otherwise, it has adopted a non-interventionist stance. Proposals for sales to sitting tenants indicate that the Dutch government is intent on turning as far as it can to the right in its policies for the social rented sector generally.

The **Soviet Union** is at first sight a very different case, although the differences themselves are enlightening. Chief among them is the continuing massive unsatisfied demand for housing, which makes the Soviet housing scene seem something of a time-warp for western observers. The persistent shortage should mean - and to a great extent does mean - undiscriminating and grateful acceptance of what eventually is offered to the many who still live in crowded and unsatisfactory conditions.

However, as was shown in Chapter 5, there is empty housing even in the cities with the greatest demand, such as Leningrad and Moscow. The location and image of different estates clearly dictate tenants' attitudes to an extent which cause the housing authorities real concern. Rent arrears are a significant problem, even with rents which are negligible by western standards.

Indeed, rent levels are now seen as one of the main issues in Soviet housing circles, not only because they are manifestly uneconomic, but also because they are in no way linked with the increasingly varied standards of quality to be found in Soviet housing - a problem which is not entirely foreign to this country either. The effect in the Soviet Union, as here, is to increase tenant dissatisfaction.

Apart from examining rent structures, the government is also encouraging people to join housing cooperatives as an alternative to the normal state rented sector. Although the motive for this policy is largely economic, it cannot but set a trend towards the two-tier social rented provision found in the other countries covered by this study. However, as has been seen in all five countries, the upper tier is - so far at least - small in relation to the mainstream social rented sector.

As elsewhere, it is notable that the Soviet housing authorities have recognised the crucial weaknesses in the management structures of their rented housing, which they are tackling by encouraging the take-over of employers' housing by the municipalities, and by developing more accountable and comprehensive local management arrangements.

Final thoughts

In all five countries, the proportion of the social rented sector which poses serious management problems is unquantified but clearly small. Nevertheless, it represents a large absolute number of dwellings, and tends to be concentrated in certain areas.

The incidence of management problems is generally greater on peripheral estates (particularly those with limited social and economic infrastructure and a poor population), and in buildings which have uncontrolled access arrangements (particularly deck or balcony access).

Such undesirable physical features merely serve to exacerbate the social strains which according to all the evidence appear to be the root cause of problem estates. Indeed, as has been shown, attractive housing in good condition can quickly become seriously rundown if it is insensitively allocated.

Moreover, social sector landlords in all five countries are increasingly facing at least some pressure from 'residualisation' as their more affluent tenants move into owner-occupation, cooperatives, or the private rented sector, and the demand from the socially disadvantaged grows.

Market forces were conspicuously absent from the development of the social rented sector. Since the early 1970s, social landlords have increasingly needed to promote a product of intrinsically limited - and declining - attractivenes to a clientèle which not only has been changing in character and expectations, but also with its sense of choice blunted by largely indiscriminate rent pricing structures and housing benefit support arrangements.

The solutions described in previous chapters have almost invariably concentrated on the physical improvement measures to make the product more attractive. In some cases they have also sought to make the back-up services more responsive to tenants' needs. Overall management structures clearly have an important part to play in achieving this effective relationship between supplier and customer, and all experience shows that monolithic landlord organisations find it difficult to create this relationship.

Ultimately, however, it is tight and effective management of human and material resources, and face-to-face human contact which make for real accountability. Where people of the right calibre and with clearly understood responsibilities are dealing with tenants, management problems seem to be containable, even on the worst estates. It is by no means self-evident that any particular form of overall management structure is always capable of providing the essential human relationships at the estate level.

In the end, more may depend on the professionalism and dedication of those discharging the management function at the 'coal-face' than on any system, if our large estates are once more to become acceptable to those who live there.

INDEX

POLICY
AND
POLITICS

POLICY AND POLITICS is the quarterly journal that gives a real insight into public policy and policy-making both in the United Kingdom and Europe.

POLICY AND POLITICS is an interdisciplinary journal which features in-depth articles on housing, social, health, education, employment, planning and environmental policy topics.

Recent articles include:

Wealth, inheritance and housing policy
Housing policy and 'special needs'
Decentralisation in Sweden
Public management in uncertainty

Volume 19 (1991) will include papers on:

The politics of race and housing
Quality and decentralisation
Unemployment and local policy-making in Germany

If you are interested in obtaining single copies or a subscription to **POLICY AND POLITICS** please contact Pam Aldren at the address below. The editor, Robin Means, welcomes articles submitted to him within the journal's areas of interest.

University of Bristol
School for Advanced Urban Studies
Rodney Lodge Grange Road
Bristol BS8 4EA Telephone 0272 741117
Editor Robin Means